The Dollars and Sense of Estate Planning

FOREST J. BOWMAN

West Virginia University
College of Law

Prentice Hall, Englewood Cliffs, New Jersey 07632

Library of Congress Cataloging-in-Publication Data

Bowman, Forest J. (date)
    The dollars and sense of estate planning

    Bibliography
    Includes index.
    1. Estate planning--United States--Popular works
2. Inheritance and transfer tax--Law and legislation--
United States--Popular works. I. Title
KF750.Z9B66. .1989   343.7305'3   88-9917
ISBN 0-13-217795-1   347.30353

Editorial/production supervision
    and interior design: Mary Rottino
Cover design: Lundgren Graphics, Ltd.
Manufacturing buyer: Mary Ann Gloriande

©1989 by Prentice-Hall, Inc.
A Division of Simon & Schuster
Englewood Cliffs, New Jersey 07632

The publisher offers discounts on this book when ordered
in bulk quantities. For more information, write:

    Special Sales/College Marketing
    College Technical and Reference Division
    Prentice-Hall
    Englewood Cliffs, New Jersey 07632

Printed in the United States of America

10 9 8 7 6 5 4 3 2 1

ISBN   0-13-217795-1

PRENTICE-HALL INTERNATIONAL (UK) LIMITED, LONDON
PRENTICE-HALL OF AUSTRALIA PTY. LIMITED, SYDNEY
PRENTICE-HALL CANADA INC., TORONTO
PRENTICE-HALL HISPANOAMERICANA, S.A., MEXICO
PRENTICE-HALL OF INDIA PRIVATE LIMITED, NEW DELHI
PRENTICE-HALL OF JAPAN, INC., TOKYO
SIMON & SCHUSTER ASIA PTE. LTD., SINGAPORE
EDITORA PRENTICE-HALL DO BRASIL, LTDA., RIO DE JANEIRO

Dedication

To my father, Forest W. Bowman, 1905-1986,
who would have been so proud.

Contents

Preface

This book is intended to provide a readable, understandable source of information about the estate planning process. While I am a lawyer, the book is not aimed primarily at lawyers - or law students - (though I would hope that both would find it beneficial) and I have deliberately tried to avoid the use of "lawyers' English," which is a contradiction in terms anyway.

The need to understand something about the use of our property during our lifetimes and to begin planning for its disposition on our deaths seems plain. The need is especially acute among life insurance underwriters, stock brokers, bank trust officers, financial planners, accountants, lawyers, and others who are in the business of helping "build" and "plan" estates.

Unfortunately, most books on estate planning are simply beyond the ken of all but the most knowledgeable tax lawyer or accountant, a fact I discovered when searching for a suitable text for my class in Estate Planning. A major problem with most of these books is that their emphasis is wrongly placed. They treat the estate planning process as a purely functional one, concerned largely with how to avoid the federal estate tax, and ignore the far more important matter of emotions. Our "things," you see, are not just assets to be moved back and forth across a balance sheet. They are part and parcel of ourselves. And what we do with them during our lifetimes and how we treat them on our deaths can have enormous consequences to our families and loved ones, consequences that range far beyond the mere levying of taxes or the valuation of assets.

In this book, then, we will look beyond the traditional concern with taxes (though this topic certainly will not be ignored) and seek to provide broad-based information about the whole matter of the ownership and devolution of property.

Of course, anyone attempting to cover estate planning in fewer than a dozen volumes runs the risk of being criticized for superficiality. My object, however, is not to cover *all* of estate planning, but to give those who need a fundamental understanding of the subject a readable, understandable source.

Forest J. Bowman

Introduction

Estate planning is easily defined in a dictionary sense. It is the process by which an individual plans for the acquisition, use, conservation, and disposition of his or her wealth.

As long as we are talking about wealth in simply the balance sheet sense, as merely the accumulation of items of certain monetary value having no sentimental, historic, or other added value, the concept of estate planning is relatively simple. But when we add the element of human nature, the problems begin to crop up. We realize that wealth consists of every imaginable type of asset, acquired from unbounded sources, with no telling what emotional baggage. And it is here that the term estate planning becomes much more difficult to define with any reasonable degree of precision.

It is, for example, one thing to suggest to the owner of a nonproductive farm that he sell the farm and convert the proceeds into corporate stocks, which will bring in a handsome dividend income and will be more easily divided up after his death than the farm. But it is quite another thing to make this suggestion to a widower for whom the farm represents memories of his happy life with his late wife, who helped him pay for the farm by scrimping and saving throughout difficult economic times. Converting the farm into stocks becomes even more difficult because the widower may well recall the "difficult economic times" in which he and his wife paid for the farm as the "best years of their lives."

An estate, then, is something more than mere assets of certain monetary value. And estate planning involves infinitely more than merely shuffling assets back and forth across a balance sheet in the quest for some sort of minimal death tax burden. This fact is the source of both much of the difficulty and, to a large extent, much of the satisfaction in the field of estate planning.

This book is an attempt to look at estate planning from the human perspective—as the owners of estates look at their assets and the management and disposition of them. The traditional estate planning concerns with taxes, ownership forms, wills, trusts, and the like will be considered; indeed, much of the book will be inevitably concerned with these matters. But always we will be viewing the accumulation, ownership, management, and disposition of an estate with an eye first on the *human* elements.

Problems of human relationships, the difficulties that attend the ownership of certain kinds of assets, and the ever-present necessity of dealing with the inevitability of death are no less the concerns of the estate planner than the burdens of income, estate, and gift taxation and the complexities of wills and trusts.

Good estate planners have always understood this. And the tax and other specialized planning that these planners do is merely a means of helping the estate owners accomplish their other (and usually vastly more important) goals. And so they use their specialized knowledge to help achieve the human ends of their clients, not the other way around. This will be the approach of this book.

Estate Planning Is Not a Dead Issue

In this life nothing can be said to be certain,
excepting death and taxes.

Benjamin Franklin

If you ask the average person what estate planning is all about, the answer will probably be something like this: "Estate planning is the process of planning how to dispose of your property when you die so that little or no death taxes will be paid." Of course, estate planning is concerned with precisely this issue. But estate planning is not concerned entirely with this topic, nor is it concerned primarily with it. Tax savings is only one of many concerns of the estate planner. Indeed, for all our concern with tax savings, estate planning would be necessary even if all the tax laws were repealed tomorrow. (Tax lawyers shudder at this possibility, however exceedingly remote and fanciful. But it remains an accurate statement.)

Moreover, estate planning is not merely concerned with planning for death and the disposition of assets or savings of monies at that time. Estate planning has a significant lifetime purpose. This is probably as good a point as any to begin.

OBJECTIVES OF ESTATE PLANNING

A good estate plan can be broken down into two major divisions: (1) lifetime objectives and (2) death objectives.

Lifetime Objectives

Replacement income. Most people tend to view estate planning solely as having to do with death and what happens to one's property on death; however, a sound estate plan can provide significant advantages during one's lifetime.

For example, since one major reason individuals work is to provide a decent standard of living for the family, an important lifetime goal of estate planning should be to assure the continuance of a decent standard of living for the family if the income earner is disabled or decides to retire.

The sudden disabling of the income earner is usually an unforeseen event, while retirement is generally anticipated. But unless adequate estate planning has taken place in anticipation of either occurrence, the normal patterns of family life may be substantially altered and many future plans may be frustrated. Social Security and other governmental programs may provide some relief, but a satisfactory solution to the problems brought about by a sudden and drastic lowering of the family income can only come about if careful planning has taken place. Failure to provide such planning may mean that important family objectives will not be accomplished.

Avoidance of income and gift taxes. At the other extreme, when a family has significant wealth and is not worried about the loss of income from a job but is concerned about its tax burden, substantial lifetime tax savings may result from careful estate planning. (These tax savings usually result from the use of devices which are often known by the unflattering term loopholes. One person's loophole is, however, another person's tax shelter. It depends on whose bank account is being raided.) The nonpayment of taxes that are legally due is, of course, tax evasion and is a crime. But there is nothing at all improper (legally or morally) about tax avoidance through the utilization of any of a number of legitimate means provided by the Congress. (It may be helpful to remember that the basic difference between tax evasion and tax avoidance is about ten years).

Improving the investment package. The necessity of listing all of one's assets in an effort to look at the estate and income tax saving possibilities will often afford the estate owner the first overview of his or her estate in many a year. It may also point out glaring inconsistencies in ownership patterns or suggest that there are certain types of assets that are now inappropriate, or at least less appropriate than in former times. The owner may then wish to dispose of these assets.

As we shall see later in greater detail, this is when the financial planner should be called into the estate planning process. For every family farm with enormous emotional baggage, there is likely to be a block of stock or some other relatively fungible asset that can be disposed of without any negative emotions on the part of the owner. Whether to sell such assets and what to replace them with is precisely the role of the financial planner.

Peace of mind. Finally, there is the sense of peace that comes from having put one's estate in good order for the protection of loved ones that is a natural and desirable objective of the estate planning process. Accepting the inevitability of death and planning for the most efficient way to leave one's assets to prevent family fights, reduce taxes, and otherwise protect loved ones is a very important estate planning goal.

Death Objectives

Reduction of death taxes. The reduction or avoidance of death taxes has long been a principal reason most people have engaged in estate planning. Indeed, avoiding death taxes remains a major estate planning objective. Just as avoidance of the income tax leaves more money for the taxpayer's enjoyment, so the avoidance of death taxes leaves a larger estate to satisfy the needs of the decedent's family.

A good portion of this book will be devoted to tax savings. This is, after all, the benefit of estate planning that is most visible to the public. But it is important to emphasize that tax saving is only one aspect of estate planning. Moreover, tax saving should always remain secondary to the carrying out of the underlying objectives of the estate owner. An estate plan that conflicts with what the owner really wants to do with his her estate is a poor plan, no matter how much is saved in taxes!

If, however, your goal in estate planning is solely to save taxes, here is a shortcut that will make it unnecessary to read the remainder of this book or engage in any further planning: give all your money to me. The money should be sent by certified check, via the publisher, whose address is in the front of this book. I will, in turn, arrange to pay any gift taxes assessed. Thereafter, there will be absolutely no tax consequences to you, either during your lifetime as a result of the income tax, or on your death, because of death taxes.

"But," you say, "I don't want to give all my money to a stranger. I'd rather keep it and pay some taxes." Good. That graphically illustrates an important lesson: some things are *worse* than paying taxes. An estate plan that does not conform to the way the estate owner wants to leave his or her assets is a poor plan, no matter how much is saved in taxes.

We will be back to this maxim repeatedly, even as we continue to inquire into ways to reduce taxes. This is not an inconsistent approach; it is merely to recognize that the "tax tail" should not wag the estate planning "dog." We will repeatedly look at ways to accomplish the goals of the estate owner. Having done that, we will then inquire into ways to reduce his or her tax burden in a manner consistent with accomplishing the other goals.

It is a curious thing that our obsession with saving taxes has blinded us to the more important aspects of estate planning and caused a serious misplacing of emphasis. But it is true. Think about it for a moment. When you have finished your work on earth and wish to provide financial protection for your loved ones after your death and avoid potential family squabbles over your assets, the most important matters facing you ought to be

(1) the drafting of legal instruments that will carefully set forth what you want to
     have happen with your assets and that give your executor the power to carry out
     your wishes,

(2) the selection of an executor who is properly suited to the task, and

(3) when there are minor children, the selection of proper guardians who have the
     necessary authority to act in the best interests of your children.

However, in our concern over saving taxes, we often ignore such matters as
these, throwing together an estate plan that concentrates on taxes to the exclusion of
these infinitely more important human matters. It is a shame that the relatively minor
business of saving taxes should spoil the much more serious aspects of the estate planning process.

Ensuring that beneficiaries receive their intended share of the estate. I n
terms of human affairs, this is probably the most important aspect of estate planning.
It is also perhaps the simplest. For reasons that are deeply embedded in our psyche,
our property becomes, in a very real sense, a part of our personalities. Assuring that
this property goes to those whom we wish to have it on our death is vitally important
to most people. (Even those who insist, "Once I'm gone, I don't care what happens to
my assets," usually don't mean this with respect to every asset they own. Talk is, after
all, a very cheap commodity.)

The failure to do any estate planning is almost a guarantee that, with notable exceptions, the assets in our estates will not go where we wish them to go. For example,
and greatly simplified, if you die without a will or other document disposing of assets
on death, the state legislature of the state where you were a permanent resident has
written a "will" for just such a circumstance. This "will" is found in the statutes of descent and distribution, a section of the laws that provides what is to happen to an estate when the owner dies without having made any provision for it.

While the statutes of descent and distribution are a legislative attempt to do with
one's estate what the average person would have done had he or she written a will,
the simple fact is that the average person doesn't exist. Real people almost always
have certain assets that require special care or attention (grandfather's portrait or an
involved interest in underwater real estate in Florida, for example). Relatives or loved
ones are almost always of unequal need. For example, one daughter might become a
well-paid corporate vice-president while the other is married quite young to a man
who will never have a steady income. And no matter what state you reside in at your
death, the statutes of descent and distribution do not provide for gifts to charity; so if
you wish to leave a bequest to your church or university or some other charitable organization, it can only be done through a will or other testamentary document. Intestacy is, then, a last-ditch estate plan on which no careful person should rely.

Satisfying this need of seeing that beneficiaries get what is intended for them is
the purpose of the much-maligned probate system. Where there has been no estate
planning, the probate system will rely on the statutes of descent and distribution to

pass your assets to whom the law says should have them. (As we have suggested, these persons may not be the precise persons whom you would prefer to have your assets.) When there has been estate planning, your will or other testamentary documents will determine where the assets go. But the overseeing of the actual passage of the assets to the proper persons is done, in either event, under the supervision of the probate system.

The book, *How To Avoid Probate**, made the best-seller list a number of years ago by purporting to show how to avoid the probate system, which was characterized as unduly slow and expensive. *How To Avoid Probate*, which is rabidly antilawyer (it doesn't matter; we lawyers don't like the author any more than he likes us) is now out in a revised edition, but the fundamental message remains: transfer all your assets to a revocable living trust and avoid probate.

No one who knows anything about the settlement of estates would deny that the American probate system has its serious defects and there is much to be said, in many instances, for avoiding probate. But anyone who has any reason to suspect that his or her wishes with respect to the disposition of property may be thwarted should make every use of the protections afforded by the system. Avoiding probate only makes sense if you are certain your estate will not need the protections of the system. On the other hand, if you do choose to avoid probate, or at least reduce your estate's reliance on the probate system, it can only be done (as *How To Avoid Probate* points out) by proper estate planning. It is possible (indeed, in many cases, preferable) to utilize the probate system to assure that certain assets go to those of your choosing and to avoid the system where such protection is not required. But, again, this can only be done with proper estate planning.

Avoiding family disputes.   It is not unheard of for a family to live peacefully or at least under conditions of an unarmed truce while the dominant parent or other wealthy family member is alive, only to erupt into open warfare when he or she dies. Very often the intensity of the hostilities is fueled by the memory of hurts brooded over for years or arguments of long standing. Family feuds can simmer for generations from greed over the possibility of inheriting money (or of not inheriting enough), jealousy over other family members inheriting assets that in normal times and under normal conditions would not be of interest to anyone, and unwillingness to accept the inevitable change of relationships among survivors once the dominant family member is gone.

If the seeds of such a situation exist, careful estate planning can help avoid or at least reduce this possibility. *Every* family should be examined for this potential problem; families that erupt into warfare when the spoils are divided cut across race, class, religion, ethnic, and all other known classifications. Without estate planning, such families would be well advised to begin arming early, because warfare will surely follow.

* Norman R. Dacey, *How to Avoid Probate,* (New York, N.Y.: Crown Publishers, 1965.)

Support for survivors in time of stress. When a loved one dies, especially when the death is sudden and unexpected, can be the worst time to make important decisions with respect to taxes, investments, and the disposition of the personal assets of the deceased. With proper estate planning, these difficult and potentially troublesome decisions can already have been made. Moreover, a set of advisers of the deceased's choosing, who are already familiar with the estate and any potential problems, can be in place, ready to help the survivors just as they helped the deceased before death. The emotional support that well-chosen estate planners can provide in these situations is perhaps one of the more important nontax reasons to engage in estate planning.

Increasing the size of the estate for survivors. The size of the estate that a decedent leaves to his or her loved ones can be substantially reduced in two ways: (1) by the expense of making the transfer to the loved ones or the loss to the estate through delay or lack of orderly planning for the transition, and (2) by the federal estate tax and state inheritance or estate taxes.

Transferring property almost always costs some money. There are deeds to be prepared and recorded, title documents have to be properly registered, and the assets often have to be located, inventoried, and prepared for transfer. When the estate is large, these costs can be substantial, even when proper estate planning has been done. But when the estate is unplanned, the problems are multiplied. For example, when care has not been taken to assure that the estate is liquid enough to meet the death tax burdens, forced sale of certain assets may be necessary to raise the money to pay the taxes. And forced sales almost never result in full value for estate assets. (A good rule for figuring the return on forced sales of tangible assets is to estimate what the assets will bring if they are sold by an auctioneer off the back porch on a rainy Saturday afternoon.) Likewise, an estate that contains assets for which there is not a strong market (such as assets in a closely held business) is particularly vulnerable to loss in transfer when the possibility of transfer has not been adequately planned in advance. Careful estate planning can help avoid these problems.

Moreover, estate planning can greatly facilitate the administration of an estate. A will or other testamentary document that confers the necessary powers on the executor or trustee can avoid costly disputes over authority and can assure that a person of the decedent's choosing is ready and able to work for the best interests of the decedent's estate. Finally, by way of repetition, an estate that has been carefully planned will usually pay reduced death taxes.

Estate planning differs from estate to estate. The goals, problems, and techniques of estate planning will vary from estate to estate, depending on such factors as the following:

Size of the estate
Nature of the assets in the estate

Family situation of the estate owner

Age, sex, and health of the estate owner

Where the estate owner resides

Personal interests of the estate owner

For example, an elderly widow with a moderate estate whose children are grown and self-supporting and who is deeply involved in the work of her church will want to do different things with her estate than the married, middle-aged family man who owns a valuable closely held business and is a rabid fan of his university's football team.

The widow will probably want to leave a simple will with perhaps a bequest to her church and outright gifts of the remainder to her children. She will not likely have any concern about death taxes or estate liquidity.

The businessman, on the other hand, will require a trust to assure that his wife and children are protected in the event of his untimely death. And, given his relatively moderate age, he may want to plan for his retirement and the possibility of disability. There may even be significant income tax savings that he can secure through proper estate planning. His estate plan should pay special attention to the operation or disposal of his business in the event of his death or disability, and he must assure that his estate is liquid enough to pay death taxes and the other expenses of settlement of his estate without having to make a forced sale of the business, particularly if he resides in a state with relatively high death tax rates. When all this has been provided for, he may wish to leave a bequest to his university's athletic program, which can perhaps be funded through a life insurance policy that will not deprive his family of any assets he now owns.

The point is that estate planning is an intensely personal business. No two clients have the same needs or interests. Even where two persons do appear to be quite similar in their needs and interests, the simple passage of time can change everything. Some children do better than others and may necessitate a change in the parents' dispositive plans. An unforeseen sequence of deaths can cause a profound alteration in the needs within a family. Children and grandchildren are born and die, businesses prosper and fail, charitable interests come and go. As with so much else in life, "the only thing that remains constant is change."

THE PROFESSIONAL ESTATE PLANNING TEAM

Estate planning, in its modern sense, is a team operation, involving the coordination of efforts of at least seven different professionals, as well as the persons whose property and family are in question. While each of the seven professionals has different duties and responsibilities, each can bring unique knowledge and skills to the estate planning process.

State licensing laws provide that certain aspects of estate planning may only be engaged in by a licensed practitioner in a specific field. For example, if the estate planning process requires the drafting of a will or a trust agreement, this may only be done by a licensed lawyer. If liquidity of the estate is a problem and life insurance is seen as the answer, it may only be sold by a life insurance underwriter. If financial statements are required, they may only be prepared by an accountant.

Despite the fact that this legal requirement of specialization prevents each profession from practicing all aspects of estate planning, each member of the estate planning team should be as knowledgeable as possible about the entire subject. Just because lawyers alone can draft wills and trusts does not mean that knowledgeable life insurance underwriters, accountants, bank trust officers, financial planners, and others should not be familiar with these documents. Indeed, to the careful lawyer, the knowledge the other professionals can bring to a review of the lawyer-drafted documents can be a valuable safeguard.

The Lawyer

Because estate planning is, to a large extent, a legal transaction that requires the special knowledge and skill of a lawyer, the lawyer should be the captain of the estate planning team. The lawyer will do the legal and tax research and draft the necessary legal instruments, interpreting the law and applying it to the client's specific personal, legal, and financial situation. In doing this, however, the lawyer must utilize not only his or her own research efforts, but must collate the information and suggestions provided by other members of the team and synthesize everything into a cohesive plan that will meet the client's needs and objectives.

The Accountant

As the tax laws have become more complex, accountants have become increasingly expert in the field of taxes. (Indeed, a competent tax accountant will be as knowledgeable about tax law as a tax lawyer.) Moreover, accountants customarily are involved in the process of making prognostications about future tax trends and their impact on the values and earning power of assets. This ability to bring together a knowledge of today's taxes, possible future tax trends, and other factors affecting an estate owner's assets is invaluable to the estate planning process. Because of this, an accountant can provide invaluable in-depth expertise with respect to the potential tax problems and possible tax saving possibilities that exist for the estate planning client.

Finally, accountants are quite frequently the persons most familiar with the estate owner's financial affairs and, thus, are frequently in the best position to advise the estate owner on the need to do estate planning or to update existing estate plans. They will often know what assets are available and what various objectives or alternatives will cost. If the estate owner is a business person, the accountant will also be in a unique position to point out the business problems that may arise on the owner's death.

The Life Insurance Underwriter

Life insurance is usually an integral part of an estate plan. Life insurance is essential in an estate when the assets are inadequate to support the decedent's family, as well as when the estate is not liquid enough to pay taxes and other costs that occur at death. Moreover, life insurance is often used for business-related purposes, such as funding buy--sell agreements and providing for retirement. The life insurance underwriter, then, can measure the estate owner's need for life insurance, determine the amount and type of insurance best suited to the owner's needs, and sell the proper insurance. He or she will also be in the best position to evaluate and recommend settlement options and provisions for annuities or other forms of life income, as well as to suggest uses of life insurance that may not have occurred to other members of the estate planning team.

A life insurance underwriter ought to be much more than merely a salesperson. Anyone can sell life insurance. (Well, *almost* anyone.) But the life insurance underwriter who is part of the estate planning team must also be skilled in estate analysis, knowledgeable of tax law, familiar with accounting procedures, and thoroughly acquainted with the multitudinous forms of life insurance now available, as well as new forms of insurance that are now appearing on the horizon. One indication that a life insurance underwriter is knowledgeable in these various areas is the designation "Chartered Life Underwriter," which is given only after the underwriter has completed an extensive and academically rigorous course of instruction. A life insurance underwriter who carries the designation CLU behind his or her name is not guaranteed to be competent, but the designation is not without its significance.

Life insurance underwriters also play an important role in the estate planning process because they are primarily salespersons. Lawyers, accountants, bank trust officers, and the like are either prohibited from soliciting business or have a strong professional bias against such activity. But the life insurance underwriter is expected to be a salesperson and to aggressively pursue the sale of life insurance. Since life insurance is an important element in almost every sound estate plan, the life insurance underwriter is frequently the person who first locates the estate planning client. As a part of the sales process, the life insurance underwriter will often lead the client into the charting or analyzing of estate planning needs. Since life insurance seldom exists in a vacuum (any more than a will or trust should exist apart from a sound life insurance program), the sale of life insurance often begins the entire process of estate planning.

The Bank Trust Officer

The bank trust officer's experience in administering estates and trusts is of great value in the estate planning process. Moreover, since bank trust departments will handle the investments for large estates, the trust officer, or someone who works for the trust officer, will likely be knowledgeable about investments and how they fit into an estate plan.

As with the other professionals on the estate planning team, the trust officer will of necessity be familiar with the nature and objectives of a will and trust, the consequences of estate, gift, and income taxes, and the evaluation of an estate owner's financial affairs.

American banking is undergoing a revolution today. The staid, columned, hush-hush institution of yesterday is giving way to aggressive, hard-sell organizations that are actively seeking clients for their services. As with the life insurance underwriter, the bank trust officer can often be the finder of estate planning clients.

The Stockbroker

Increasingly, stockbrokers are becoming involved in the estate planning process because of their knowledge of investments. The estate owner who is concerned about the ravages of inflation or the possibility of economic depression (and this should include all estate owners) will call increasingly on the services of the stockbroker, whose business it is to know about investments that can help avoid economic losses caused by such factors as fluctuations in interest rates, inflation, and depressions. The stockbroker is primarily a salesperson who makes his or her living from commissions on sales. But truly professional brokers recognize that long-term awards can be gained by foregoing the temptation to suggest unnecessary trades and concentrating on investment suggestions that will be best for the long run. The stockbroker can be of enormous help to the estate owner by continuing to monitor the assets in the estate and suggesting changes in the makeup of the estate as the economic climate changes.

The Financial Planner

The financial planner is a relatively recent addition to the estate planning team, if only because financial planning as a distinct profession is a fairly recent development. The financial planner brings together knowledge of the various disciplines of life insurance, investments, taxes, and law and attempts to apply an overview to the client's situation. Increasingly, bank trust officers, life insurance underwriters, stockbrokers, and mutual fund salespersons are obtaining additional schooling and earning the designation Certified Financial Planner or Chartered Financial Consultant, which reflects their increased knowledge of personal financial affairs. A financial planner may well replace one or more of the members of the estate planning team or may serve as an additional member. The important thing is to understand that the financial planner can bring a unique and invaluable overview approach to the estate planning process.

The Physician

While not a member of the estate planning team in the sense that the other members serve the client's needs, the physician can be important when there are questions with respect to the present mental capacity of the estate owner or when the estate owner wishes to build into his or her estate plan a fail-safe mechanism in the event of future mental or physical incapacity. We will inquire into this in greater detail later when we discuss the techniques of avoiding the consequences of one's future incapacity.

Others

The preceding list is by no means exclusive. Given the unique nature of a client's estate or personal or family situation, others may well play an important role. An estate owner who is deeply involved in a specialized business such as oil drilling may require the advice of an expert in the oil business to adequately plan the estate, whose family is scattered throughout the world may require the services of an international lawyer, and so on. But whatever the combination of professionals required, the team concept is absolutely essential to effective estate planning today. No one person and no one discipline can possibly be aware of all the problems and opportunities that are present in an estate.

An interesting reaction to this fact is the fairly recent phenomenon of estate planning councils that have begun to appear throughout the United States over the past 15 years or so. These organizations offer the opportunity for the various disciplines involved in the estate planning process to gather together in a social forum for study and discussion.

APPLYING THIS CHAPTER TO *YOUR* SITUATION

Proper estate planning requires, as we have seen, careful attention to the specific needs of the individual client. For each client, then, you need to determine precisely what comprises the estate; what are the personal lifetime goals and needs of the client; what are the needs and goals of the client's family, both before and after the client's death; what will be the tax consequences of different courses of action; and what, if any, unique personal problems exist within the client's family that should be addressed in the estate plan.

Armed with this information, you then call on the services of others on the estate planning team and, together with the client, build an "estate plan".

CASE PROBLEMS

1.1 Evaluating the Greens' Estate. John and Mary Green have been married for 17 years. John is a chemist with a drug manufacturing concern that has major offices in 12 states. Mary is a buyer for a local department store. Their combined annual income is in the high 70s and they have accumulated assets (including the equity in their home) in excess of $125,000. They have three children, John, Jr., 13, Marie, 11, and Donna, 5. Marie suffers from Downs syndrome. The couple's combined bonus for the past year came to over $12,000 and they are wondering how they should use this money, along with their others assets, to help secure a better future. John has approached a life insurance underwriter friend of his about purchasing life insurance. The Greens have never done any formal estate planning except to have a simple will drafted shortly after their marriage when they lived in another state.

Questions
1. What questions will have to be answered before you can advise the Greens about their estate plan?
2. What problems do you see in the Greens' situation that should be addressed in an estate plan, regardless of what the Greens decide to do?
3. What disciplines would you bring into the planning of the Greens' estate?

1.2 Helping the Widow. Nancy Everett is a 78-year-old widow with two grown children, a daughter, 54, who teaches school and is married to a postal worker, and a son, 50, who is a master sergeant in the United States Army. The son's wife is employed as a secretary for the Army. Ms. Everett has a pension of $400 a month from her husband's former employer and Social Security income of $320 per month. Both will cease on her death. She has savings of $42,000 and owns her home, which is valued at $38,000. Since her daughter has looked after her since her husband's death she wants the bulk of her estate to go to her, but she wants to do so in a way that will not offend her son or cause trouble between her son and daughter.

Questions
1. What additional information do you need to advise Ms. Everett about her estate plan?
2. How would you advise Ms. Everett to handle the passage of her estate to her daughter without causing hard feelings on the part of the son?
3. What problems that were present in the Greens' estate plan are absent in Ms. Everett's estate plan?
4. What disciplines would you bring into the planning of Ms. Everett's estate and what disciplines would be unnecessary?

SELECTED READINGS

CRUMBLEY, D. LARRY, and MILAM, EDWARD E., "Personalizing the Estate Planning Process," 116 *Trusts and Estates* 8, 1977.

FARR, JAMES F., and JACKSON, W. WRIGHT, JR., *An Estate Planner's Handbook.* Boston: Little, Brown and Company, 1979, pp. 1-11.

LUTON, JAMES P., "Accountants Can Play Key Role in Initiating and 'Selling' Estate Planning to Clients," 5 *Estate Planning* 40, 1978.

STRENG, WILLIAM P., *Estate Planning.* Washington: Bureau of National Affairs, Inc., 1981, pp. 3-29.

TWEED, HARRISON, and PARSONS, WILLIAM, *Lifetime and Testamentary Estate Planning.* Philadelphia: American Law Institute-Professional Education, 1983, pp. 1-3.

2

Nonestate
Planning

There are some others that account wife and
children but as bills of charges.

Francis Bacon
Of Marriage and Single Life

Almost the entire literature on estate planning deals with clients who have sufficient assets to worry about taxes or other problems in the disposition of their estates. The texts are full of discussions of the marital deduction, generation-skipping trusts, powers of appointment, and the like, all devices designed to assist clients with sizable estates either to avoid taxes or to deal with other problems in passing on their assets at the time of their death.

But there is a whole class of clients for whom these devices and their discussioins are meaningless, but whose concerns with their estates and the families they wish to protect are just as real. These are the owners of what we will call the nonestates, those whose fortunes are made up, in one writer's words, "principally of children and debts" (Shaffer, 1979, p. 191).

In raw numbers, the members of this class make up perhaps the largest potential group of estate planning clients (a fact that is not as inconsistent as it appears at first glance). For the estate planner, this group offers an opportunity to "get in on the ground floor" with a client who is not yet wealthy. By performing valuable service at this stage in the client's life, the planner may well maintain the client's loyalty and business as the client climbs up the socioeconomic ladder. (For every wealthy estate planning client who walks through the practitioner's door, there are three or four potentially wealthy estate planning clients who originally came through the door as the owners of nonestates. Not everyone is born a Rockefeller.)

But what can be done for these people? If you have a wife and young children and own little or no estate, how can the family be protected in the event of your untimely death? What legal devices, if any, ought to be employed? How can you get blood out of a turnip?

Let's assume we are asked to help plan the "estate" of Roger Everyman, a 30-year-old appliance salesman with a 28-year-old wife named Rhonda and two children, a girl, 1, and a boy, 3. Roger has had two years of college and would like to finish his college education some day. His wife, likewise, has had two years of college, but possesses no marketable skills. She stays home and cares for their children. Roger earns $18,000 a year and he and Rhonda spend all of it (on, as you might suspect, not particularly riotous living). They "own" their home (in the sense that possessing an equity of $8,000 in a $50,000 home can be called owning the home), a 3-year-old Plymouth that was recently paid for, and their household furnishings (the house is done in "early conglomeration") valued at perhaps $1,000 if it doesn't rain on the day of their sale, and have a savings account the balance of which varies from a high of $450 to a low of $0. Roger as $10,000 of whole life insurance on his life. His wife and children are uninsured.

WHAT ESTATE PLANNING DOES THE OWNER
OF A NONESTATE NEED?

The Will

As we will see later in a different context, Roger and his kind will most likely need a will, because the operation of the intestate laws will almost certainly give a substantial share of his estate to his minor children, to the exclusion of his wife, who is going to need all the assets she can find if Roger should die unexpectedly. At least this is one of the rationalizations we can give Roger for drafting a will. In truth, since Roger and Rhonda no doubt own their home in joint tenancy (which means that it will automatically pass to Rhonda on Roger's death) and since they have so little else, the specter of their children owning an intestate share of Roger's estate on his untimely death is not especially frightening. Still, a will would leave Roger's pitiful estate to Rhonda in somewhat "cleaner" fashion than the laws of descent and distribution.

Roger and Rhonda may argue (probably because an uninformed adviser has told them so) that they do not need a will because they own everything jointly. Indeed, if they live in a community property state of if they own most of their major assets in joint tenancy with right of survivorship, they will not need a will to pass these jointly owned assets on to the surviving spouse. But depending on joint ownership as a will avoidance technique has two severe limitations. First, it is highly unlikely that *all* of their respective estates will be owned in joint tenancy. And these separately owned assets will pass by intestacy. Second, joint ownership only works to avoid the necessity of a will for the first spouse to die. If Roger should die and Rhonda should follow him within a short time, the joint ownership that Rhonda had enjoyed with Roger will be meaningless, since Rhonda will have owned these assets entirely in her own name at the time of her death. So joint ownership is not a practical substitute for a will as an estate planning device.

Roger and Rhonda also need a will as a means of designating the person who is to settle their estates and take care of their two children in the event of Roger and Rhonda's untimely death. And they will be keenly (and somewhat painfully) aware of this need. Indeed, it is likely this very question that has led the couple to seek estate planning advice in the first place.

If Roger and Rhonda should die without a will while their children are young, the authorities would appoint a guardian for the children anyway and they would name someone to settle Roger and Rhonda's estates. In the great bulk of cases, the person(s) named as guardian of the children and administrator of the parents' estates will likely be the same person(s) that Roger and Rhonda would have named in their wills.

So, unless Roger and Rhonda wish to assure that an otherwise likely candidate for the guardianship of their children and the management of their estates (a wayward sister or black sheep brother, for example) is *not* appointed guardian, the need for a guardian or administrator does not exactly necessitate the drafting of a will. However, by naming a guardian for the children or executor of the estates in their wills, Roger and Rhonda can direct that the surety bond for these persons be waived. Since the cost of the bond will be born by the estate, the waiving of this bond is a savings to the estate, which leaves a little bit more to pass on to the beneficiaries. Waiving the bond does not necessarily place the children or the estate in any jeopardy since the person selected as guardian or executor will obviously be someone Roger and Rhonda trust. Waiving the bond merely avoids eating into the assets of an already meager estate.

In a psychological sense, however, the drafting of a will to designate a guardian for their children is particularly important, not because the will is so necessary to the designation of the guardian, but because the necessity of formally selecting a guardian causes Roger and Rhonda to *think* about the problem, to consider who is available to serve as guardian, and to approach the person of their choice and ask her or him to serve as guardian. (Indeed, this is the *real* reason that persons like Roger and Rhonda should have a will, not so much for what the will does for them as for what the process of drafting a will causes them to do.)

Overplanning the nonestate. The drafting of a will for Roger and Rhonda is not without its own peculiar problems. To begin, once they have cleared the hurdle of resistance to drafting a will, they will likely want to try to anticipate every possible eventuality and provide for the passage of their property under those conditions. Leaving their property to each other and their children is easy. But when they begin to consider the possibility that their children may not survive them, the problems mount. Roger and Rhonda need a will that will pass their property to each other and, in the event that both are dead, to their children. They may wish to provide for the passage of their assets to their parents or others in the event that they and their children die. But they should be encouraged not to try to provide for every possible sequence of deaths. (As I write this I recognize that I am spitting into a wind of considerable velocity. The bare possibility, however remote, that "my husband's sister" or "my wife's nephew" may someday end up with all or part of a small estate can lead to some of the most convoluted drafting since the Treaty of Versailles.)

Inappropriate dynastic planning. Then there is the nearly universal problem in our society (particularly on the part of males) to tend to think in *dynastic* terms. At the extreme, the dynastic planner wants to assure that his children, and his children's children, and his children's childrens' children, ad infinitum, keep the family property intact and use it as the original owner decreed. And he wants this for reasons that are intensely psychological.

Something in the American psyche—it may have been the national experience of "opening the West" or "conquering a continent"—has caused most American property owners (even the owners of precious little property, such as Roger Everyman) to think of themselves as the progenitors of a great body of descendants. And these modern-day Abrahams, with their descendants destined to be as numerous as the stars in the sky, see their property as a chance to speak to their succeeding generations of descendants. This need is inexorably intertwined with the quest for immortality, which affects us all to some extent, and it may be in part a necessary offsetting of the recognition of mortality that must accompany the decision to draft a will.

Whatever the reasons, the problem is very real. So we face the client with few assets, who has accepted the fact that he or she is going to die someday and who wants to use a will to buy a piece of immortality. And he or she proposes to do this by tying up property for generations of descendants.

Usually it is not quite this plain, but the problem is a persistent one. In addition to the difficulties raised by the Rule Against Perpetuities (about which more later), there is the simple fact that the nature of property changes over time. An estate that cannot be readily altered or disposed of by its owners as conditions change is doomed to face substantial losses. If the estate planner does not talk the client out of tying up his or her property with dynastic planning, no one else will. Roger and Rhonda's property should, then, with few exceptions, be passed cleanly, that is, outright, to whomever it is going (unless a simple trust is provided for the children. If, for example, it is left to their parents, they should be permitted to do what they wish with it. There is too little property here to bother the beneficiaries with any legal ties that prevent their using it as they see fit.

Designing a will for the future. Then, too, there is the problem that once Roger and Rhonda write their wills they are unlikely to return to their estate planners and update the instrument as changed conditions dictate. So their wills must be drafted, insofar as this is possible, with the couple's future in mind. This, of course, can only be done in a broad, general sense.

Their wills, for example, should contain language that will include in the distribution of their estates children born or adopted after the execution of the wills to the same extent as those children already in existence when the wills were executed.

Or, if Roger and Rhonda insist, they may wish to exclude these after-born and after-adopted children from sharing in the estate. What is important is that the issue be addressed. If it is not, any children born (and, in some states, adopted) after the wills were executed will take a share anyway (Kentucky Revised, Statutes Sec. 394.382[1]).

If there are reasons that certain children need special care, this should be provided, perhaps by a simple unfunded life insurance trust (which we will discuss in detail later). Alternate executors and guardians should be provided for to cover the eventuality that the first choices die or are otherwise unable to serve. If Roger and Rhonda's parents have been selected as guardians or executors, some thought should be given to the possibility of the parents' incapacity due to advancing age, and the couple should seriously address the question of whether they want their parents to be guardians or executors after a certain age. (A grandmother aged 55 may be the perfect guardian for a compliant tyke of 2 whom the grandmother cares for on occasion now. But the parents must consider whether it is fair to the child or the grandmother for her to be guardian of the child at the rebellious age of 17 when the grandmother is 70.)

If Roger dies now, his estate will clearly not have any tax problems. But if he lives to the time when the actuaries say is likely, he may die with an estate that will require tax planning. Indeed, the possibility is that if Roger does well he will likely have tax problems long before he decides to seek professional help in redesigning his estate plan. So the wills drafted for Roger and Rhonda should attempt to solve what tax problems they can. Under the present law, for example, any assets left to the surviving spouse are exempt from the federal estate tax by reason of the marital deduction (Internal Revenue Code, Sec. 2056). So, unless there are compelling reasons not to leave the bulk of the estate to one another, Roger and Rhonda should be advised to do so because such a transfer will be free from the federal estate tax on the death of the first spouse, no matter how large an estate is left.

Some states specifically exempt life insurance left to a named beneficiary from state death taxation (Revised Statutes of Nebraska, Sec. 77-2004). If Roger and Rhonda reside in such a state, they should be advised to name one another or their children as beneficiaries of their life insurance policies, and not to leave the proceeds of the policies to their estates. (An estate is not a "named beneficiary" and policy proceeds left to the estate would be subject to death taxes.)

Roger and Rhonda should be warned of the necessity to coordinate future estate planning activities (such as the purchase of life insurance or the change of designation of beneficiaries in life insurance) with the plan designed in the will. And they must be made aware of the advisability of reviewing all their estate planning documents on the happening of certain events and, in any case, after the passage of years.

If Roger and Rhonda's is a second marriage and there are children from previous marriages, special care should be taken with respect to the protection of the children of the deceased spouse. Can Roger be certain Rhonda will care for his children after his death, and can Rhonda be equally certain of Roger's concern for her children after her death? This is a touchy subject to bring up in a will conference, but it needs to be addressed and dealt with in the will and other estate planning instruments.

Life Insurance

Roger's most profound need is for a larger estate to protect his family in the event of his untimely death. If Rhonda is to be expected to support the family in anything other than a poverty level position after Roger's death, she will have to develop a marketable skill. Depending on the nature of her first two years in college, she will need two or more years of schooling to get a degree. The family's financial needs on Roger's death, then, will include the cost of Rhonda's education. And this is only the beginning.

The possibility of inheritance aside, Roger's only chance of leaving an adequate estate for his family in the event of his untimely death is life insurance. We will discuss this topic and how to determine precise life insurance needs in Chapter 13. Suffice it to say for the present that Roger needs life insurance, that he needs to begin a balanced, well-thought-out program, and that he needs to do it now! If the estate planner whom Roger and Rhonda has sought out does not sell life insurance, it is the planner's duty to advise the couple in general terms of their needs and to assist them in finding a qualified life insurance underwriter who can help them fulfill these needs in a professional manner.

APPLYING THIS CHAPTER TO *YOUR* SITUATION

While estate planning is traditionally concerned with the needs of clients who have considerable assets and who wish to avoid death taxes, persons with few assets also have needs that require the assistance of estate planners. The estate planner can provide invaluable assistance to persons of limited means by assisting them in avoiding unnecessary costs at death and in the handling of their estates thereafter, and by helping them come to grips with some vital personal decisions that should be made in contemplation of their premature deaths.

While a small estate will likely require much less complicated planning and the use of simpler instruments, a will and life insurance probably represent the minimum in planning documents. As we will see later, a simple life insurance trust may also be a valuable estate planning tool for the client with a small estate.

CASE PROBLEMS

2.1 Assisting the Everyman Family in Estate Planning. Assume the same factual situation set forth in the text for Roger and Rhonda Everyman.

Questions
1. What additional information do you need to advise the Everymans and what disciplines would you call on to assist them?

2. If the Everymans own their house, car, furniture, and bank account jointly with right of survivorship, and if they have an agreement with Rhonda's sister and her husband that they will take the Everyman's children if Roger and Rhonda die, why should they go to the trouble and expense of drafting a will?

3. What special provisions would you make in Roger and Rhonda's wills and in their insurance planning to protect them in the event that they make no changes in their estate plans over the next 20 years?

4. As the estate planner that Roger and Rhonda used to draft their wills or provide their insurance coverage, what should you do if you learned from a newspaper article that they had won $1,000,000 in the Pennsylvania lottery?

2.2 Helping the Lamberts Plan.   Carl and Mary Lambert are a married couple in their mid-sixties. Both are retired and drawing a small pension that will end upon their deaths. They have a $55,000 home, totally paid for, $25,000 in savings and investments, two cars valued at $6,000 total, and $25,000 of whole life insurance on each of them. Their only son died six years ago; he is survived by a daughter who is 19 and lives with her mother and stepfather in modest circumstances in a neighboring town. The Lamberts live in a common law state (i.e., one that does not recognize the concept of community property).

Questions

1. What different problems does the Lambert estate raise that were not present in the Everyman estate?

2. Given the fact that the Lamberts have their home paid for and have accumulated some savings, in what ways can this estate be considered similar to the Everyman estate?

3. Do the Lamberts need a will? Why?

SELECTED READINGS

GERHART, EUGENE C., "A New Look at Estate Planning: The General Practitioner and Mr. Average," 50 *American Bar Association Journal* 1043, 1964.

MARTIN, JOHN H., "The Draftsman Views Wills for a Young Family," 54 *North Carolina Law Review* 277, 1976.

SHAFFER, THOMAS L., *The Planning and Drafting of Wills and Trusts*. Mineola, N.Y.: Foundation Press, Inc., 1979, pp. 191–197.

WEINSTOCK, HAROLD, *Planning an Estate*. Colorado Springs, Colo.: Shepard's/McGraw-Hill, 1982, pp. 39–44.

3

The Nature of Property Interests

Property has its duties as well as its rights.

Benjamin Disraeli

The process of estate planning begins with a simple question, "What is the size of the estate of the person for whom we are planning?" But if the question is simple, the answer is not. A person's estate will consist of different assets, depending on who is asking the question and for what purpose.

If the Internal Revenue Service is asking the question, it will want to know "What is the size of the *taxable* estate?" If it is the local probate court that is making the inquiry, the question will be "What is the size of the *probate* estate?" There are, you see, estates, and then there are estates.

For federal estate tax purposes, we begin with the concept of the *gross* estate, which is a listing of all the assets owned by the decedent at death. The gross estate consists of everything the decedent owned at death, plus a number of asets that he or she may have thought were disposed of before death but that the IRS includes in the estate for tax purposes. The Internal Revenue Code, in its inimitably blunt fashion, states that a decedent's gross estate includes the value at the time of death of "all property, real or personal, tangible or intangible, wherever situated."

For our purposes at this point, we can simplify the problem by saing that, for federal estate tax purposes, assets are included in the gross estate because:

1. They are owned by the decedent at the time of death, or
2. They were transferred by the decedent and either
   a. the transfer was made too close to the date of the decedent's death, or
   b. the decedent retained certain prohibited benefits or rights in the property.

What is in the estate for purposes of state death taxes may also be different from the federal estate tax estate. For example, life insurance, as we have seen, is not included in the decedent's estate under certain circumstances in some states. On the other hand, it is included in the federal gross estate unless certain steps have been taken to exclude it. In some states, then, an estate with life insurance could have one value for federal estate tax purposes and another value for state death tax purposes.

For probate purposes, only those assets that must go through the probate process are considered to be part of the probate estate. Probate, as we discussed in Chapter 1, is a court procedure designed to assure that the assets of a decedent pass on the decedent's death to those who should have them, either because the decedent has said so in her or his will or because the state law provides where they go when the decedent leaves no will.

It is possible, then, for an asset to be included in a decedent's gross estate for federal estate tax purposes and not be included in the decedent's estate for state death tax purposes or for probate purposes. Indeed, in the average estate the tax estates (federal and state) and the probate estate will usually be quite different. Primarily, this is because of the different ways property is owned.

HOW PROPERTY IS OWNED (AND HOW OWNERSHIP FORM AFFECTS THE ESTATE PLANNING PROCESS)

Sole Ownership

The simplest way to own property is to hold title in your name alone. Except in the eight community property states (about which more later), property owned in this fashion belongs to the person in whose name it stands: if it is held in your name alone, it belongs to you. Period. For both tax and probate purposes property held in sole ownership is includable in your estate.

Joint Ownership

There are three principal forms of coownership of property:

1. Tenancy in common
2. Joint tenancy and tenancy by the entirety
3. Community property

Tenancy in common. This is a form of joint ownership between two or more persons in which each person owns an undivided interest in the property. The interests need not be equal, but each co-owner (known as a *tenant in common*) has an equal right to occupy or manage the entire property. The distinguishing feature of a tenancy in common is that, on the death of one of the tenants in common, his or her interest passes according to the deceased tenant in common's will or, if there was no will, according to the state law. The interest does *not* pass to the surviving tenant(s) in common (unless the deceased coowner willed the property to them or the interest passed to them by state law). Thus, if you and your business partner own a piece of land as tenants in common, on your death your interest in the property will pass to your family (or anywhere else you may will the property) and not to your business partner who owned the property in common with you.

Tenancy in common is an attractive way for investors to hold property when they do not wish to have the surviving investor or investors inherit the interest of the deceased investor.

Community property states recognize the concept of tenancy in common, and an interest that a spouse owns as a tenant in common with someone other than his or her spouse is considered to be separate, not community, property.

At death, any interest owned in property as a tenant in common is included in the estate of the deceased tenant in common for probate as well as estate tax purposes.

Joint tenancy and tenancy by the entirety.   Joint tenancy is the most common form of joint ownership today, particularly among married couples. While the legal characteristics of joint tenancy may vary depending on the peculiarities of state law, the following characteristics are fairly typical. During their lifetimes the rights of the coowners (known as *joint tenants*) are essentially the same as with tenancy in common, with each joint tenant having an equal right to occupy or manage the entire property. A joint tenancy differs from a tenancy in common, however, in that, on the death of one joint tenant, his or her interest in the property passes automatically to the surviving joint tenant or tenants. And it passes without the necessity of going through the probate process. Thus, there are the advantages that come with being able to avoid probate: avoidance of publicity, avoidance of probate delays, reduction of administration expenses, and convenience. For this reason, joint tenancy property is *not* considered to be a part of a decedent's probate estate, although it will be considered to be part of the estate for federal estate tax purposes.

Thus, if you and your business partner own a piece of property as joint tenants, on your death the property will pass automatically to your business partner, regardless of how you may provide in your will or what the state law may provide for the passage of property when you have left no will. And this joint tenancy property will not have to go through probate administration. When you exhale and fail to inhale again, this property passes by operation of law to your business partner as your joint tenant. Nothing further need be done to effect the transfer. But your estate may still have to pay tax on this property, because it was an asset you owned at death for tax purposes. Joint tenancy property, then, is "in" your estate for federal estate tax purposes and "out" of your estate for probate purposes.

This automatic passage of joint tenancy property to the surviving joint tenants can be both a blessing and a curse in the estate planning process. It is a blessing in that it is a will substitute. When you purchase the property as a joint tenant you have, in effect, already decided how you want this property to go on your death. And whether you die with a will or without a will, the joint tenancy property will pass on your death to the surviving joint tenant(s). And it will pass without having to go through probate administration.

Moreover, property held in joint tenancy often enjoys preferential treatment for state death tax purposes, particularly where the joint owners are husband and wife. Thus, in many states, the decedent spouse's share of property held in joint tenancy by a husband and wife will *not* be part of the taxable estate or the probate estate (Code of Iowa, Sec. 450.2-.3).

Finally, property held by husband and wife in joint tenancy is usually free from the claims of creditors of either spouse. Because of this and the other advantages, couples with few assets often hold most of their assets in joint tenancy and are frequently heard to say, "We don't need a will, we own everything jointly." And this, of course, is true with respect to the property held in joint tenancy. But any property not held jointly will pass according to the state's laws of descent and distribution. And, since it is unlikely that *all* of a person's assets will be held in joint tenancy, there may be a need for a will to take care of those assets that are owned by the decedent separately.

A more serious problem is that joint tenancy only works as a will substitute for the FIRST joint tenant to die. If you own a piece of property in joint tenancy with your wife and do not have a will because you are depending on the joint ownership feature to take care of the passage of this property on your death, think how you will feel when your wife unexpectedly dies first. (To say nothing of how she may feel about all this!) You will then own the entire property, and if you are unable to draft a will before your death (as when you and your wife are in a serious accident and she dies immediately and you linger a few days before dying), on your death it will pass according to the statutes of descent and distribution, which may not be exactly how you would wish it to go.

Moreover, if you own property in joint tenancy with a minor or someone who becomes incompetent, you have set in motion the inevitability that the property will pass on your death to someone who should not own it. You cannot change the passage of this property by your will. Joint tenancy property, remember, passes *automatically* to the surviving joint tenant.

While ownership of property in joint tenancy can, as we have seen, reduce death taxes in some circumstances, it is also possible that holding property in joint tenancy with another may result in *increased* death taxes. If, for example, you and your husband own estates that are valued at $400,000 each, there would be no federal estate tax payable on the death of either of you. But if you own your assets in joint tenancy, when you die your $400,000 will pass to your husband, and on his death (say, in 1990) his estate will be valued at $800,000 (ignoring any possibility that the estate values will grow with the passage of time) and a tax of $75,000 will be due the IRS. As we will see later, there are ways to let your husband enjoy the benefits of your $400,000 and still avoid having to pay federal estate tax on his death. But joint tenancy is not one of these.

Tenancy by the entirety is essentially a joint tenancy that exists solely between husband and wife. It was once a favored type of ownership in the law but is declining in popularity (Powell, Real Property, Sec. 621). None of the community property states, for example, recognize tenancy by the entirety. Moreoever, where it does exist is has often been severely modified by statute. In some states, for example, a tenancy by the entirety can only be created in land (*Polk* v. *Allen*, 19 Mo. 467, 1854). In others it may be created in both real property and personalty (*Bailey* v. *Smith*, 89 Fla. 303, 103 So. 833, 1925). In all instances, there is the question of whether tenancy by the entirety can exist where a state has adopted a Married Women's Act or Married Women's Property Act, the effect of which is to provide for separate estates for married women (Annot. 141 A.L.R. 179).

Tenancy by the entirety, then, is an anachronism that has little place in modern estate planning. The facts that the popular right of survivorship is available through the joint tenancy and that the disadvantages of the tenancy by the entirety (including the discrimination against women) do not exist in the joint tenancy make the joint tenancy a much preferable device for those seeking the advantages of survivorship.

Community property. Eight states (Arizona, California, Idaho, Louisiana, Nevada, New Mexico, Texas, and Washington) have adopted the system of marital property known as community property, under which each spouse owns a one-half interest in most property acquired during marriage, no matter which spouse first acquired the property. Five of these states, Arizona, California, Nevada, New Mexico, and Texas, were former Spanish-Mexican colonies. A sixth, Louisiana, came to the United States in the Louisiana Purchase from France in 1803. While France purported to own the Louisiana Territory at that time and sold it to the United States, this title was by no means uncontested. And the territory had come to France from Spain. The community property law of these states is derived, then, from the civil law marital property system of Spain (as opposed to the "common law" system of marital property, which came to the eastern states from Great Britain). Community property systems were later adopted in Idaho and Washington, perhaps because of the influence of California. Curiously, seven of these states (all except Louisiana) have abandoned the civil law in favor of the English common law as their basic system of jurisprudence, but have retained community property as their system of marital property.

It is important to understand, however, that there is no single system of community property in these eight states. The legal fundamentals are similar in all eight states, but the law has developed differently in each state over the years by reason of legislative enactments and court decisions.

The fundamental attribute of community property ownership is that each spouse owns a one-half interest in all property acquired during marriage by either spouse, except property received by inheritance or gift. The earnings and reinvestments of community property are also community property. In all community property states, a married person may also own separate property, which remains the separate property of the owning spouse and may be disposed of by that spouse as he or she wishes during lifetime or at death. In most states, the earnings of separate property also remain separate property. If separate funds are commingled with community funds to the extent that they can no longer be identified as separate funds, they are usually regarded as community property.

For probate and tax purposes, community property is treated as being owned one-half by each spouse. Thus, if while married and living in a community property state, you purchase cattle with the earnings from your business, on your death your spouse is considered to be the owner of one-half of those cattle. Only one-half of the value of the cattle need be included in your estate tax return, and only one-half of the value of the cattle will be subject to probate administration. (The remaining one-half, remember, did not pass to your spouse on your death. Your spouse already owned it under the law of community property from the moment you purchased it.)

Joint ownership forms are summarized in Table 3.1.

TABLE 3.1   Characteristics of Joint Ownership Forms

	Included in Taxable Estate	Included in Probate Estate
Sole ownership	Yes	Yes
Tenancy in common	Yes	Yes
Joint tenancy	Yes	No
Community property	One-half	One-half

THE PSYCHOLOGICAL ROLE OF PROPERTY

Speaking of property as assets and attempting to plan an estate by making suggestions with respect to these assets as though they were dry figures on a balance sheet is a mistake, as every estate planner worth his or her salt will instinctively realize.

Indeed, the very concept of estate planning is grounded in a fundamental misunderstanding. The idea somehow conjures up the picture of a planner who makes recommendations to a client, who then goes out and makes certain that his or her estate is composed of the sorts of assets and in the exact proportions the planner recommended. Then, when the client dies, the estate has been so planned that there is no tax payable to the state or federal government and no difficulties arise in the passage of this property to the family and loved ones of the deceased.

But it doesn't happen that way. Clients come to planners with the assets they have acquired and to which they are psychologically attached. They have no intention of getting rid of these assets, even if it would help their estate planning "posture." They have definite ideas about who should get what on their deaths (or, occasionally, they have absolutely no idea at all who should get what and need help working through this problem). They may want to control the use and disposition of their estates for generations to come. Almost always, they have no idea what their estates are worth.

The raw truth is that, for most of us, our assets—our "things"—are in some deep-seated psychological sense a part of ourselves. The estate planner who does not understand this is asking for big trouble.

Property is much more than merely something we use. It is that, to be sure, but it is also much more. In a very real sense, property is a part of our personalities. Ask the American businessperson, "Who are you?" and he or she will likely answer by telling you what he or she does. "I'm the life insurance underwriter," "I'm the butcher," "I'm the meter reader." Note that they are not telling you what they *do*; they are telling you who they *are*. Who they are and what they do are the same thing.

The property we use to do whatever we do (whether for our livelihood or as an avocation) is not just a collection of "things"; it is a part of our personalities. The carpenter who brings his toolbox to the job cannot be fully understood until you look at his tools and how he takes care of them. The woman who drives a Porsche to work is making a statement about herself—about who she is—just as much as she is utilizing a means of transportation. People who decorate their home in a certain fashion are using their property to say, "This is who we are."

Several years ago I took a continuing education course in estate planning. One interesting thing that emerged from this study was that businesspeople who had built their businesses "from scratch" were almost always very concerned about who would inherit the business and what would be done with it. But they seldom had any idea at all what the business was worth. The reason for this is that the businesses were not assets of certain value in their estates; the businesses were in a very real sense a part of "who they were." (My experience in this respect parallels the findings of others, most notably Shaffer, 1979.)

I am deeply interested in the rich past of America. American history has been my consuming passion for as long as I can recall. But I can't run around and say to people, "Hi, I'm Forest Bowman. I'm deeply interested in the rich past of America." (There are padded rooms for people who act like this.) So, instead, I use my possessions to make my statement for me.

Take my office, for example. On one wall is a photograph of Abraham Lincoln and his youngest son, Tad, taken in Mathew Brady's Washington studio on February 10, 1864. It's my favorite Lincoln photograph because it's not "the president of the united states," but simply "Tad Lincoln and his dad." On another wall I have a reproduction of a Kurtz and Allison print of General Phil Sheridan at the Battle of Cedar Creek, Virginia. My great-grandfather was there that day in October, 1864, and, although he lived nearly 50 years to the day after that battle, that day, and what he and his comrades had done on the bloody banks of Cedar Creek, remained the high point of his life. In some mystical way, you see, I am using this print to say, "This is a part of me. This is who I am." And, although it is worth very little in dollars and cents, that print of the Battle of Cedar Creek is one of the most valuable things I own. In truth, I care more about what happens to that print on my death than I care about certain assets of considerably more monetary value.

So, also, I have a copy of Porte Crayon's steel engraving "The Cliffs of Seneca." Seneca Rocks, as that magnificent limestone formation is now known, is one of the finest climbing faces in the eastern United States. But when Porte Crayon sketched that picture in the backwoods of what would soon become eastern West Virginia, my family owned those rocks. The log house in the foreground of the picture is my ancestral home. Like the print of the Sheridan at Cedar Creek, this engraving makes a statement about who I am that I cannot make myself. My property is not just something I own or something I use; it is a part of "who I am."

The estate planner who approaches clients and their possessions with the callow attitude of "I am the expert and I know what is best for you" is doomed to failure. Indeed, as we have seen, what is best for the client will vary from person to person and attitude to attitude. The most important factor in estate planning, then, is an appreciation of what is important to the people being served and some understanding of how to translate this sense of importance into a rational plan that meets the clients' needs. Then, when all this has been accomplished, you look to saving taxes.

Using the Psychological Views of Property
for Nonpsychological Purposes

If we accept the fact that property has important psychological significance to all of us and that the needs of the property owner with respect to these needs must come first with the estate planner, why do estate planners continue to pay so much attention to taxes? If the role of estate planning is not to save taxes, but first to accomplish the other goals of the client and then to save taxes if possible, why is most estate planning approached from the tax angle? Answering these questions for all people at all times is impossible. But there are at least three reasons estate planners continue to place so much emphasis on taxes.

First, some estate planners simply don't know any better. They approach estate planning taxes first because that's where the emphasis is placed in everything they read. They assume that all clients want to minimize costs and save death taxes. But a significant percentage of people simply do not care whether their heirs have to pay more tax after they are gone. They conclude (and it is difficult to argue with this position) that they are not going to do any lifetime planning that will restrict their ownership and use of their property just so that their heirs will have to pay a little less tax on the property they are inheriting. Concern with death taxes for a client of this sort is not only wasted but unsound. Even where the client *does* care what death taxes will be payable after his or her death, this is only one of the considerations.

Second, the possibility that, by careful planning he or she can save taxes, will often lead the client to consider what would otherwise be an unpleasant task, that is, facing up to the inevitability of death and what happens to one's property after death.

There is something in-built in the human psyche that tells us if we delay drafting our wills and taking other estate planning steps we cannot die. Conversely, once we have executed wills and other documents and completed the necessary planning, we *can* die. So we tend to put it off. Even if we do begin the estate planning process, we do so under false colors. No one "dies" anymore. We "pass away", "go to our rewards", or "succumb." (In some estate planning circles, believe it or not, the phrase "when the will matures" is now being used as a euphemism for dying. I have not yet reached the point where I can talk about the "will maturing" with a straight face, but I am trying. Perhaps if *my* will does not mature too soon, I will learn to use the phrase without giggling.)

Life insurance salespeople, especially, will understand the human reluctance to face up to even the remote possibility of death. Trying to determine what the spouse and children will require to live on after the income earner has died, and thus calculating what life insurance is needed, is not exactly the most upbeat way to spend an evening. That is why most life insurance today is sold by means of computerized gimmickry that creates charts of future earnings or as an investment instead of as a protection for loved ones after the client dies.

But the human dislike of paying taxes is so great that it can actually be used to overcome this reluctance to plan for one's death. (This suggests that the human fear of taxes is even greater than the fear of death. I have never seen this argument presented anywhere, but it is an intriguing idea. Death is, beyond question, less frightening than taxes in one respect; death does not get worse everytime the Congress or the state legislatures convene.)

But, to continue, a client who under normal circumstances would never think of drafting a will or disclosing what he or she owns to an estate planner will leap at the opportunity once it becomes clear there is a possibility of cutting the government out of a few dollars of taxes. And when you explain that the savings can come not only later in death tax savings but *today* in reduced income taxes, clients will fall all over themselves in an effort to discuss their property holdings and anything else the planner thinks is necessary.

In this respect, then, some emphasis on taxes can be very helpful to the estate planner. The tax savings, however real to the client, are used to accomplish the other, and much more important, goals of the client, even if the client sees the tax savings as a paramount goal.

Finally, savings in taxes can help justify the expense involved in estate planning. So much of what is done in estate planning appears to have no present value (if you discount the peace of mind that should accompany the knowledge that one's affairs are in order), and it is often difficult to justify charging a client for work done that has a value only in the future—and then only if the plan is not changed later, as is likely to be the case.

This apparent lack of any product with present value is a very serious problem in estate planning. It can lead to underplanning by the professional who does not feel that she or he can charge for the time necessary to do a complete plan and who is understandably unwilling to do extensive work without being adequately compensated. In the legal profession, then, we have a great many "fifty-dollar" wills, which are totally inadequate for the clients' needs but which are drafted because the lawyer does not believe the client will pay the $500 to $1,000 that may be necessary to prepare an adequate estate plan.

Being able to show the client immediate and long-term tax savings (usually in excess of the estate planner's fee) can make the planner's fee a great deal more palatable. So taxes are used, again, to accomplish other goals of the client that are actually more important than tax savings.

APPLYING THIS CHAPTER TO *YOUR* SITUATION

As an estate planner or an estate planning client, it is essential to know the makeup of the estate, both in dollars and cents, for tax planning, and in the emotional sense. To properly plan an estate one must know the following:

1. Whether any tax planning is necessary and, if so, the nature and extent of the planning required.
2. Regardless of the tax situation (and sometimes in spite of it), whether there are assets that must be treated in any special way because of their emotional value.

Anyone undergoing the estate planning process must make a complete inventory of assets, which should be periodically updated. (The inventory forms found in Appendix F are a good place to start.) The inventory should reveal the gross estate for both death tax and probate purposes. This is the logical starting point for the estate planning process.

Next, the client must candidly detail those assets that are not fungible; that is, they cannot readily be substituted for other assets of equal value. Then the planner can work around these specific emotional needs.

CASE PROBLEM

3.1 Who Owns What (and Why Does It Matter)? Tom and Gloria have been married 20 years. They have four children, ages 12 through 18. Tom is an electrical engineer and Gloria teaches kindergarten. They own a $150,000 home in Philadelphia, where they have lived for seven years. The home is owned in joint tenancy with the right of survivorship. The mortgage balance is $20,000. Tom and Gloria each have a car titled in their names, although Tom paid for both cars with his salary. Their investments consist of $30,000 in stocks and bonds, $20,000 in Tom's name, and $10,000 held in joint tenancy. Their bank accounts are jointly held and have an average balance of $6,000. Tom has $250,000 term life insurance and Gloria has $125,000 term life insurance. Before moving to Philadelphia they lived in Los Angeles (where they had grown up, gone to school, met, and were married.) While there, they accumulated all their stocks and bonds. When they left there, they sold their home and a beach house they owned. With this money they purchased their home in Philadelphia and also bought a cabin cruiser, which Tom has titled in his name alone. The boat is valued at $40,000. They also own a house full of antiques that they have collected during their marriage. The collection is valued at $80,000. Gloria expects to inherit her father's summer cottage on the Pacific just north of Los Angeles. The value of the cottage is $175,000. Tom and Gloria are only children and their parents are still living.

Questions

1. What additional information do you need to advise Tom and Gloria?
2. From the information given:
    a. What is the value of Tom's present taxable estate for federal estate tax purposes?
    b. What is the value of Tom's probate estate?
3. If you determine that there will not likely be any federal estate tax liability on Tom's death, how can you use "tax savings" to encourage Tom and Gloria to pursue the estate planning process?
4. Should Tom and Gloria own their home in joint tenancy? Should they own their other assets in joint tenancy?

SELECTED READINGS

Bowman, Forest J., *The Complete Retirement Handbook*. New York: Putnam Publishing Co., 1983, pp. 124–127.

Kahn, Arnold D., *Family Security Through Estate Planning*. New York: McGraw-Hill Book Co., 1979, pp. 7–11.

Powell, Richard R., and Rohan, Patrick J., *Powell on Real Property*. New York: Matthew Bender, 1968, pp. 619–627.

Shaffer, Thomas L., *The Planning and Drafting of Wills and Trusts*. Mineola, N.Y.: Foundation Press, Inc., 1979, pp. 19–26.

Weinstock, Harold, *Planning an Estate*. Colorado Springs, Colo.: Shepard's/McGraw-Hill, 1982, p. 20.

4

Intestacy:
The Estate Plan
Created
by Operation
of Law

*No man's life, liberty or property are safe while the
legislature is in session.*

1 Tucker (N.Y. Surr.) 249 (1866)

If you die without a will you are said to die *intestate*. Intestate is a Latin word meaning, not surprisingly, "not having made a will." (Occasionally, you see, the law *does* make sense. But don't get excited. It won't happen very often.)

INTESTATE STATUTES

When you die without a will, as we saw earlier, your property passes according to the intestate statutes of your state, which are also known as the laws of descent and distribution. These statutes make up a "legislative will," which is designed to leave your property pretty much as you would have if you had left a will.

Since the legislature will not know precisely how anyone might want to leave his or her property, the legislative will is designed to reflect what the average person would have done with his or her estate. (Actually, the legislative will is designed to reflect what the average man would do with his estate. This is only one of its problems.)

It should be obvious, then, that permitting your property to pass under the intestate statutes is a perfectly viable estate planning alternative. That is, if you are aware of what your state's intestate laws provide and wish to have your property pass that way, deliberately leaving no will permits your property to pass under the intestate statutes. (However, it is fair to say that most people who die intestate do so by default rather than by design.)

The laws of intestacy vary from state to state. So before consciously selecting intestacy as your estate plan, you must be aware of the specific intestate scheme of your state. And there are other problems, mostly stemming from the nature of intestate statutes. The major shortcoming of the "legislative will" is that it is a totally inflexible estate plan designed for a mythical average man with no room for any disposition of property in any way other than that provided by the intestate statutes.

For example, as we have already noted, the intestate statutes are designed to distribute the estate of a man, not a woman. Thus, these laws routinely provide protection for a surviving spouse who is a female and who (in the eyes of the old English land law, from whence much of our modern property laws are derived) should not inherit the husband's lands.

So, too, the intestate statutes are designed to dispose of a moderate estate, one that is neither very large (and, thus, requires tax planning) nor very small (where everything should go to the surviving spouse, to the exclusion of any children who may survive). The legislative will is helpful only for the estate that is composed of nothing unusual or out of the ordinary. Yet, in point of fact, there is no such thing as a typical estate, except in the calculations of the statistician, and almost all of us own at least one asset that is out of the ordinary and requires some special attention, whether it be an involved interest in underwater real estate in Florida, Grandpa's Civil War sword, or Uncle Henry's collection of unpatented inventions.

Intestacy under the Uniform Probate Code

The problems that can arise when an estate passes by intestacy can best be understood by looking at a specific intestate scheme. The intestate provisions of the Uniform Probate Code (which are in effect in 11 states) is a good place to start.

The Uniform Probate Code provides that if you are survived by your spouse alone (i.e., no children or parents survive), the spouse takes everything. If, on the other hand, your spouse *and* children* survive you, and if the children are also the children of your surviving spouse, the surviving spouse takes the first $50,000 of your estate and divides the remainder with your children. If your surviving children are not also the children of your surviving spouse, the spouse does not take the first $50,000 of your estate but divides the entire estate with your children.

If you are survived by a spouse and no issue but one or both of your parents survive, your spouse takes the first $50,000 and splits the remainder with your parent(s).

Confused? Maybe this will help. Under the Uniform Probate Code a surviving spouse (regardless of sex) takes:

1. The entire estate if no issue or parents survive the decedent.
2. The first $50,000 and one-half of the balance of the estate if:

---

*Actually the law says "issue," not "children." Issue includes children, grandchildren, great-grandchildren, and so on. So if you are survived by grandchildren and no children, the grandchildren would take as "issue." Ancestors always cut off descendants, so if you are survived by children *and* grandchildren, the children would take and not the grandchildren.

    a. Parent(s) survive(s) but no issue survive, or

    b. One or more issue survive who are also issue of the surviving spouse.

  3. One-half of the estate if the decedent is survived by one or more issue who are not also the issue of the surviving spouse.

If no spouse survives you, your intestate estate will be disposed of in this order :

    1. If children survive, they will share equally in your entire estate. If there are no children but grandchildren survive, the grandchildren will share equally in your estate. If some children survive and others are dead but have left children surviving them, your estate will be divided among your children and the children of your deceased children (i.e., your grandchildren). The grandchildren will take the share that would have passed to your deceased children. For example, assume that you die intestate and leave three living children. Two other children have died before you. One of your deceased children (child A) left two children surviving and the other (child B) left three children. Your estate will be divided into five shares. One share will go to each of your three surviving children. The remaining two shares will pass to the children of child A and child B. The children of child A will each take one-tenth of your estate (one-half of one-fifth) and the children of child B will each take one-fifteenth (one-third of one-fifth).

    2. If you are survived by no issue, your entire estate will pass to your parents.

    3. If you leave no issue or parent surviving, your estate passes to the issue of your parents (i.e., to your brothers and sisters, nieces and nephews, grandnieces and grandnephews, etc.).

    4. If no issue, parent, or issue of parents survive you, your estate will pass as follows:

    a. One-half of your paternal grandparents, or to their issue if the paternal grandparents do not survive, and one-half to your maternal grandparents, or to their issue if the maternal grandparents do not survive.

    b. If there are no surviving grandparents or issue of grandparents on either the paternal or the maternal side, the entire estate passes to the relatives on the other side.

    c. If you are survived by no issue, parents, issue of parents, grandparents, or issue of grandparents, your estate will pass to the state.

This scheme of disposition of an intestate estate is in effect, with some local modifications, in the 11 states that have adopted the Uniform Probate Code and in 3 other states that have adopted substantially similar intestate patterns. In the other 36 states, however, the intestate distribution scheme will vary in many particulars. In the author's state of West Virginia, for example, an estate *never* passes to the state. Some relative, however remotely related, is always found. (Persons who are so distantly related that they did not even know the decedent but who take because they are the closest surviving relative are known as "laughing heirs." The idea is, I suppose, that they laugh instead of cry when they learn of the decedent's death and that they will inherit the estate. I have always wanted to be a laughing heir.)

Schematically, this is how the intestate scheme of the Uniform Probate Code looks

TABLE 4.1. Intestate Distribution under the Uniform Probate Code

If no spouse survives:

Grandparents

Escheats to state if no close relatives

Parent

Issue

Dependent

Issue

Issue

Issue

Issue

Issue

Issue

West Virginia also adheres to the old English idea that the surviving spouse (the intestate laws presume it will be the wife) should not inherit the husband's lands. So West Virginia law provides that, if a spouse and issue survive, the issue take title to the decedent's real estate, *subject to the surviving spouse's life estate in one-third of all the real estate*. It is a complicated and entirely out-of-date concept, but a land owner who dies intestate in West Virginia survived by a spouse and issue can expect to have his or her real estate pass in this fashion. And West Virginia is not unique in this respect.

PROBLEMS WITH INTESTACY

Intestacy, then, is not always (or even often) a practical solution to the problem of estate planning. Intestate schemes, no matter how carefully designed, cannot avoid certain problems.

Personal Effects

The division of one's personal effects is a major source of family discord. The difficulties appear to have very little to do with the size of the estate or the value of the personal effects.

If, for example, a mother dies intestate and one daughter believes that she should have a certain cut glass vase and another believes she should have it, it will be difficult to avoid hard feelings no matter which daughter ultimately gets the vase. All this can be taken care of by a simple will in which the mother designates which daugher is to receive the vase.

The reason a will is so effective in this instance is that neither daughter will resist (or, in most cases, even resent) the passage of the vase to the other *as long as that decision has been made by their dead mother.* Psychologically, the dead mother's personality has attached to the vase. The passage of the ownership of the vase to one daughter instead of the other is the doing of the mother and the daughters will accept that. However, if the matter were left to the two daughters alone, each would resent the other's claim.

One major reason for writing a will, then, is to avoid family squabbles after you are gone. If you leave an item of property to one child, the others may resent it, but the resentment will most likely be directed to you. Since you are dead, all your angry children can do is come to the cemetery and kick your tombstone. They will not start a family blood feud that simmers for three generations.

Gifts to Charity

The intestate laws of every state are quite precise as to who shall take the estate of an intestate. And in every instance those persons designated are relatives. There is no way that a charity, no matter how attached you may be to it, will share in any part of your intestate estate. If you wish to leave all or part of your estate to charity, you must do so by a will or other estate planning document. There are no exceptions to this rule. The legislative will does not provide for charities.

Nonrelatives

The legislative will also makes no provision for nonrelatives. Thus, if you wish your estate to pass to a dear friend on your death, you cannot rely on the intestate statutes. You must leave a direct bequest, by will or other estate planning document, to the person of your choice. Otherwise, your intestate estate will pass to relatives alone. If you have, for example, raised a child from tender years and think of the child as your own, but have never formalized the relationship by an adoption proceeding, this child is not (except in a few states and under a rather complicated doctrine that you should not rely on) your heir for purposes of intestate succession.

You will also recall from the outline of the intestate scheme of disposition discussed earlier that in-laws do not share in an intestate estate because in-laws are not relatives. Thus, if you are fond of your daughter-in-law and are pleased that she will be sharing in your estate through your son's inheritance, you must understand that, if your son dies before you do, your daughter-in-law will take nothing from you under the intestate statutes. If you wish to provide for your daughter-in-law, you must do so in the same fashion as you would provide for your favorite charity—by a will or other estate planning document.

Near-Simultaneous Death

One major problem with the operation of the intestate statutes is that they are fixed and rigid. Assume that Ralph, a medical student in the second year of his residency, and Hilda, an emergency room nurse, are married and have no children. They are struggling to get Ralph through his residency and established in a medical practice. Hilda's parents disapproved of their marriage and have contributed nothing to the couple. But Ralph's parents have helped the young couple generously, buying them a car, paying the rent on their apartment, helping them with their groceries, and generally assisting in any way they can. They even paid for a $100,000 insurance policy on Ralph's life. Ralph has named his wife beneficiary of the policy, providing that the $100,000 is to be paid to her in a lump sum on his death. His parents have been named alternate beneficiaries.

One day Ralph and Hilda are in a terrible automobile accident. Ralph is killed and Hilda is badly injured. Three weeks later, Hilda dies from the effects of the accident. Assuming that neither Ralph nor Hilda have a will, what will happen to their property if they die in a state that has adopted the Uniform Probate Code?

The answer is starkly simple and harsh. When Ralph died, survived by his wife and no children, the intestate statutes provided that his wife would take the first $50,000 of Ralph's estate and divide the remainder with his parents. If we assume that Ralph's estate, excluding the life insurance proceeds, did not exceed $50,000, Ralph's parents took nothing and the entire estate passed to Hilda. (The life insurance proceeds passed, not by intestacy, but according to the provisions of the policy. That is, Hilda, as the primary beneficiary, took the entire $100,000.)

Now, when Hilda died three weeks later, what happened? You guessed it! Since she was not survived by a spouse or issue, Hilda's entire estate, including the $100,000 she received from the life insurance company, passed to her parents—the ones who opposed the marriage and contributed nothing to the couple—to the exclusion of Ralph's parents, who provided much of what made up the couple's estate.

(It is true that Ralph's parents were named alternate beneficiaries in the life insurance policy, but, since Hilda, the primary beneficiary, survived Ralph, the $100,000 went to her at that time and there was no need to pass anything on to the alternate beneficiaries. Of course, had the settlement provision been left to Hilda to determine after Ralph's death, and had she been unable to make such a determination during the three weeks she lived, the proceeds of the policy would never have become payable to Hilda and Ralph's parents would take the $100,000 as alternate beneficiaries.)

The problems that arise in an intestate estate because of near-simultaneous death are there not only for the young couple with no children, but for any childless couple, regardless of age. In addition, the couple with children can face an accident where the children and one parent are killed and one parent lingers a while before dying, and the entire family estate passes by intestacy to one set of parents to the exclusion of the other set of parents, simply by the "luck" factor of which parent died last. The results are almost always unfair, and such situations tend to be unusually messy. But a simple will or other estate planning document can avoid this problem entirely.

Advancements

The common law doctrine of advancements, which is in effect today in many states, seems almost designed to cause undue friction among the heirs of an intestate estate. For example, assume that you die intestate survived by two daughters, ages 15 and 18. You purchased a $10,000 automobile for the 18-year-old two years ago, but have not purchased a car for 15-year-old since she isn't old enough to drive.

The doctrine of advancements provides that significant lifetime gifts to an heir are *advancements* to that heir, to be set off against the heir's intestate share. The idea is that a parent would want to even up his or her estate among the heirs. Thus, where a child receives a large lifetime gift, the doctrine of advancements assumes that the parent would want that child's share of the parent's intestate estate to be reduced accordingly so that all the other heirs are treated fairly. The idea is grounded in a commonsense proposition. But it is exceedingly difficult to carry forth the idea in real life.

Applying the doctrine in our example involving the $10,000 car when your intestate estate is divided up, the daughter who received the $10,000 car will receive $10,000 less than the other daughter (since the daughter who got the car has already received that $10,000 from you as an advancement).

The problem with the doctrine of advancements is that, unless it is very clear that the lifetime gift *was* intended as an advancement or equally clear that the gift was *not* intended as an advancement, the heirs are bound to be on opposite ends of a family dispute. In our example, the daughter who got the car will likely insist that the car was an absolute lifetime gift and not intended to be an advancement against her share of your intestate estate. The other daughter, on the other hand, will likely insist that the $10,000 car was an advancement and that she should take $10,000 more of your intestate estate. Which one is correct? Who knows? The only person who can say for sure is dead and the daughters are left to fight it out (literally). It's a nasty problem that can be avoided with a simple bit of estate planning.

The law of advancements varies from state to state. In some states *any* unexplained lifetime gift to an heir is presumed to be an advancement. In other states, gifts must be specifically described in writing as advancements to qualify. (I wouldn't want you to get the idea that it's simple.)

Gifts To Children

When an individual dies intestate leaving a spouse and children, ordinarily, especially with smaller estates, the surviving spouse should inherit the entire estate. However, you will note that the intestate scheme set forth in the Uniform Probate Code (as well as most other intestate schemes) provides for a division of the decedent's property between the surviving spouse and children. While most married couples will own the family home in joint tenancy with right of survivorship, other significant assets may be owned by one spouse or another as separate property. In this instance, the children will share ownership with the surviving spouse. If that is what the decedent would want to have happen, fine. But if the decedent would prefer to have the entire estate pass to the surviving spouse, the intestate statutes will not receive this result.

For larger estates, the problem can be just as acute since the federal estate tax law provides that any property left to the surviving spouse is exempt from taxation because of the marital deduction. When property is left to pass by intestacy, the result may be that some of the property will pass to children (and be subject to the estate tax) instead of passing to the surviving spouse (where it would avoid the estate tax).

Executors and Guardians

If you die intestate leaving children but no spouse surviving, the court will appoint a guardian for your children. The court will make an effort to select the person you would have most likely chosen, usually a close relative. But the selection may well be the one person you would *least* like to have as guardian of your children.

Likewise, someone must manage your estate after your death, paying all the bills and collecting the debts due you. If you do not make such a selection in your will, the court will select someone for you. Again, the person selected may be the last person you would trust with your estate assets.

The real question, then, is this: Who writes the rules under which your children will be raised and your estate assets managed, you or the legislature of your state?

Partial Intestacy

It is important to understand that intestacy does not mean simply "dying without a will." It means dying without a will that covers all your assets. Thus, it is possible to leave a will that specifically disposes of certain assets, but fails to mention others. In this case you are said to have died *partially intestate*. In such event, the assets you disposed of in your will pass according to the provisions in your will, while the other assets that were never mentioned in your will pass according to the intestate statutes. All the shortcomings of intestacy that we have listed previously apply equally to partial intestacy.

Since it is unlikely that any testator will be able to list all of his or her assets in a will and keep the will up to date by changing it to include other assets as they are acquired, a simple way to avoid partial intestacy is by use of a *residuary clause* in the will. Such a clause merely states something like "All of the rest, residue, and remainder of my estate, I leave to my son John." Then when you die (or, if you prefer, "when your will matures"), your estate will be distributed as you have directed in your will, with specific assets going as you have provided. Any assets you have acquired after executing the will or which you have not otherwise provided for in the will will pass to your son John under the residuary clause.

WHICH STATE'S LAWS CONTROL WHAT ASSETS?

Disposition of the Estate

If you die owning assets in several states, you could have the taxing authorities of each state claiming the right to tax these assets. Moreover, since state intestate laws vary considerably, who inherits some of your intestate property may well depend on which state's law controls.

Generally, the law of a decedent's permanent residence (known in the law as the *domicile* of the decedent) controls the disposition of the decedent's personal property, whereas the law of the state where real estate is located controls the disposition of the real estate.

Thus, if you have written your will while living in Ohio and later die while permanently residing in New Jersey, owning real estate there and in Vermont and having a considerable personal estate in New Jersey, the laws of Ohio will have nothing to do with the disposition of any of your property. The states of New Jersey and Vermont will determine how your real estate passes, and New Jersey will control the passage of your personalty.

That the disposition of your Vermont real estate will be determined by the law of Vermont does not mean that you must "write a Vermont" will or anything of the sort. It merely means that the state of Vermont will look to how you have disposed of your Vermont real estate and determine if it is proper under Vermont law. If, for example, you have left a will drafted in Ohio that leaves your Vermont real estate to your sister, Vermont will merely look to the will to see if it is a proper one under Vermont law. If it is, your Vermont property will pass to your sister.

(Vermont requires three witnesses to a will. Ohio, like most American states, requires only two witnesses. But since your will was executed properly according to Ohio law while you were a permanent resident (domiciliary) of Ohio, Vermont will, under the full faith and credit clause of the U.S. Constitution, recognize the Ohio will as having been validly executed.)

If you died intestate, the Vermont real estate will pass according to the laws of intestacy of Vermont, despite the fact that you died a permanent resident of New Jersey. On the other hand, your New Jersey property, both real and personal property, will pass according to the New Jersey intestate statutes.

If we take this example one step farther and assume that you died in Florida while on an extended vacation and that a substantial portion of your personal property (your car, your bank account, your clothing, and most of your personal effects) were with you in Florida, the law of New Jersey will still control the disposition of this personal property, since New Jersey is the state of your domicile and the state of domicile controls disposition of one's personal estate. (If you left a substantial estate that may produce some death tax revenues for the state, Florida may contest the question of your New Jersey domicile and insist that you were domiciled in Florida at your death. That, of course, is another question, but it does point up the need to carefully establish your domicile so that your estate may not have to carry on an expensive fight to establish your domicile after you are gone.)

Administration of the Estate

In the preceding discussion we have been concerned with which state's law controls who gets what from your estate. An equally important question is which state's laws will control the administration of which assets. We will delve into this question in some detail in Chapter 7.

APPLYING THIS CHAPTER TO *YOUR* SITUATION

Anyone who engages in estate planning must understand the intestate statutes of his or her state and must be aware of the potential problems that can arise if intestacy occurs. As with other aspects of the estate planning process, the problems and their intensity will vary depending on the family situation, the personalities involved, what the owner of the property wants to do with it on his or her death, and the types of property to be passed on. A single woman in her sixties who has a comfortable estate has different problems and concerns from that of a man in his thirties with a wife and two children and precious little property. Dying intestate will mean different things to each of them, but, despite the differences, it will mean *problems* for both.

CASE PROBLEMS

4.1 Is Intestacy a Viable Alternative? George Armstrong is 62 years old, retired, and has never been married. He has a comfortable pension from the company for which he worked, which will have no residuary value on his death. He owns a modest two-bedroom home valued at $60,000, with its undistinguished furnishings included, and a car valued at $8,000, and has stocks, bank accounts, and CDs valued at $45,000. The only special asset he owns is a small stamp collection valued at $12,000. George has one sister living and a brother who has died leaving two children, a son and daughter. George is not close to any of his family.

Questions
1. Assuming that George does not care who gets his estate, are there any reasons he should no rely on intestacy as an estate plan?
2. In a state that has adopted the Uniform Probate Code, how would George's estate be divided up in the event he died intestate?

4.2 The Dangers of Intestacy. Earl Day is in his late fifties and in declining health. He and his wife have been married for over 25 years and have three children:

a son, 24, who is in his second year of dental school; a daughter, 22, who will enter law school in the fall; and a son, 20, who is married, has one child, and is an enlisted man in the army. Earl and his wife live in Virginia where they own their home, valued at $125,000, in joint tenancy with right of survivorship. They have stocks and bonds and other savings valued at $75,000 and raise Arabian horses as a hobby. Earl's wife has an extensive collection of cut glass and Earl has a collection of antique airplanes that he maintains in flying condition. At least once a month Earl and his wife fly in their modern airplane to visit one of the children or to attend a horse auction. Earl's entite estate will probably be valued at $750,000 and his wife's at $250,000.

Questions
1. What problems does Earl have with intestacy?
2. What is the greatest single problem that Earl's intestacy would cause?

SELECTED READINGS

BEHRENFELD, WILLIAM H., *Estate Planning Desk Book*. Englewood Cliffs, N.J.: Prentice-Hall, Inc., 1977, p. 94.

BOWMAN, FOREST J., *The Complete Retirement Handbook*. New York: Putnam Publishing Co., 1983, pp. 80–84.

SHAFER, THOMAS L., *The Planning and Drafting of Wills and Trusts*. Mineola, N.Y.: Foundation Press, Inc., 1979, pp. 60–64.

5

The Will:
The Cornerstone
of Estate Planning

Let's choose executors, and talk of wills.

Shakespeare, *King Richard II* Act III, Scene 2

A will is a written instrument, executed according to certain legal formalities, by which an owner of property disposes of his or her property on death.

RESTRICTIONS ON THE RIGHT TO DISPOSE OF PROPERTY BY WILL

The right to dispose of your property at death according to your wishes is a rather fundamental right in this country. But there are some limits on this right, founded for the most part in certain social and economic considerations and reflected in the legislation of the various states.

Protection of the Family

First there are restrictions that are designed to protect members of the family from disinheritance. For example, in every state a married person must leave a certain amount of his or her estate to a surviving spouse. If this amount is not left to the spouse, the spouse has the right to take it from the estate anyway, despite what the will provides. The amount the surviving spouse is guaranteed varies from state to state (and often is not very much), but the fact remains that a married spouse does not have total freedom with the disposition of his or her estate; some of it must go to the surviving spouse.

Moreover, while no state's law requires that children be left anything under normal circumstances, the law of some states provides that children born or adopted before or after a will is executed have the right to claim a *forced share* of a parent's estate unless the parent's will clearly excludes them. The idea is that children can be disinherited, but the law will protect them against being overlooked. Thus the will that makes it clear that the children were not overlooked can leave them nothing. But if the will is unclear on this matter, the children can take a forced share of the estate even though the will purports to leave them nothing.

Excessive or Untimely Gifts to Charity

Many states invalidate testamentary gifts to charities that exceed a certain percentage of the estate or that are made in wills executed shortly before death. Theological implications aside, statutes of this sort are designed to prevent a decedent with an undue concern for the hereafter from disinheriting the natural objects of her or his bounty by leaving all or most of the estate to charity.

Governments' Right to Tax

The right of the state or national governments to tax the transfer of one's assets at death has been settled for a long time among all but the lunatic fringe. Surprisingly, there is a split of opinion in this country with respect to whether the right to pass one's estate by will is a "natural" or God-given right, on the one hand, or a right granted by the legislature, on the other. But the law is clear that, regardless of whether the transfer of one's estate by will is a natural or legislatively granted right, the government has a right to regulate and tax such transfers.

National Social Policy

You cannot leave your property in such a way as to violate public policy. For example, the U.S. Constitution guarantees to all citizens the equal protection of the law. Thus, if you were to leave your estate to the city to establish a park for the use of "citizens of white Anglo-Saxon protestant background" only, the courts would strike down this provision. [They would either let the money pass by intestacy (or under the residuary clause of your will, if there is one) or let it be used for a park for *all* citizens, depending on a number of factors and legal principles. We will delve into this aspect of the problem in more detail later (*Evans* v. *Abney*, 396 U.S. 435, 1970).] The same principle would apply if the park were to be for the use of "females only" or if it excluded persons of certain religious or ethnic backgrounds.

Unworthy Heirs

Moreover, although you may leave your property in a perfectly legal manner to, say, your wife, if she were to kill you after you executed your will and be convicted of murder, in most states and under most circumstances she would not be permitted to inherit from you under the legal principle that one should not be permitted to benefit from a wrong [*Bird* v. *Plunkett*, 139 Conn. 491, 95 A.2d 71, 1953]. This, of course, is not so much a limitation on your right to leave your property to your spouse as it is a limitation on your spouse's right to inherit from you. But the effect is the same; your spouse cannot inherit from you despite the provisions of your will.

Control of an Estate from the Grave

To prevent an owner of property from controlling the use of the property for many years after death, the law places a limit on the duration of time that a testator can control the use of his or her property. The theory is that the wealth of this world should be controlled by the living (who must bear the consequences of their stewardship of this wealth) and not by the dead. The Rule Against Perpetuities, which has given law students more heartburn than all the hot Mexican food and cheap beer ever consumed, is the principal means of achieving this goal. We will confront this rule in Chapter 10.

WILL FORMALITIES

The limitations on the disposition of one's property at death just set forth are, however (with the exceptions of the government's right to tax and the spouse's right to a share of the estate), of little consequence to the average testator. Most of us do not seek to violate public policy, or disinherit our spouses, or tie up our property for generations to come. For most of us, a will is simply a device to achieve our purpose of leaving our hard-earned property as we wish.

Age and Mental Capacity

Generally, any person who has attained the statutory age (usually 18, but it will vary in one or two states) and is of sound mind may execute a will. The soundness of mind required to execute a will is known as *legal capacity* and the test is not very severe. For the most part you are considered to have the necessary capacity if the following are clear:

You are aware that you are executing your will.

You know and understand the nature and extent of your property.

You know who are the natural objects of your bounty and appreciate the claims they would have upon your assets.

You are capable of formulating an orderly plan for the disposition of your estate.

Eccentricity, many of you will be relieved to know, has of itself no effect on testamentary capacity, nor is old age alone sufficient evidence of incapacity. And the capacity to make a will must exist *at the time the will is executed*. If you are incompetent before or after the execution of the will, but competent at the time of execution, the requirement for capacity has been met.

Formalities

The laws of the various states that set out the requirements for wills (known in each state as the Statute of Wills) set forth the formalities required for a valid will. Generally, they require that a will be

in writing,

signed by the testator, and

witnessed by two competent witnesses.

Nuncupative Wills

To all this generality, however, there are many exceptions. For example, a few states permit an oral will (known as a *nuncupative will*) under very limited circumstances. Usually, nuncupative wills are limited to military personnel on active duty or mariners at sea and they must be reduced to writing by the persons to whom the testator orally related the will within a specific (and usually quite brief) period of time. Moreover, they may only be used to transfer personal property, not real estate. For the most part, oral wills are not worth the paper they aren't written on.

Holographic Wills

In 28 states, certain wills need not be witnessed if they are written entirely in the handwriting of the testator. Handwritten wills, which the law calls *holographic* wills, were once commonplace in rural America, but they are seen less and less frequently today. Nonetheless, their validity in those states that permit them is beyond question. A difficulty that often arises with respect to holographic wills is when a testator uses a form or handwrites a will on a paper that also contains other typed or printed provisions. The law varies from state to state, but most states that recognize holographic wills also recognize what is known as the *substantial compliance* doctrine, which provides that if the handwritten portions of the will can be read without reference to the typed to printed portions, the holographic will is valid notwithstanding the state Statute of Wills requirement that the will be "entirely in the handwriting of the testator."

The Signature

If a testator is unable to write, his or her signature can be affixed to the will by another person, in the presence of the testator and acting at the testator's direction. This was once common when a considerable portion of the population was illiterate. Now, however, it is more likely to occur when the testator is physically unable to write. In either event, however, it is sufficient if the testator's "signature" is affixed to another person in the testator's presence and at his or her direction.

Witness Competency

The requirement for competent witnesses is also frequently watered down. Competency of a witness does not refer merely to mental capacity to understand what the witness if witnessing, but also to being an objective or impartial observer. Thus, a witness who is also a beneficiary under a will is considered to be an "incompetent" witness because he or she has an interest in having the will declared valid. But, in most states, if an incompetent witness is necessary for the proving of the will, the witness can merely be required to give up any gift under the will and is then considered a competent witness.

Number of Witnesses

Note, too, that while most states require only two witnesses, three states (New Hampshire, South Carolina, and Vermont) require three witnesses. But if a will is properly executed in a two-witness state and the testator later dies a resident of a three-witness state, the latter state is required, under the Full Faith and Credit clause of the U.S. Constitution, to recognize the will with two witnesses as a valid will, assuming all other requirements have been met.

Undue Influence

Another requirement for a valid will is that it be executed freely by a testator who is not under the undue influence of another person. The undue influence rule is one about which a good deal has been written but which is, in fact, of limited application. Who knows why a person will leave property to another? When does the love and affection one feels for another cease and become the undue influence of the beneficiary over the testator?

Generally, one is under undue influence when the wishes of another are substituted for the wishes of the testator. But if the testator, notwithstanding the influence of another, is able to carry out her or his own wishes, there has been no undue influence.

There is frequently a close relationship between allegations of undue influence and allegations of lack of capacity to make a will. Certainly, a testator who is of somewhat diminished mental capacity, but competent nonetheless to make a will, is more likely to be the potential victim of the undue influence of another than a person of strong mental capacity.

BASICS OF A WELL-DRAFTED WILL

A well-drafted will should meet the three following objectives of the testator at a minimum:

1. It should dispose of the testator's property in accordance with the testator's wishes.

2. It should dispose of the testator's property in such a fashion as to avoid conflicts among the testator's family and friends.

3. It should, if consistent with the objectives of the testator, avoid death taxes.

Such a will should contain, then, the following provisions at a minimum.

Exordium Clause

The exordium clause serves to identify the testator and sets forth her or his intention that this paper serve as a will. It affords the testator the opportunity to declare the place of domicile. (While such a declaration will not be conclusive of the question of domicile, it is one additional factor that will be taken into account by the courts in determining the domicile of the testator should this matter come under question.) Finally, this clause will formally invalidate all former wills or other testamentary instruments. The following is a sample exordium clause.

> I, DANIEL CLAY WEBSTER, domiciled and residing in Charleston, Kanawha County, West Virginia, make this Will and revoke all Wills and other testamentary documents previously made by me.

Note that the clause contains none of the "being of sound and disposing mind and memory and aware of the inevitablility of death" language found in many older wills. Stating that you are of sound mind is absolutely no evidence whatsoever that you *are* possessed of sound mind. Such language adds nothing, so why use it? Moreover, the clause is very straightforward about what is being done: Daniel Clay Webster is "making his will." He is not, as was often the case in former times, "enumerating the following Articles Testamentary."

Calling the instrument a "will" is sufficient, as opposed to calling it a "Last Will and Testament." The distinction between a will (a word of Anglo-Saxon origin that described an instrument by which a decedent disposed of real estate) and a testament (a word of Latin origin that described an instrument by which a decedent disposed of personal property) has been meaningless since the eighteenth century, although some lawyers insist on using the archaic forms.

Note, also, that this clause provides some assistance in resolving the question of testamentary capacity. It states clearly that this instrument is the testator's will. An understanding that he or she is executing a will is, you will recall, one of the requirements for testamentary capacity. Once a testator has signed an instrument with this clause at the beginning, it will be difficult for one seeking to set the will aside on grounds of testatmentary incapacity to argue that the testator thought he or she was autographing a napkin or performing any other act except that of executing a will.

Identification and Definitions Clause

This clause allows you to get certain matters out of the way and avoid the necessity of having to use convoluted definitions and names later. For example, you can identify your wife and children specifically and thereafter need only refer to them generically as "my wife" or "my children" instead of "my wife, Martha Eleanor Todd Webster" or "my children, Mary Todd Webster, John Adams Webster," etc. You can also settle the matter of survival and avoid the necessity of repeatedly using the language, "if he survives me by at least sixty days." Moreover, if you have a person who is not really a child or other relative but has been informally taken into the family in a relativelike status, this clause is the place to identify the person and set straight the relationship. Such a clause can tell the executor volumes about family names and relationships.

The identification and definitions clause also clearly establishes the first requisite of testamentary capacity, that the testator knew his family, the "natural objects of his (or her) bounty."

An identification and definition clause would read as follows:

ARTICLE I. IDENTIFICATION AND DEFINITIONS

A. "My wife" is Martha Eleanor Todd Webster. We have two adult children, Mary Todd Webster, and John Adams Webster. We have also raised from infancy Andrew Jackson Webster, the son of my late brother Millard Fillmore Webster. Although we have never formally adopted him, Andrew Jackson Webster is regarded by every member of my family as our son. Whenever reference is made to "my children" in this Will, Andrew Jackson Webster is to be included in the definition of "children."

B. "Survive me" or words of like import are to be construed to require that the person referred to survive me by sixty (60) days.

Payment of Debts Clause

A clause providing for the payment of the testator's debts is almost universally recommended for inclusion in all wills. At the risk of bringing down the wrath of a majority of writers on this topic, let me suggest that such a clause is (1) unnecessary, and (2) inadvisable in all but a limited number of wills.

To begin, creditors are protected nearly everywhere in the law with respect to priorities and methods of recovery. The probate process is a perfect example of such a creditor protection system. Legal debts of the decedent must be paid whether the will directs their payment or not. Similarly, expenses of administration, last illness, funeral, and burial will have to be paid whether there is a legal direction to pay them or not. The same can be said of all sorts of taxes. It may give the testator a good feeling to know that he will go to his spiritual reward with all debts paid, but the probate process will take care of this need without any specific direction from the testator and without creating any unnecessary problems.

And it is possible that a clause directing their payment will actually cause some difficulties. The typical language employed in such a clause requires the executor to pay "all my *just* debts." It may be that a debt is no longer a legally enforceable one (because the statute of limitations has run, for example) or that the testator has refused to pay the debt during lifetime as a matter of principle (believing, for example, that the creditor has not completed the work for which he or she had contracted). But now the debt, notwithstanding that it is no longer legally enforceable or that the testator did not feel it should be paid, is arguably a just debt and must be paid under the payment of debts clause. Moreover, even where the word just is not used, a creditor could conceivably take the position that the payment of debts clause has created a trust for the benefit of creditors.

In short, it seems best to omit any reference to debts except for the following:

1.If it is important to the testator that debts be paid from some specific fund to the exclusion of other funds, this should be clearly expressed. Often, for example, a testator will want the debts paid from the residuary estate. This wish should be specifically expressed, but it need not be done in a separate payment of debts clause. The clause describing the powers of the executor would be an appropriate place to set forth this direction. (If the will contains no provision with respect to payment of debts, usually the debts will be paid by taking proportionately from the persons who received assets from the estate, whether under the will or otherwise. The testator must decide whether he or she wants this result or whether the expenses are to be paid by the residuary legatees.)

2.If the testator wishes to establish as debts certain items that might not otherwise appear to be obligations of the testator, such as a loan from a child, this should be clearly expressed. A payment of debts clause would be the appropriate place to set forth this matter.

3.The payment of taxes should be expressly provided for in most wills. This should be done, however, in a separate clause relating only to taxes.

A payment of debts clause would read as follows:

ARTICLE II. PAYMENT OF DEBTS

Several years ago, at the time when I had undergone considerable business reverses, my son John loaned me Ten Thousand Dollars ($10,000). Although he never thereafter mentioned this money, it was my clear understanding that this was a loan and not a gift. I therefore direct that this debt be paid, with interest at eight percent (8%) per annum, compounded annually from the date of the loan, by my executor from my residiary estate.

Payment of Taxes Clause

As previously stated, it is normally advisable to provide the source of payment of death taxes. Normally, a testator will want taxes paid from the residuary estate. But if nothing is said with respect to this wish, under local law taxes may be apportioned on a pro rata basis to all property that is included in the estate for death tax purposes, whether such property passes under the will or outside the will.

If the marital deduction is being claimed for federal estate tax purposes and the marital deduction gift is to be provided from the residuary estate, you need to take care that the tax payment clause provides that taxes are paid out of the *nonmarital* gift. Otherwise, the marital deduction may be reduced by the amount of any tax liability.

A fairly typical payment of taxes clause would appear as follows:

ARTICLE III. PAYMENT OF TAXES

I direct that the burden of all estate, inheritance, and similar taxes of whatever nature which are imposed by reason of my death with respect to any property, whether disposed of by this will or not, shall be borne without apportionment by the residue of my probate estate.

Directions as to Remains and Funeral

Some wills contain elaborate directions with respect to the disposition of the decedent's remains and the funeral. In truth, the will is just about the worst place imaginable to put such directions. Most families will, out of respect for the deceased and in an effort not to appear too "grasping" with respect to the decedent's estate, not read the will until after the burial. By then it will be too late to carry out any specific requests regarding the remains or the funeral.

Certainly, if there are directions as to the disposal of the decedent's body, as, for example, where the decedent has provided anatomical gifts for transplant, time is of the essence. The appropriate medical facilities should have been alerted in advance of the potential gift and for the removal of the body, or the specific organs, to the medical facility before decomposition sets in. Obviously, the will is not the place for such directions.

Moreover, any specific requests the decedent may have with respect to the funeral (or the absence of one) should be set forth in a document that will be certain to be opened before the burial. The best place for such documents is with a copy of the will, which is placed in the executor's hands before the decedent's death, or which is placed in a convenient location and the executor and others are informed of its presence and, especially, of the desire of the decedent that the document be read "as soon as possible after my death."

Disposition of Tangible Personal Property Clause

The clause by which the testator disposes of tangible personal property is one that must be carefully watched lest the testator "run amock" and attempt to list every little thing owned and where it will go, along with alternative dispositions depending on the possibility of different sequences of deaths. Nonetheless, for psychological reasons explained earlier, this clause is a most important one for most testators.

If a major reason for drafting a will is to avoid family disputes once the testator has died, the place to avoid those disputes is obviously in the disposition of personal property clause. This is where you say who gets what. And, if you are careful, it is here that you set up the beneficiaries for a dispute-free resolution of the question of who gets what of the property you have not specifically left to any one person.

Perhaps the best way to understand the workings of the disposition of personal property clause is to look at an example.

ARTICLE IV. DISPOSITION OF PERSONAL PROPERTY

A. If she survives me, I give to my wife all of my tangible personal property.

B. If my wife does not survive me, I direct that the following items of my tangible personal property be distributed as indicated:

1. My stamp collection, including all books and records relating thereto, to my daughter Mary;

2. My grandfather's Civil War sword to my son John;

3. My restored 1923 Model A Ford to my stepson Andrew;

4. My collection of antique fishing tackle to my grandson John Adams Webster, Jr.

If any of my children or my grandson shall not survive me, the specific bequest to such deceased child or grandchild shall lapse and pass in accordance with paragraph E of this article.

C. I may leave, with the original or a copy of my will, a letter containing a list of certain items of my personal property, with a request that these items be distributed as this letter provides. I recognize that this letter, not having been executed in compliance with the West Virginia Statute of Wills, has no legal effect. But it is my wish that my requests in this letter be carried out.

D. If my children cannot agree as to the distribution of my tangible personal property, I direct that an independent appriaser be appointed to establish a value for these items and that one of my children be selected by lot to make the first selection from among these items and that the items thereafter be divided among my three children with each alternating in selecting items until the personal property has been divided among them in such fashion that each has selected items of approximately the same total value. It is, however, my fondest wish that my children, out of respect for my memory, make an amicable division of my tangible personal property, remembering always that the family relationship that their mother and I have sought to nurture is vastly more valuable than any item of mere property.

E. Should any child not survive me but leave issue surviving him or her, the deceased child's heirs shall take the share of the deceased child, by right of representation.

There are several important things to note about this clause. First, all tangible personal property was left to the surviving widow. To do otherwise would risk causing a profound disruption in her lifestyle at precisely the time when she may need to be surrounded by the comfortable memories of the past. She may well want to give away the stamp collection, Model A, grandpa's sword, and the like. But, in the absence of a compelling reason to the contrary, this should be *her* choice. Leaving everything to her leaves her the option of distributing her deceased husband's personalty or keeping it around her.

Second, we didn't try to provide for the disposition of all of the decedent's personal property. There is no way this can be done without a will of monumental proportions and, if the decedent continues to collect items of personalty, the risk is great that the will is gong to be out of date at the time of death. The letter that "may" accompany the original or a copy of the will gives the testator an opportunity to revise her or his plan of disposition as the mood strikes and as items are added to the collections.

If the letter had been written before the will were executed, it could be considered a part of the will by virtue of the doctrine of incorporation by reference. Incorporation by reference has four requirements:

1 The document referred to must be in existence at the time the will is executed.
2. The document must be identified in the will so that there can be no mistake about its identity.
3. The document must be clearly intended to be incorporated into the will.
4. The document, when found, corresponds to the identification in the will. If these four tests are met, most states will permit it to be incorporated into the will, which means that it is actually a part of the will and is as binding on the executor as any other part of the will.

The letter we have referred to does not meet the first test of the doctrine of incorporation by reference; it is not in existence at the time the will is executed. This was deliberate. We do not want a list that is incorporated into the will because such a list cannot thereafter be amended except by amending the will. The list we have referred to can be amended at any time without anything at all being done to the will.

The fact that it has no legal effect is of little import because of something we discussed in Chapter 3, the psychological role of property. Once the father in our example is gone (i.e., his will has "matured"), his personality has attached to his property. And if he leaves behind a letter which says, "I want Mary to have this, and this, and this; and I want John to have this, and this, and this; and I want Andrew to have this, and this, and this;" the children are very unlikely to dispute what the father wants done with his property. After all, it *is* father's property, and father has made clear his wishes with respect to the property. (Of course, it isn't father's property at all. Father is dead and gone. But you get the point. Psychologically, father is speaking from the grave about this property and the children are very unlikely to dispute his wishes. (I have warned my children that I will be coming back to haunt them if there are any disputes over my property. And I have every intention of doing so!)

Third, note the provision for the appraiser. The importance of the appraiser here is not so much that she or he will referee the division of the spoils but that father has made it plain that he wants no dispute and has prepared a mechanism to carry out this wish.

Finally, note the "sermon" in the last sentence of paragraph D. Father has, in the terminology of today's youth, "laid a guilt trip" on the kids. In essence, he has said, "Shame, shame on you if you can't make an amicable distribution of my personal property. What's the matter with you? Don't you understand that no amount of property is as valuable as the loving family relationship that your mother (also dead by now, remember) sought to nourish? Now, stop being so 'grabby' and do this thing in a peaceful, pleasant fashion."

Disposition of Real Estate Clause

The disposition of real estate is really no more difficult than the disposition of personal property. It is included here merely because the testator may wish to dispose of real estate to different persons than those who received the personal estate. If so, it should be done plainly and succinctly.

ARTICLE V. DISPOSITION OF REAL ESTATE

I give my farm in Grant County to my friend, Oliver Cromwell, of Charles Town, West Virginia.

Note that, in this clause, as in the clause disposing of personal property, Webster simply "gave" the assets away. There was none of the old (or "olde") language by which the testator would "give, devise, and bequeath" the property. Distinctions between "devising" (which is how real estate was disposed of in former times) and "bequeathing" (which was how one passed on personal property) have been unnecessary for generations. (Help me pass the word to America's lawyers, will you?)

Residuary Clause

The residuary clause of a will is simply what the name suggests, the clause wherein you dispose of the residue of your estate that is left after all the specific devises and bequests have been made. Usually, such a clause can be mercifully brief.

ARTICLE VI. RESIDUE OF ESTATE

I give the rest, residue, and remainder of all of my interest in any property, wherever located, to my three children, and any after-born or after-adopted child or children, share and share alike.

Note that we have included the possibility of any after-born or after-adopted children sharing in the decedent's estate. Since he is old enough to have a grandchild, there may be little possibility of any more children being born, but perhaps not. In any event, there is always the possibility that he may later adopt a child. If the decedent does not expect either event to occur, he can clearly avoid the remote possibility that such children may be born or adopted and "force" a share of his estate by saying, "I have considered the possibility that other children may be born to me or adopted by me and I do not wish them to share in my estate." Period. This excludes the possibility of these children taking a forced share.

No Contest Clause

Suppose the decedent has one child who has always given him trouble and who is likely to cause trouble in the settlement of the decedent's estate. What can he do to reduce the possibility of friction?

First, he should *not* use the attached-list-with-no-legal-significance. This is just the sort of situation when he will want to have everything "nailed down" very clearly. If at all possible, the personal gifts should be listed in the will and a provision (such as the one requiring the use of the appraiser) should be established to assure that the unmentioned personal property can be divided with proper supervision and a minimum of discord.

Second, the decedent could make a gift of the troublemaking child in his will and then use what is known as an *In Terrorem* or *No Contest* clause. Such a clause would read as follows:

ARTICLE VII. DISQUALIFICATION OF CERTAIN BENEFICIARIES

All devises and legacies contained in this will are given upon the express condition that the respective beneficiaries shall not oppose the probate of this will or contest the validity of any provision in this will or any provision from being carried out in accordance with its terms. If any such beneficiary shall oppose the probate of the will or contest the validity of any provision of this will or any terms, I revoke all devises and bequests given to such person and direct that the devises and bequests to this person pass to the remaining beneficiaries under this will, in equal shares.

Note that we provided what should happen to the troublemaking child's devises and bequests if this clause should take effect. This is because some states invalidate such a clause unless there is such a "gift over" on breach of the condition (*Fifield* v. *Van Wyck*, 94 Va. 557, 27 S.E. 446, 1897). Also, some jurisdictions render the clause ineffective if the devisee or legatee is found to have contested the will with "probable cause" (*South Norwalk Trust Co.* v. *St. John*, 92 Conn. 168, 101 A. 961, 1917).

Our decedent could have further strengthened the operation of this clause by leaving all his children a specific bequest of, say $20,000. Then, when the troublemaking son is considering whether to try to have the will set aside or to attack some provision of it, he must determine whether the risk of losing the bird-in-the-hand $20,000 is worth the possibility of taking more if he can prevail in a contest of the will.

If the decedent has had a less than satisfactory relationship with his wife and does not want to leave everything to her, he has the same sort of decision to make as with respect to a potentially troublemaking child. He must, you will recall, leave his spouse a certain specific portion of his estate, depending on the law of the state where he is domiciled. If it is his intention to leave her nothing more, he must carefully assure that he has, at least, left her that much. Otherwise, she can "take against the will," which means that she can force the executor to pay her at least the minimum to which she is entitled, which may have the effect of upsetting the estate plan set out in the rest of the will.

The Executor

The selection of the executor is one of the more important provisions in a will, since this is the person or institution that will be responsible for the management of the decedent's estate in the postmortem period. If, as noted earlier, no executor is named or if the one named is unable or unwilling to serve, the selection of the executor will be left to the probate court, an unattractive alternative at best.

Moreover, there may be certain specific powers that the executor should have to properly administer the estate and that are not automatically provided by the general law of the state of the decedent's domicile. The following executor clause is an example.

ARTICLE VIII. EXECUTOR

A. I nominate the GOTHAM NATIONAL BANK OF CHARLESTON, West Virginia, Executor of this Will.

B. I direct that neither bond nor security be required of my Executor appointed hereunder.

C. In addition to the powers conferred by law, my executor shall have the following discretionary powers:

1. To join with my wife or her estate in the filing of Federal income tax returns for any years for which I have not filed such returns prior to my death without requiring her or her estate to indemnify my estate against liability for the tax attributable to her income; and to consent, for Federal gift tax purposes, to having gifts made by my wife during my lifetime as being made half by me for Federal gift tax purposes.

2. To use administration expenses as deductions for estate tax purposes or income tax purposes and to use date of death values or the alternate valuation date for Federal estate tax purposes, regardless of the effect thereof on the interest of any beneficiary of my estate, without reimbursement or equitable adjustment.

Note that the selection of the executor is only a "nomination," not an "appointment." The actual appointment will be made by the court, but if the nomination is otherwise proper the court will appoint the party the decedent has nominated. The possibility that the designated executor may not be able to serve suggests that the decedent should in most cases name an alternate. We did not name an alternate in this case since the Gotham National Bank is likely to be around for a long time and will certainly be willing to serve.

Also, our example dispenses with the requirement for bond or security. Banks are strictly supervised and the fiduciary responsibility (an executor is a fiduciary) is one of the highest responsibilities in the law. Should the bank act in such a fashion that the estate suffers a loss because of the bank's conduct, there is adequate remedy under the law for the estate to recover. The cost of bond or other security is a cost that is borne by the estate. Therefore, if it is not absolutely necessary, it should be waived.

Had the decedent named his brother-in-law (the one with the thin mustache and the alligator shoes, with the teeth still on them), it would probably be advisable *not* to waive the requirement for a bond. In any event, our clause waives the requirement only for an executor appointed under the will. If it is necessary to name another executor (the Gotham Bank has gone under, for example), an alternate executor will have to post a bond or other security.

The tax provisions included in this clause are there to simplify matters for the executor and perhaps save the estate some money. Note, however, that provision C.2 protects the executor (1) in the allocating of administration expenses as deductions for estate tax or income tax purposes, and (2) in the decision of whether to use the alternate valuation date from the claim of any beneficiary that his or her interest was affected. In making each of these decisions, it is possible that some beneficiaries will benefit and others will suffer. The executor, however, mut make these decisions with the interest of the *entire estate* in mind. Thus, our provision protects the executor from the claims of any beneficiary that he or she has been harmed by the decision.

Guardian of Minor Children

If the decedent had minor children at the time of execution of his will, he should have selected a guardian for the children. The process is similar to that of selecting an executor and the language is much the same. As noted earlier, the real importance of the selection of a guardian in a will is that the couple will have confronted the issue and made the necessary arrangements that the will is merely verifying.

Testimonium Clause

The testimonium clause establishes that the testator executed the will with full and complete knowledge that the instrument was, in fact, his or her last will and testament. It establishes the date the will was executed (which may be important if there is another testamentary instrument) and provides a place for the formal signature of the testator. The following is a fairly standard testimonium clause:

IN WITNESS WHEREOF, I, DANIEL CLAY WEBSTER, have signed this will, consisting of this page, three preceding typewritten pages, and one subsequent typewritten page, on the preceding and subsequent typewritten pages of which I have signed my name in the left-hand margin for purposes of identification, at Charleston, West Virginia, on this the ___ day of _____ 198__.

_____
DANIEL CLAY WEBSTER

Attestation Clause

The attestation clause is signed by the witnesses and sets forth their understanding of what has taken place. It assures that the will was executed in compliance with the state law relating to witnesses and other formalities and can be a key clause if the will is challenged for lack of observance of execution formalities.

> Daniel Clay Webster stated to us that this instrument was his Will and signed it in our presence. We now believe him to be of sound mind, of at least the age of eighteen, and not under duress. We now, at his request, and in his presence, and in the presence of each other, sign our names as witnesses, all on this ___day of _____, 198__

_____   _____

                                         _____

_____   _____

                                         _____

_____   _____

Self-proving Clause

A question often raised by persons about to execute their wills is, "What happens to the probate of our wills if the witnesses cannot later be located to come before the court and identify the will?" In an increasingly mobile society, the question becomes more important every day.

Someone who was familiar with the witnesses must come in and swear before the appropriate official that he or she is familiar with the witness's signature, that the signature in the will is, indeed, the witness's signature, that he or she knew the witness at the time the will was executed, and that the witness was of sound mind and not likely to participate in a fraudulent will execution. The process is, as you might suspect, somewhat unwieldy.

Because of this, many states permit the use of a *self-proving affidavit*, a document that is, in effect, a deposition signed by the witnesses before a notary public describing what took place at the execution of the will. Such a document, made in compliance with the appropriate state law, can be presented to the proper authority when the will is probated. This eliminates the necessity of having the witness come in to testify as to the execution of the will (the self-proving affidavit contains their sworn testimony on this matter). Here is a sample self-proving affidavit designed to be used in West Virginia:

STATE OF WEST VIRGINIA

COUNTY OF KANAWHA, to-wit:

This day personally appeared before me, the undersigned Notary Public in and for Kanawha County, _____, _____, and _____, the three subscribing witnesses to the foregoing writing purporting to be the will of Daniel Clay Webster, bearing date the ___ day of _____, 198__, who, after being duly sworn, do depose and say:

That Daniel Clay Webster signed, declared, and acknowledged the writing to be his Will in their presence on the ___ day of _____, 198__, and at the time Daniel Clay Webster was of sound mind and disposing memory and of at least the age of eighteen years; that at the request of Daniel Clay Webster, and in his presence and in the presence of each other, each signed his or her name to the Will; and that at the further request of Daniel Clay Webster they each do now make this affidavit to be preserved with the Will by Daniel Clay Webster and to be produced and offered in evidence whenever this Will shall be offered for probate, pursuant to the statutes of the State of West Virginia provided for such cases.

_____

_____

_____

Taken, subscribed, and sworn to before me this ___ day of _____, 198__, as witness my hand and official seal.

_____
Notary Public In and For
Kanawha County, W.Va.

My commission expires_____.

APPLYING THIS CHAPTER TO *YOUR* SITUATION

To prepare a will that properly disposes of your assets and sets the stage for postmortem family harmony, you *must* be familiar with the law of your domiciliary state regarding wills. If, for example, you wish to leave the bulk of your estate to charity, you must know if your state is one that places limits on such gifts. Similarly, you must be aware of what the law of your state guarantees your spouse and how it views children who are not mentioned in the will.

You must also be certain to observe all the formalities required of your statute of wills with respect to executing a valid will, from age and mental capacity to whether your state recognizes holographic wills.

The final product need not be a convoluted will done in "Lawyers' English" (another contradiction in terms); indeed, it ought to be a perfectly readable document. Language set forth in this chapter, or something very close to it, can serve as a guide for most of the provisions of the average simple will.

CASE PROBLEMS

5.1 Special Solutions for Special Problems.   What special solutions are available to the estate owner with the following problems?

1. A wife who does not want to leave her entire estate to her husband but who also does not want her will contested.
2. A couple with valuable antiques to be divided among several children and grandchildren.
3. A father who wishes to leave nothing to one child but does not want the child to contest the will.
4. A testator who wants to be certain that his executor pays all his bills before distributing the estate among the heirs.
5. A testator who does *not* want her brother-in-law to serve as executor of her estate.

5.2 A Simple Estate with Complex Problems.   Richard and Ellen VanDyke have acquired, through a lifetime of hard work and frugal living, an estate in excess of $1,000,000. They have two children, a son age 40 and a daughter age 38. An older daughter was killed some years ago in an automobile accident and is survived by three children, all of college age. The VanDyke's estate consists mostly of rental real estate and corporate stocks; there are no personal collections of any particular value.

Questions
1. What are the three major reasons the VanDykes need a will?
2. If Mr. VanDyke has suffered a stroke and there is some question as to his mental capacity, how can this question be resolved in order for him to execute a valid will?
3. If the VanDykes live in a state that requires only two witnesses and never plan to move to another state, do they need to use three witnesses?

SELECTED READINGS

BOWMAN, FOREST J., *The Complete Retirement Handbook*. New York: Putnam Publishing Co., 1983, pp. 84–86, 96–100.

PRICE, JOHN R., *Contemporary Estate Planning*. Boston: Little, Brown and Company, 1983, pp. 168–186.

SHAFFER, THOMAS L., *The Planning and Drafting of Wills and Trusts*. Mineola, N.Y.: Foundation Press, Inc., 1979, pp. 169–190.

STRENG, WILLIAM P., *Estate Planning*. Washington, D.C.: Tax Management, Inc., 1981, pp. 335–341.

6

Some Practical Questions About Wills

In some instances homemade pies are superior.
Wills never.

Matter of Douglas
195 Misc. (N.Y.) 661, 662 (1949)

WRITING YOUR OWN WILL

In some states you may, as we noted earlier, write your own will entirely in your own hand and avoid the necessity of dealing with witnesses and the expense of having a lawyer draft your will. And in every state you may familiarize yourself with the statute of wills and draft your will in compliance with the statute. In some states (California is a notable example) the State Bar will even provide you with forms that will assist you in the process of drafting your will.

It no doubt appears self-serving for a lawyer to suggest that a layperson should not draft his or her own will. But I do. I recommend that a nonlawyer seek the services of a lawyer for the preparation of one's will for the same reasons that I recommend that a nonphysician seek the services of a physician for the performance of a prefrontal lobotomy. (Indeed, it is not too far-fetched to suggest that nonlawyers who insist on doing their own wills should also seek a prefrontal lobotomy, but I digress.)

All the reasons listed earlier in support of having a will also suggest that one should have a *valid* will. A lawyer with any experience in probate matters can relate horror stories of estates that have been overtaxed, distributed to the "wrong" persons, or otherwise horribly mutilated because the testator left a will that was invalid or, worse, incompetently done.

A perfect example from the author's experience is that of a man who wanted to cut one son out of the will, since the son had deserted the father years before. The father carefully left all his assets to his remaining children and put the will in his safe deposit box. In the ensuing years, however, the father acquired additional assets that were not mentioned in the will. When the father died, the runaway son returned to claim his share of the father's estate. Although the father's will specifically "disinherited" the boy, the will contained no residuary clause and so disposed of only those assets that were listed in the will. As to the assets acquired after the will was executed, the father died intestate and the son took his share of those assets. Since the father had acquired the great bulk of his estate after executing his will, the son shared in most of his father's estate, despite his father's wishes to the contrary.

In a fairly recent West Virginia case, a very wealthy bachelor left a considerable estate by means of a dubious handwritten will. The estate has been before the Supreme Court of Appeals of West Virginia on two occasions and is likely to go there again, with the result that the estate will be much depleted by lawyers' fees before anything can be distributed as the testator wished. (This fact will be worth at least two nasty editorials in the antilawyer media, neither of which will make note of the fact that hiring a lawyer could have prevented the whole problem in the first instance.) For a very small legal fee, this man could have had a will drafted that would have accomplished his wishes. More money would have passed to his beneficiaries than will be the case with the will he drafted himself.

Lawyers like the author wait in vain for the day when lawyers will be respected for what they do. But that is not the point here. The point is this: in drafting wills, as in so many other matters relating to the estate planning process, lawyers are a necessity (a necessary evil some would say, but the point is the same; they are necessary to the effective carrying out of the process). So don't write your own will.

WHERE TO KEEP YOUR WILL

The proper place to keep a will is where it will not be inadvertently destroyed and where it can be retrieved quickly when the testator dies (and the will has matured). In many states, a bank safe deposit box is sealed by the state tax authorities when the boxholder dies. In those states, the safe deposit box would obviously be an inappropriate place to store one's will. But in states where the safe deposit box is not sealed, the box may be the perfect place to maintain the will if someone else (the surviving spouse, for example) has access to the box. Often, the lawyer who drafted the will might agree to keep it in the firm's safe or, if a bank is serving as executor, it may store the will.

Regardless of where the original is kept, a copy of the will should be readily available to the executor. I often recommend that clients keep a copy of their will in a certain drawer in the desk in their den or in their nightstand. On this copy I suggest they write the words, "Original in safe deposit box" or other information as to the location of the original. Then I suggest that the client inform the executor, the spouse, and perhaps the children where this will is kept and that they be informed to read the will immediately to assure that the client's wishes are being carried out. (It is with this copy that the decedent will want to leave the "unofficial" letter regarding the disposition of certain items of personal property and any other instructions that he or she may wish to leave.)

AMENDING AND REVOKING WILLS

A will is a transitory document with no legal effect until the testator dies. Therefore, any will can be revised or revoked by the testator (assuming the testator is of sound mind) anytime before death.

Codicils

The simplest means of amending a will is to draft an addendum specificially designed for the existing will. Such a document, known in the law as a *codicil*, must be executed with the same formality required of the will itself. That is, it must be in writing, executed before the requisite witnesses (unless it is wholly in the handwriting of the testator in a state that recognizes holographic wills), and signed by a testator who has the legal capacity to do so.

Note, however, that the codicil does not have to be in the same form as the will itself; it must merely meet the requirements of the Statute of Wills of the state where you are domiciled when the will is executed. Thus, if your state recognizes holographic wills, you can write a holographic codicil to your typewritten will. Or, on the other hand, you can have a typewritten (and properly witnessed) codicil to a holographic will. The only requirement is that the codicil, like the will itself, be made in compliance with the state's Statute of Wills.

At the time the testator dies, both the will and the codicil must be separately presented for probate. Obviously, then, if you have the will and more than one or two codicils, the possibilities for confusion with so many documents is multiplied. For this reason, most lawyers recommend that a will have only one or at most two codicils. If, after having twice amended your will by codicil, you wish to amend it again, you should redraft the will itself to include all the changes you have made in the past and wish to make at this time. Having multiple codicils only adds to the difficulties of probate.

As a practical matter, if your changes to your will are significant, it will often be simpler to draft a new will than to make substantial amendments to your existing will be means of a complicated codicil. The idea of a codicil is merely to permit you to make small changes to your will without having to redraft the entire will. If the changes you want to make are significant, there is no advantage to using a codicil.

Revoking Your Will

A will is revoked by any unequivocal act that indicates that the testator no longer intends the document to be a lawful will. The key word here is "unequivocal."

The Uniform Probate Code provides, for example, that a will may be revoked by the following:

1. A subsequent will that revokes the prior will or part thereof, expressly or by inconsistency.
2. Being burned, torn, canceled, obliterated, or destroyed with the intent and for the purpose of revoking it by the testator or by another person in his or her presence and by his or her direction (UPC Sec. 2-507)

This provision is fairly representative of most state laws on the question of revocation of wills.

If you think about it for a moment, the only *safe* way to revoke a will is by executing a later will that expressly revokes the earlier will. The reason is that all the means of revoking a will listed in item 2 are inherently ambiguous. If your will is discovered after your death with the signature obliterated, who is to say that you obliterated the signature or that it was done by one of your heirs who was disappointed with the will? Unless you obliterated the signature in the presence of witnesses (who should be totally disinterested, that is, they should not benefit whether the will is found to be valid *or* revoked), or unless the signature was obliterated at your direction in your presence and in the presence of witnesses, there will always be some question, particularly if some heirs suffer if the will is *not* probated and others suffer if it *is* probated. (And the witnesses will only resolve the matter if they survive you, which witnesses have an uncanny way of not doing when most needed.)

Moreover, you will notice that item 2 also requires that the burning, tearing, canceling, obliterating, and so on, be done "with the intent and for the purpose of revoking" the will. Intent is a highly subjective matter. Unless you have made the matter clear to your disinterested witnesses, who is to say what your intent was when you destroyed the will?

Obviously, then, by revoking a will by any means other than the execution of a later valid will, you are setting your loved ones up for the sort of suspicion and back-biting that can only lead to the in-fighting that a well-drafted will should avoid. With rare exceptions, the only safe and proper way to revoke a will is by a later will that unequivocally revokes all earlier wills.

Dependent Relative Revocation

What if you revoke your current will with the intent of drafting a new one immediately but are struck and killed by a meteorite on your way to the lawyer's office? Is there any way that the old will can still be held valid?

The law, with the fine precision we have come to expect from it, answers clearly, "It depends." And what it depends on is the doctrine of Dependent Relative Revocation, a doctrine that is certainly one of the "shakiest" in the law of wills.

According to this doctrine, if

(1) the testator has effectively revoked a valid will; and

(2) the revocation was expressly done on the condition that a new will was to be drafted; and

(3) the new will is not made (or, if made, it is not valid because not properly executed, or for any reason) the old will will be considered valid (*Lacroix* v. *Senecal*, 140 Conn. 311, 99 a.2d 115, 1953.

The idea is that the revocation was conditional on the later will being drafted, and when this will was not drafted, the testator would have preferred that the old will be in effect rather than to die intestate. The fallacy in the doctrine should be obvious. How do we know that the testator would have preferred the old will to intestacy? Obviously, in most cases we do not. Thus the doctrine of Dependent Relative Revocation has little application in real life.

This doctrine is included at this point for two reasons:

1. To show, although the rule exists and will on rare occasions "revive" a revoked will, no testator should ever depend on it.

2. To point out again that the business of drafting and executing wills is a precise and complex matter worthy of more care and attention than the offhand manner in which it is often treated.

Revocation of Wills by Operation of Law

Under the laws of most states, certain changes in your marital status have the effect of revoking your will unless the will was drafted with the change in marital status in mind. For example, if you marry after drafting a will, the will is revoked in most states unless it was drafted with the marriage in mind. So, also, a divorce or annulment of a marriage will revoke a will (unless, again, your will was drafted with the divorce or annulment in mind, which is extremely unlikely). So, if you have undergone a significant change in your marital status since writing your will, check with your lawer to be certain that the will is still valid. You could be intestate and not know it.

Outdated Wills

A problem that is often more serious than intestacy is that of dying with a will that is out of date. For example, assume that your will gives your estate in equal shares to your three daughters and provides that, if any of the daughters do not survive you, her share will pass to her children. You are thinking, naturally, that you love your daughters equally (even though children never understand or believe this) and want your estate divided among the three of them or their families. But if all three of your daughters die before you, leaving seven grandchildren, unequally spread among the three daughters, you will most likely want to leave your estate in seven shares, one to each grandchild, since you love your grandchildren equally. (You are unlikely, for example, to love the only child of one daughter twice as much as you love one of two children of another daughter.) But your will leaves the estate in three equal shares, precisely as your original family was structured. Unless you do want your estate to be divided in three shares among the seven grandchildren, your will is out of date and does not reflect your wishes with respect to your property.

Or consider the tax consequences of an out-of-date will. Before the Economic Recovery Tax Act of 1981, a husband could only leave a wife, sheltered from taxation by the marital deduction, the greater of one-half of the adjusted gross estate or $250,000. Anything over this amount was subject to taxation at some very steep rates. Many wills were drafted at that time leaving the spouse only so much as would qualify for the maximum marital deduction under the federal estate tax law at that time.

Now the marital deduction is unlimited; any property left by one spouse to another is free of the federal estate tax because of the marital deduction. You may wish to leave your spouse all of your estate. If your will was drafted before the 1981 tax act, it may well not do so because of a tax provision that is no longer a part of the law. An out-of-date will in this instance can cost the estate considerable tax dollars and prevent the surviving spouse from inheriting what you would otherwise prefer he or she take.

Or let's say that you left your estate in equal shares, outright, to your three children. Now, 15 years later, you can see that the children (who were tiny when you wrote your will) are going to have unequal needs. It may be clear, for example, that one son will never hold a steady job. Another son may be a brain surgeon with no financial problems. A daughter may be doing well as a stock broker, but has a child who will need considerable medical attention over the years. Your old "everything-to-the-children-in-three-equal-shares" will is not just out of date; it is a definite hazard.

The illustrations are endless, but the point is simply this: Every will, no matter how carefully considered and drafted, should be reviewed every few years to assure that your estate will not pass contrary to your current wishes.

Updating Your Will Yourself

Clients often bring a will to their lawyers on which they have interlined, usually in indelible ink, certain changes, striking out other provisions. "Here," they say, "this is how I want my will to be redrafted." In the meantime, of course, they intend that their present will remain in effect.

Unfortunately, in most cases a will that has been interlined and stricken through is now a revoked will, and if the client dies before the new will can be prepared, the client dies intestate. *Never* make any kind of marks whatsoever on a will that you do not intend to revoke by doing so. Otherwise, you may very well have revoked the will unintentionally.

FORMALITIES OF EXECUTION

The formal requirements for execution of wills vary considerably in detail from state to state. Because ours is a mobile society with people often owning property in many states, most lawyers seek to draft and execute a will that will be valid in all the American states.

For example, most states require the testator to sign the will in the presence of witnesses, so usually the signing of a will is actually done with all witnesses present, even in those states that permit the testator to acknowledge to the witnesses that the signature already on the will is the testator's.

For the most part (and that is a caveat of some consequence in this particular instance), a will should be (note, again, the qualification) valid in all American states if the following ten safeguards are observed:

1. If the will consists of more than one page, the pages should be fastened together and specified, that is, "PAGE ONE OF SIX PAGES, PAGE TWO OF SIX PAGES," and so on.

2. The lawyer should be certain that the testator has read the will, understands it, and approves of its contents.

3. The lawyer, the testator, three disinterested witnesses, and a notary public enter the room where the execution is to take place. The door is closed and *locked*. The lawyer explains that the reason the door is closed and locked is that the law of some states requires that there be no interruptions of the execution process. By locking the door, the fact that there were no interruptions is impressed on the witnesses.

4. The lawyer asks the testator three questions:
    a. Is this your will?
    b. Have you read it and do you understand it?
    c. Does it dispose of your property in accordance with your wishes?

The testator should answer yes to all three questions in a voice that can be heard and understood clearly by all three witnesses.

It is neither necessary nor customary that the witnesses know the contents of the will. It is only necessary that they understand that they are witnessing a document that the testator has explained to them in his or her will. If, however, there are unusual provisions in the testator's will that may well lead to a will contest, this is the point at which the lawyer would raise them. For example, if one son is being disinherited and the lawyer foresees a will contest in which the son will assert his mother was not of sound mind when the will was executed, the lawyer should alert the witnesses to the fact that there may later be some questions raised as to the testator's capacity and ask the following questions of the testator :

1. Is there anything unusual about your will? (To which the testator will respond by describing the fact that she is disinheriting her son.)

2. Why are you doing this? (To which the testator will respond by explaining in such detail as necessary the reasons why she is disinheriting her son. This is im-

portant because it will show that the testator did recognize that her son was a "natural object of her bounty" and that she did not leave him anything for reasons that he understood and which were, we hope, perfectly rational.)

3. Is anyone putting any pressure on you to disinherit your son?

At this point the lawyer will ask the witnesses if they have any questions they would like to ask the testator in order to establish that she is of sound mind. The lawyer asks the testator if he or she would like to have the three witnesses, whom he now identifies, serve as witnesses to the will. The testator should respond yes in a voice that can be clearly heard and understood by the witnesses.

The testator signs the left-hand margin of each page except the signature page of the will. The signature page is signed on the line there provided. All witnesses are directed to lean forward and watch the testator sign.

Each witness initials each page of the will except the signature page and the self-proving affidavit. Each witness then writes his or her name and address on the lines provided on the signature page and signs his or her name on the lines provided on the self-proving affidavit. One witness reads aloud the attestation clause, which attests to what is being done. (This is so the witnesses will have no question as to what they are signing and why.)

The notary public completes the self-proving affidavit.

The ceremony being completed, the door to the room is opened and witnesses and the notary leave. The lawyer then reviews with the client what should be done with the original will and the copy of the will that the lawyer provides. (In the real world, this may also be the time when the bill is presented.)

The necessity for making a ceremony of the execution of a will cannot be overemphasized. It is, of course, one of life's rituals, involving as it does the recognition of one's mortality and the preparation one has made for death. The ceremonial aspects of the execution also impress on the client that this is a serious matter. This not only makes the bill more palatable (no minor matter on occasion), but it also reinforces the importance of what has been done through the will.

Occasionally, clients (or even witnesses) will be ill at ease during the execution of a will. There will often be awkward banter between some of the parties. This is perfectly natural, and the lawyer supervising the execution of the will should patiently guide the discussion and the tenor of the occasion back to the dignified business at hand.

JOINT AND MUTUAL WILLS

Wills, like everything else, go through fads. In the 1940s the "in" thing in the will business was a joint will, which is a single document involving two or more testators, usually a husband and wife. By such documents, husbands and wives routinely left their entire estates to one another and then to their children or elsewhere on the death of the survivor.

There is a certain sentimental appeal to the joint will, but it is a practical nightmare. To begin, once the first party dies and the will is probated, it is a matter of public record what will happen to the estate of the surviving spouse. Moreover, and even more troublesome, is the fact that the joint will is often held to imply a promise not to revoke. Thus, when the first party has died, the second party can never change the will, even though the second party may die years after the first party and even though the value and nature of the joint estate may have changed radically in the interim *(In Re Estate of Wiggins,* 45 App.Div.2d 244, 360 N.Y.S.2d 129, 1974).

Even mutual wills (i.e., separate instruments by which husband gives to wife and wife gives to husband and each, if survivor, gives to the children) have been held to contain or imply a contract not to revoke *(Turner* v. *Theiss,* 129 W.Va. 23, 38 S.E.2d 369, 1946).

The mischief caused by a joint or mutual will is hardly worth the advantage that the simplicity of the devices afford. So stay away from joint wills entirely. As to mutual wills, a simple clause that states that no contract has been made on the subject of revocation will suffice.

APPLYING THIS CHAPTER TO *YOUR* SITUATION

If your state's law permits it, you can write your own will entirely in your own hand and eliminate the necessity for witnesses and the lawyer's fee. But undertaking to draft your own will should only be done when your estate is not complex and when you expect no problems among your heirs in the division of your estate. Paying a lawyer to draft a will is always cheaper than having to litigate the question of whether your purported will is valid.

The problem of an invalid will is the same as that of no will at all: intestacy. But dying with an out-of-date will can be even worse than intestacy. You need, then, to carefully review your will and other estate planning documents from time to time to assure that they are not out of date.

CASE PROBLEMS

6.1 Writing Your Own Will. Mary Chestnut, a widow with two grown children, wishes to write her own will to avoid a lawyer's fee. Her estate consists of her bank accounts, corporate stock, three pieces of rental property, her household goods, and some antiques. The total value of her estate is approximately $750,000. She wants to divide it equally between her two children.

Questions
1. List three reasons why she should *not* draft her own will.
2. Assuming she insists on drafting her own will, what formalities should she be certain to follow?

3. If she already has a valid lawyer-drafted will and merely wants to update it, how can she do this herself?

4. If, after writing her will (and executing it), Mary meets and marries Robert Lee, what problems, if any, does this cause with respect to her will?

6.2 A Joint Will.   George and Martha Jefferson executed simple wills on the same day by which they left their entire estates to one another and to their children on the death of the survivor. George died in 1970 and Martha inherited everything from him. Now Martha has remarried and wants her new husband's children to share in her estate (at least part of which she inherited from George).

Questions
1. Can Martha leave all or part of her estate to her new husband's children?
2. If George and Martha had wished to make it clear that they were not in any way limiting the survivor's right to dispose of the entire estate as he or she should see fit, how could they have done this?
3. Would a joint will be better or worse for George and Martha?

SELECTED READINGS

KURTZ, SHELDON F., *Family Estate Planning*. St. Paul, Minn.: West Publishing Co., 1983, pp. 45–65.

PRICE, JOHN R., *Contemporary Estate Planning*. Boston: Little, Brown and Company, 1983, pp. 168–169.

SHAFFER, THOMAS L., *The Planning and Drafting of Wills and Trusts*. Mineola, N.Y.: Foundation Press, Inc., 1979, pp. 70–78, 184–185.

7

Probate

*Surely the probate of a fraudulent or forged paper
is a fraud on the living as much as the suppression
of the last Will.*

Gaines v. Chew, 2 How. (43 U.S.) 619, 651 (1844)

The term probate has several meanings. For the most part it is viewed as the process by which a deceased person's assets are inventoried, all debts due the decedent are collected, all debts owed by the decedent (including taxes) are paid, and what is left over is distributed according to the decedent's will or the intestate statutes of the state where the decedent was domiciled at death.

Probate is also a part of the process of providing clear title to assets. For example, if you die owning Blackacre, a car, 500 shares of Amalgamated Buggy Whip Corporation stock, and some money in the bank, your heirs and loved ones will take these assets, either through your will or by reason of the intestate statutes of your state.

However, let's say you also died owing some debts—a mortgage on Blackacre, six month's of payments on the car, and the usual monthly bills to the phone company, water company, and the like. Assuming that your assets are sufficient to pay all these debts, someone must assure that they are paid before the titles to Blackacre, the car, the stock, and any money left in your bank account are passed on to your heirs. The person who does this is your personal representative, known as an *executor* if you named the person in your will and an *administrator* if appointed by the court.

The process of probate is such that your executor or administrator can only transfer the title to these assets after all your debts have been paid. Thus, when the title is passed to your heirs, it is a *clear* title, a title that is unencumbered by any debts you may have left.

To the layperson (and to many lawyers), this process is slow, cumbersome, and unduly expensive. As a result, there has been a growing movement across the country for probate reform (with "reform" having substantially different meanings depending on who is proposing what).

PHASES OF THE PROBATE PROCESS

The probate process has five phases:

1. *Filing the will* with the appropriate governmental body (usually known as the probate court) and appointment of the representative of the estate (the executor or administrator): This process is typically known as *admission of the will to probate*. If there is no will, this step consists of filing a statement to the effect that the decedent left no will and appointing a representative of the estate.

2. *Inventorying and appraising the assets* of the estate: In this phase of the probate process, the personal representative takes possession of the assets in the probate estate. If it appears that the assets may not be sold or disributed in relatively short order, the personal representative will arrange to have title transferred to him or her in his or her official capacity. If, on the other hand, quick sale or distribution is expected, the personal representative will probably allow the assets to remain titled in the decedent's name. In most cases, although it is not required, the personal representative will provide the heirs and beneficiaries of the decedent with a copy of the inventory of assets. At this stage the personal representative will also place a value on the assets that the decedent owned at death, an important responsibility where death taxes are a concern.

A concern in this phase of the probate process is the determination of what is included in the probate estate and what is included in the taxable estate. As we saw earlier, assets that may be included in the decedent's estate for death tax purposes may not be included for probate purposes. Since the two estates have entirely different purposes, the personal representative must carefully determine precisely what assets make up each estate.

3. *Collecting debts* owed to the estate and paying debts owed by the estate: The procedure for this phase of the process is usually spelled out in considerable detail in the probate statutes. Some form of notice will be given to the decedent's creditors to present their claims against the estate, usually by a notice of publication. The personal representative must then review each claim to determine its validity and pay the claim if it is valid. When a claim is disallowed, the personal representative must give the creditor a notice of disallowance, which will also inform the creditor of a means of appealing the disallowance.

4. *Paying taxes*, including the federal estate tax, any state estate or inheritance tax, and the income tax owed by the decedent for the portion of the tax year during which she or he was alive: In large estates, the determination of estate and inheritance tax liability is a major responsibility of the personal representative and the lawyer for the estate. Unlike other creditors, the taxing authorities do not need to file a claim for taxes due but, rather, the personal representative must file the appropriate death tax

returns in a timely fashion. (I know. They ought to wait in line like every other creditor, but they don't.)

5. *Distributing assets of the estate* to those who are entitled to them: After the assets have been collected and liabilities against the estate have been settled, the personal representative must tender an accounting disclosing the assets collected, liabilities paid, and distributions to be made. Upon receiving judicial approval of the accounting (at which time the personal representative also gets her or his fee approved), the assets remaining in the estate can be distributed to the appropriate heirs. (In many cases the distribution to the heirs takes place before the final accounting is made to the court. But the approval of the probate court is necessary to assure that the assets have been properly distributed. When title examiners are searching for clear title to realty or any other substantial asset, they always look for the final settlement. This tells them that all creditors have been satisfied and that the property that was passed on to the heirs was free of liens.)

DISADVANTAGES OF PROBATE

Delay

In simple terms, probate exists to assure that the decedent's debts are paid and that his or her assets pass to those who are entitled to them. Unfortunately, however, the supervision of the probate court over the process of settling a decedent's estate has become an often complex, unwieldy, and time-consuming process.

When property does not have to go through probate, the transfer can normally be accomplished as soon as the tax releases have been obtained from the state death tax authorities. But when assets are subject to probate, not only must the tax clearances be obtained, but the procedures of the probate process must be followed.

The length of time required to probate an estate will depend on the nature of the assets in the estate, the complexity of the disposition plan of the estate, and any tax problems involved. But even relatively simple estates can take a long time to settle under most state probate systems. Much of the reason for this lies in the nature of the role of the personal representative (an individual whose appointment itself may take some considerable period of time to accomplish).

The personal representative is, in effect, a short-term fiduciary whose duty it is to protect the assets in the estate and wind up the affairs of the decedent. However, certain practical limitations on the personal representative render this role less than terribly efficient:

1. In most cases the personal representative can exercise his or her powers only with court approval, necessitating the slow and costly business of petitioning the court before anything of significance is accomplished.

2. The personal representative lacks broad general powers to administer the estate, unless the decedent's will specificially confers such broad authority on him or her.

3. The liabilities that the personal representative faces if he or she acts without proper court authorization can only be described as draconian.

Consequently, the personal representative who is even the least bit careful will always seek probate court approval before taking action that affects the estate. Given the snaillike pace of most probate court systems, delay is inevitable.

Expense

Petitioning the estate for permission at every step in the probate process is expensive, if for no other reason than that the estate must bear the cost of the personal representative's time expended in preparing the necessary petitions and presenting them to the court.

In addition, the compensation of the personal representative and the lawyer for the estate have historically been based on the value of the probate estate, regardless of what duties are required to settle the estate. (Indeed, it is not uncommon for an estate of considerable value to be quite simple to settle. For example, the estate of a decedent who left a million in stocks and bonds may be considerably simpler to settle than a much smaller estate that consists of assets to which the title may be in dispute and where there may be substantial debts that can only be paid by the sale of some of these assets.)

The fees of the personal representative and the lawyer may be set by statute or established by "general practice in the area." In either event, the fees often have little connection with the efforts involved by the personal representative and the lawyer, and they are often quite unreasonably large. (To be fair it should be pointed out that the corollary of this is also true. An estate with limited assets may require considerable effort to settle but have very little assets on which to base a fee that will adequately compensate the personal representative and the lawyer. Human nature being what it is, however, no one seems to get very excited over this aspect of the problem.)

A typical payment schedule for the services of the personal representative or the lawyer could be calculated as follows:

5% of the first $100,000
4% of the next $200,000
3% of the next $200,000
1% of the next $500,000
Over $1,000,000, not to exceed 1%

The minimum fee would be, in any case, $1,000.

Under this schedule, if an estate is valued at $600,000, a fee of $20,000 would be payable to the personal representative ($5,000 for the first $100,000, $8,000 for the next $200,000, $6,000 for the next $200,000, and $1,000 for the last $100,000).

However, since probate fees, commissions, and expenses are deductible from the income tax or estate as a cost of administration, the actual fees would be somewhat lower. Moreover, since the fee and commission rates under the process outlined become smaller on each successively higher increment in the amount of the estate, unless probate is avoided with respect to every asset the decedent owned, only the lower portion of the fee or commission is saved by avoiding probate. For example, if probate were avoided on $100,000 of our sample estate, the savings would only be $1,000.

Nonetheless, the lack of any relationship between the effort expended by the personal representaive and the lawyer for the estate and the fees to which they are often entitled is a cause for serious complaint and continues to be one of the major gripes against the probate process.

Lack of Privacy

Because probate is a court proceeding, all the documents filed in the proceeding are a matter of public record, and there is often considerable publicity surrounding the details.

It is not uncommon for newspaper stories to relate the intimate details of the will of a wealthy or prominent decedent (often under garish headlines such as "Jones Leaves $50,000 to Secretary"). Confidence men who prey on heirs who have just inherited from a decedent often use this public information to seek out their victims. It is a small matter, but in a society that values its privacy, the lack of privacy must be counted a disadvantage.

Prolonging the Grief

Keeping a decedent's estate open for an undue length of time often prolongs the grief of the survivors who feel the need to settle the decedent's affairs and "get on with life." This complaint is often heard in connection with the death of a younger person who has suffered a sudden, violent death. The prolonged settlement of the estate keeps reminding the survivors of the traumatic experience of the death of the loved one and interferes with wrapping up of the decedent's affairs and putting the decedent to rest.

Proposals for Reform

As a result of dissatisfaction over these shortcomings of the probate process, a number of reforms have been suggested. The most common change recommended is to permit estates of certain sizes or certain degrees of simplicity to avoid probate supervision. The Uniform Probate Code, a product of the National Conference of Commissioners on Uniform State Laws, is perhaps the most widespread and detailed effort in this direction. This code, which has been adopted in 14 states and has been partially adopted by or influenced the revision of probate statutes in at least six other states, permits noncontroverted estates to be administered free from judicial supervision if the parties so choose.

A more recent product of the National Conference of Commissioners on Uniform State Laws is the Uniform Succession Without Administration Act, which permits an estate to avoid probate, regardless of the size of the estate, when the estate is simple and the heirs of the decedent are willing to assume responsibility for all the debts of the decedent.

This latter act is based on the long-standing practice of settling estates in the European law systems. There, when a decedent dies, if his or her heirs are willing to assume responsibility for debts, the decedent's assets can pass to the heirs (with the decedent's debts "attached," as it were) in a matter of days or, at most, weeks. The creditors of the deceased are protected in that, in most cases, they have the right to object to this simple process if they believe they will have difficulty collecting from the heirs of the decedent. To keep creditors from objecting, the heirs usually move quickly to pay the decedent's debts or to make arrangements to satisfy the creditors that they will be paid.

It is too early to tell, but the Uniform Succession without Administration Act does not appear to be meeting with much acceptance throughout the states. It is a curious thing that we Americans resist any governmental interference while we are living, but are willing to put up with expensive and time-consuming governmental interference in the transfer of our assets after we are gone. In Europe, on the other hand, governmental interference in the daily lives of the citizenry is commonplace, but the government generally stays out of the process of settling a decedent's estate once he or she is gone.

ADVANTAGES OF PROBATE

Despite its shortcomings, the probate process is not an unmixed evil and the cost and delay of probate may be more than offset by some of its advantages. First, the primary advantage of probate is that the process does precisely what it was designed to do: it assures that the estate will, in fact, be properly transferred to those whom the decedent wished to receive it.

Also, the probate process makes it mandatory for the claims of creditors to be filed within a statutory period or they are forever barred. This protection can be especially meaningful when the decedent was engaged in a business or profession that might generate lingering contract or tort liabilities. The necessity of filing the claim within a fairly brief period can provide some certainty in a situation where much uncertainty may have existed.

Then, too, while the probate process can aggravate the grief of the decedent's family in some instances, it can also offer some opportunity for the members of the decedent's family to work through their grief in a healthy fashion. In this connection, the settlement of the estate is seen as a chance to tidy up the affairs of the decedent and "do right by them."

Also, the family awards and allowances that are available to a surviving spouse and minor children under most states' laws will protect a small amount of property from the claims of creditors.

Finally, the fact that the estate is a separate taxpayer for income tax purposes may offer some income-splitting tax savings in larger estates. If there is no estate administration, there is no separate taxable entity known as the "decedent's estate" and no opportunity for income splitting.

HOW TO AVOID PROBATE

Simply speaking, an asset is not subject to probate when, on the decedent's death, the title vests by law in another person or when the decedent's death does not cause any shifting in the title to the asset. But when the decedent is the sole owner of an asset and title is vested completely in his or her name, the asset is subject to probate.

Joint Ownership

Obviously, then, as we have seen earlier, the simplest means of avoiding probate is through some form of joint ownership in which the title of the decedent passes automatically on death to the surviving co-owner. Joint tenancy is, as we discussed in Chapter 3, the most commonly utilized form of joint ownership as a probate avoidance device. But, as we noted in Chapter 3, joint tenancy only works when there are other joint tenants surviving. If the other joint tenants have already died, the surviving joint tenant will own the property in its entirety and probate will not be avoided. Moreover, once a joint tenancy is established it is difficult to sever, and an owner of property should never transfer assets into joint tenancy unless absolutely certain that she or he will not regret the transfer later.

When assets are owned by a husband and wife as community property, the surviving spouse's one-half may or may not be subject to probate depending on the law of the state where the decedent was domiciled.

Totten Trust

The Totten Trust, which takes its name from the case of *Matter of Totten*, 71 N.E.748 (N.Y. 1904), is a deposit of money in a bank or other savings institution in the name of the depositor in trust for a beneficiary. The trust is revocable during the depositor's lifetime, and upon the death of the depositor the proceeds are payable to the beneficiary. The Totten trust is not subject to probate.

An advantage of the Totten trust is that the depositor can retain complete control over the account and can close it out or change the designation of the beneficiary anytime he or she wishes. He need not tell the beneficiary about the trust (and in most instances the beneficiary of a Totten trust does not know of the existence of the trust until the death of the depositor). The difference between a Totten trust and a simple joint bank account is that the beneficiary of a Totten trust has no right of withdrawal of the funds during the depositor's lifetime. With a simple joint bank account, however, the noncontributing joint owner can withdraw the funds anytime.

The major disadvantage of the Totten trust is that it applies only to bank accounts. Other types of property cannot be placed in a Totten trust.

Revocable Living Trust

We will examine the revocable living trust in greater detail in Chapter 10. But it is important to understand that one of the principal purposes of this trust is to avoid probate. The idea is that during your lifetime you convey property to a trustee who manages the property and pays the income to you. Upon your death, this property is not considered to be part of your estate for purposes of probate since your trustee owns the property, not you. (You may even be both the trustee and the beneficiary. But as long as you do not own the property outright, but "own" it merely as trustee for yourself, you are not considered the owner for probate purposes.) On your death the property is distributed by the trustee (or, if you have been trustee until your death, by your substitute trustee who was appointed to take over on your death) in accordance with the terms of the trust agreement. As we will see later, the revocable living trust is a very popular probate avoidance device.

Disposition by Contract

It is possible to enter into a contractual arrangement during your lifetime providing for benefits to be paid after your death. Life insurance is a typical example of such an arrangement. Unless the proceeds of a life insurance policy are specifically payable to your estate, these proceeds are not subject to probate on your death. Thus it is possible to convey substantial sums of money to a life insurance company by means of premium payments and then have the life insurance payout pass outside your probate estate on your death.

Another such contractual arrangement that will avoid probate is the pension plan or profit-sharing plan under which you designate who is to receive the benefits upon your death. If you designate anyone other than your estate as the beneficiary of these benefits, the assets will not be subject to probate. The same rule applies to proceeds payable under a deferred compensation contract, which is used to defer payment of salary to an employee in years in which the employee has other substantial income and is in a high tax bracket and to pay these benefits later (such as after retirement), when the employee is in a lower tax bracket. The contract of payment can provide for a beneficiary other than the estate of the decedent, and the benefits payable under this contract will likewise not be subject to probate.

Finally, certain United States securities, such as savings bonds, may be registered in the form of "John Doe, payable on death to Mary Doe." This is an ownership form similar to the Totten trust in that, during John Doe's lifetime, he is the owner of the savings bond, but upon his death the bond automatically goes to Mary Doe and does not pass through probate.

APPLYING THIS CHAPTER TO *YOUR* SITUATION

Probate is not an unmixed evil. While there are disadvantages to the system, such as delay and expense, when assuring that a decedent's assets pass to the parties who are entitled to them is of paramount concern, the probate system should be utilized, not avoided. It can provide a valuable protection to the eestate and the heirs of the decedent.

But when there is no concern over the decedent's property going to the proper parties, probate can be avoided by means of a number of devices that can provide privacy, lower the costs of settlement of the estate, and help avoid the delay that necessarily accompanies probate. From the simplest probate avoidance device, joint tenancy, to the more sophisticated revocable living trust, they all have one thing in common: they seek to avoid the inclusion of assets in a decedent's probate estate.

But there is no all-inclusive answer to the question "Should I attempt to avoid probate?" The decision to avoid probate is a personal one that must be made only after considering all the particulars of the decedent's estate, his or her desired plan of disposition, the parties involved, and the prospects of any conflicts over the estate.

CASE PROBLEMS

7.1 Helping Duane Salmon with Unequal Distribution to His Children.
Duane Salmon is a 72-year-old widower with three sons: Charles, 45, an orthopedic surgeon living in New York City, married, with three teenage children; Edward, 42, an aging hippy and a drummer with a rock band having no discernible domicile, unmarried, with a live-in "friend" and one child; and Richard, 38, a Presbyterian minister living in Philadelphia, married, with no children. Charles and Richard are close, but Edward has had little contact with the family for over 15 years. Duane's estate will be valued at approximately $450,000. He has a will leaving his estate 2/5 to Charles, 2/5 to Richard and 1/5 to Edward. The reason he wants to leave Edward less than the other two boys is that he has expended thousands of dollars on Edward over the past 20 years and wishes to "even up" his gifts to his sons by means of his will. However, his will does not mention the reason for the reduced gift to Edward.

Questions
1. Since the probate process will take a goodly piece of Duane's estate and delay the disbursement to the boys, should Duane consider conveying his assets to a revocable living trust in order to avoid probate? What are the reasons he *should* pursue this course and what are the reasons he should *not* do this?
2. Would you suggest any changes in Duane's will?
3. What special steps should Duane have taken when his will was executed in order to avoid a will contest?
4. Would it be advisable for Duane to convey his assets to his three sons, in the proportions he wishes them to take on his death, and avoid probate that way?

SELECTED READINGS

BOWMAN, FOREST J., *The Complete Retirement Handbook*. New York: Putnam Publishing Co.,
    1983, pp. 101–107.
FELLOWS, MARY L., "The Case against Living Probate," 78 *Mich. Law Review* 1066 (1980).
FISHER, JACOB, "Human Drama in Death and Taxes: The Bad Seed," 116 *Trusts and Estates*
    595 (1977).
JAWORSKI, LEON, "The Will Contest," 10 *Baylor Law Review* 87 (1958).
PRICE, JOHN R., *Contemporary Estate Planning*. Boston: Little, Brown and Company, 1983, p.
    165.

8

Death Taxes

Death's a debt.

Richard Brinsley Sheridan
The Rivals

One distressing aspect of teaching estate planning is the overwhelming resistance many students have to anything dealing with taxes. Mention "taxes" or the "Internal Revenue Code" and the eyes begin to gloss over, the voice dims, and a sense of helplessness starts to set in. Tax, students say, is a foreign language, the Internal Revenue Code a Mesopotamian clay tablet incised with cuneiform. There is no hope.

Students who relish the opportunity to confront the Common Law Rule against Perpetuities or who will not shrink from interpreting an insurance policy's subrogation clause, wither in the face of taxes. It was thus when the author attended law school (back in the days before the Louisiana Purchase). Today, at least six major Internal Revenue Code revisions later, it remains one of the major student phobias. They want to learn about estate planning, but without any taxes, if you please. The same sentiment pervades the practicing bar.

Yet, for all its convoluted syntax and special interest created exceptions, the Internal Revenue Code remains at least as readable as many widely read and (supposedly) understood sections of any of our state codes, and one need not be a tax expert to understand the basics (and even considerably more) of federal tax law. To a degree not widely understood or accepted, tax law follows certain rational patterns. A person seeking to understand the taxation of lifetime gifts or of decedents' estates needs to seek out and understand these patterns. The rest is easy. (Well, perhaps not "easy," but at least manageable.)

THE UNIFIED FEDERAL ESTATE AND GIFT TAX SYSTEM

The federal estate tax is a tax on transfers at death. The federal gift tax is a tax on transfers made during one's life and complements the estate tax. The way they work is as follows: You acquire assets during your lifetime. If you give them away during your lifetime, this transfer is taxed by the gift tax. If you die owning the assets, they pass, as directed in your will or by the intestate statutes, and your estate pays the estate tax on this transfer. The Internal Revenue Services has you, dead or alive. (At first glance it appears that the only way to avoid either tax is to spend all your money during your lifetime or arrange to have it spent on your funeral. But even then, in most states, you will be taxed on these ventures by the sales tax. As we will see later, however, there *are* ways out of this seemingly hopeless situation. Identifying these ways and implementing them is one of the roles of the estate planner.)

Death taxes have a long, if not necessarily distinguished, history. The Egyptians, Romans, and Greeks all had them. (We will ignore any comments about the possible relationship between the decline of these three civilizations and the existence of death taxes in their tax structure.) Pliny the Younger complained in ancient Rome that the death tax was "an unnatural tax, augmenting the grief and sorrow of the bereaved." In 1898, Senator William Vincent Allen of Nebraska argued bitterly against the adoption of a federal death tax, painting the picture of the tax collector standing "with the widow and children at the grave side of a dead father to collect a tax" (Eisenstein, 1956).

But the Congress was unmoved. On three occasions between 1797 and 1902, the federal government imposed an inheritance tax in order to meet temporary financial emergencies. Then, in 1916, the federal estate tax was adopted in a form recognizable today, largely to finance the United States' preparations for World War I.

The federal estate tax had not been in operation very long when it became apparent that persons wealthy enough to be subject to the tax could avoid it by giving away their estate during their lifetimes. On death, having no estate, the estate tax would not apply. So in 1924 the Congress adopted the federal gift tax.

But the gift tax was seriously flawed. It was calculated annually on a noncumulative basis and had an extremely large annual exclusion. So the tax was repealed two years later.

Then, in 1932, the federal gift tax, without the noncumulative feature and with a substantially lower annual exclusion, was brought back as a revenue raising measure to supplment the income and estate taxes, which had suffered greatly with the onset of the Great Depression. The gift tax was independent of the estate tax and taxed lifetime gifts at 75 percent of the federal estate tax rates.

Given the difference in rates between the gift tax and the estate tax, it was still substantially less expensive in tax terms to give one's money away during lifetime and pay the gift tax than to die with the money and pay the estate tax. So, in the Tax Reform Act of 1976, the gift tax and the estate tax were unified into one tax structure.

It should come as no surprise to learn that when the estate and gift taxes were unified into one transfer tax system, the gift tax rates were raised to equal the estate tax rates, rather than the estate tax rates being reduced to equal the gift tax rates.

STATE DEATH TAXES

State death taxes, for reasons that are more historical than rational, are typically inheritance taxes. (Fewer than a dozen states impose an estate tax.) An *inheritance tax* is a tax imposed on the beneficiary's right to inherit the money, and the tax rate is applied against the inheritance of the particular individual and not against the entire estate. The tax is imposed on the beneficiary of an inheritance, with the tax rate being lower for close relatives of the decedent. For example, a spouse might be taxed at 3 percent of all inheritance over $50,000, a child might be taxed at 5 percent on all inheritance over $30,000, a brother or sister might be taxed at 7 1/2 percent on all inheritance over $20,000, and a beneficiary who is not related to the deceased might be taxed at 10 percent on the entire share inherited.

Thus, there are *two* variables that affect the amount of tax paid under an inheritance tax: (1) the relationship of the beneficiary to the decedent, and (2) the size of the gift to the beneficiary.

An *estate tax*, on the other hand, is levied against the entire estate and not against the various portions of it that are passed on to certain individuals. It is a tax levied on the estate's right to transfer the money. There is only *one* variable affecting the amount of tax paid under an estate tax: the size of the taxable estate.

Most state death tax laws have the additional provision that if their inheritance or estate taxes on any particular estate amount to less than the maximum credit for state death taxes allowed by the federal estate tax law, the amount payable to the state is automatically increased to absorb the difference. For example, if the maximum credit for state death taxes in a particular estate comes to $8,000 but the state death taxes actually paid amount to only $5,000, the state death tax would be automatically increased to $8,000. This does not increase the amount of tax, federal and state, paid by the estate but only means that, in our example, $3,000 more will go to the state treasury and $3,000 less to the federal treasury. This additional state tax is known as the *pickup* tax.

HOW THE FEDERAL ESTATE TAX IS STRUCTURED

The Gross Estate

The starting point for the calculation of estate tax liability is the size of the estate, a concept known as the *gross estate*. As we saw in Chapter 3, the gross estate includes everything the decedent owned at death, plus a number of assets that may not normally be considered to be in the estate, but which the IRS includes in the calculation for one reason or another. (Generally, property is includable in the gross estate if it fits into one of the categories enumerated in Internal Revenue Code sections 2033 to 2044.)

For example, in addition to the assets a decedent owns outright at the time of death, the IRS will include the following as assets in the gross estate.

Life insurance. The gross estate will include amounts payable to the estate or beneficiaries under a life insurance policy, unless the decedent has taken certain specific steps to keep life insurance out of the estate for tax purposes, a matter we will discuss in greater detail later (Code 2042).

Gifts with strings attached. The gross estate will include the value of gifts the decedent made during his or her lifetime in which he or she retained either

(1) the right to the income, possession, or enjoyment of the property or the power to say who will possess or enjoy the property or its income (Code 2036), or
(2) the power to alter, amend, revoke, or terminate the gift (Code 2038).

These gifts are included in the gross estate under the theory that the decedent didn't really give this property away. For example, if the decedent gave her farm to her son John but reserved to herself the right to enjoy the income from the farm for her lifetime, John's interest *really* didn't begin until the decedent's death; so the decedent can reasonably be said not to have parted with the farm until her death. Or if the decedent had created a trust with John as the beneficiary but retained the right to change beneficiaries and name her daughter Susie, it is not unreasonable to consider the decedent the owner of the trust property since the right to say who will enjoy the property is one of the privileges of ownership.

Property subject to a general power of appointment. It is possible, as we will see later in greater detail, for the owner of property to make a gift under conditions that another person can have the right to say who will enjoy this property. Under certain conditions, this right to say who will enjoy the property is the equivalent of ownership.

For example, if a father leaves property in trust and gives his daughter the right to designate who will have the income from the property (or the property itself) and there is no limitation on whom the daughter can designate, the daughter has the equivalent of ownership since she could name herself as the owner. The only thing that stands in the way of complete, outright ownership of the property on the part of the daughter is a note that she could write saying "I appoint to myself." Under these circumstances, the daughter has what is known as a *general power of appointment*. When she dies, the value of any property over which she has a general power of appointment is included in her gross estate, just as is any other property she owns (Code 2041).

Jointly owned property. Property that the decedent owns jointly with another person (even if owned with the right of survivorship) is included in the decedent's gross estate up to the amount of the decedent's fractional share. (If the joint property is owned in joint tenancy or tenancy by the entirety, Code 2040 makes it taxable. If the property is owned in tenancy in common, it is included in the gross estate under Code 2033.)

Claims against others. Any claims that the decedent has outstanding against others at death, such as for rent, interest, dividends, and debts, are includable in the gross estate (Code 2033).

Annuities and pension and profit-sharing benefits. Pension and profit-sharing benefits are included in the gross estate:

(1) if the proceeds are payable in a lump sum, unless the decedent elects to forgo some very attractive income tax advantages that are otherwise available for pension and profit-sharing distributions.
(2) if the payments are made to the decedent's estate.
(3) if the proceeds are attributable to the decedent's contribution rather than to the contributions made by the decedent's employer (Code 2039).

Qualified terminal interest property. The gross estate also includes the value of all property in which the decedent had a "qualified terminable interest" for life that passed to the decedent by prior transfer from the decedent's spouse and that qualified at that time for the marital deduction. Don't worry about this concept right now; we'll cover it in detail later. Just understand that it is one more type of "asset" that is included in the gross estate (Code 2044).

Life insurance transferred within three years of death. When the decedent has made a gratuitous transfer of a life insurance policy or policies within three years of his or her death, the value of these policies is included in the gross estate (Code 2035). Thus, for estate tax purposes, a decedent's gross estate is often much larger than one would think. And since the higher the gross estate, the higher the estate tax, one of the tax goals of estate planning is to keep the gross estate as low as possible.

Deductions from the Gross Estate

In calculating the estate tax, a number of items are deducted from the gross estate to arrive at the *adjusted gross estate*, a figure that more nearly reflects what the decedent actually owned at death. For example, if you owned (i.e., it was titled in your name) a building worth $1,000,000 and had a mortgage of $700,000 against the building, you really didn't own a $1,000,000 asset. You owned a $300,000 asset, the value of the building that was free and clear of the mortgage. So, in arriving at the adjusted gross estate, you are permitted to deduct the amount of the mortgage against this building.

The largest group of items that can be deducted from the gross estate in arriving at the adjusted gross estate are found under Section 2053 of the Internal Revenue Code. These are:

1. *Funeral expenses*: This category includes a reasonable expenditure for a tombstone, monument, mausoleum, or burial lot, reasonable expenditure for future care of these items, and the cost of transportation for bringing the body to the place of burial. (See also Internal Revenue Regulations, hereafter cited as Regs., Sec. 20.2053-2.)

2. *Administration expenses*: These include those expenses "actually and necessarily incurred in the administration of the decedent's estate." What is contemplated here is the cost of collecting the decedent's assets, paying the decedent's debts, and transferring the property of the decedent to the proper beneficiaries. Usually they include executor's commissions, attorney fees, and expenses such as court costs, accountants' fees, and appraisers' fees. If the decedent's estate must be sold, the expenses of sale are deductible under this category (Regs. 20.2053-3).

3. *Claims against the estate*: These are the personal obligations of the decedent that exist at the time of his or her death, including taxes and pledges or subscriptions for charitable purposes (Regs. 20.2053- 4, -5, and -6).

4. *Unpaid mortgages on property included in the value of the gross estate*: Mortgages are deductible only if the property subject to the mortgage is included as part of the value of the gross estate undiminished by the amount of the mortgage. In the example used earlier, the $700,000 mortgage would be deductible from the gross estate only if the building were included in the estate to the extent of its full value of $1,000,000 (Regs. 20.2053-7).

Section 205 of the code permits the deduction of losses from casualty or theft during the administration of the estate if the losses are uncompensated for by insurance or otherwise. If the loss is partially compensated for, the excess of the loss over the compensation is deductible. For a loss to be deductible under this section, the loss must occur during the settlement of the estate. (If an uncompensated loss has occured earlier, the lost asset is simply not included in the decedent's gross estate.)

Administration expenses and casualty losses are deductible either on the income tax return of the decedent, which is filed for the year of his or her death, or on the decedent's estate tax return, but not on both. The decision on which return to claim these expenses on can only be made after comparing such factors as the marginal estate tax and income tax rates that will apply, considering the advantages of splitting them between the two returns or claiming the deductions all on one return or the other, and inquiring into the possibility of carrying out to the estate's beneficiaries the estate's excess income tax deductions in its final taxable year (Code 642).

Notice, again, what these deductions do. They permit the personal representative of the estate to deduct those expenses or losses that reduce the actual value of the decedent's estate. If an estate lists assets of $1,000,000 in the gross estate but there are expenses and losses in the amount of $400,000, the decedent's *true* estate (i.e., the estate that will actually be available for the payment of taxes and to pass on to heirs) is $600,000, not $1,000,000. Thus, the deduction of these expenses to arrive at the *adjusted gross estate* reflects more accurately the true value of the estate.

There are, however, two additional deductions permitted from the gross estate in arriving at the adjusted gross estate that do not reflect any congressional belief that these items are not properly part of the decedent's true estate. Rather, they reflect the congressional belief that the assets in these two categories do not properly belong in the adjusted gross estate where they will be subject to taxation.

Charitable deduction. Section 2055 of the code permits the deduction from the gross estate of all transfers to qualifying governmental, charitable, or religious organizations. These deductions are permitted because Congress wants to encourage charitable contributions. Thus, if a decedent leaves an estate of $1,000,000 and her will gives $400,000 of this estate to the Salvation Army, the personal representative will deduct this $400,000 charitable gift from the gross estate and there will only be an estate of $600,000 subject to taxation. (The charitable deduction provisions of the estate tax law are similar in many respects to the charitable deduction provisions of the income tax law, Code 170, and the gift tax law, Code 2522.)

If the gift to the charity is only of a *remainder* interest, only the value of the remainder may be deducted. (As the name suggests, a remainder is what remains after another interest is terminated. If you give your farm to your wife for life and provide that on her death your son is to get the title to the farm, your son is said to have a remainder interest in the farm.)

Using the charitable deduction example, assume that you leave your farm (which has an annual income of $100,000) to your sister for her life and provide that on her death the farm is to pass to the Salvation Army. On your death, the personal representative of your estate will deduct from your gross estate the value of the Salvation Army's right to the farm after your sister's death. Since the Salvation Army's right to the farm sometime in the future is worth less than the right to have the farm immediately, the deduction will be less than if the farm went to the Salvation Army immediately upon your death. Exactly how much the farm is worth to the Salvation Army on your death will depend on how long the Army will have to wait to get possession of it. Thus, if your sister is elderly and the Salvation Army is likely to get possession of the farm rather soon (and your sister will probably get to enjoy the income from the farm for a relatively brief period of time), the charitable deduction will be higher than if your sister is young and likely to live many years.

For reasons we will discuss later, the use of various types of trusts is often an effective way to make charitable gifts, particularly charitable remainder gifts. For the present, however, it is sufficient to know that the gifts a decedent makes to charity are deducted from the gross estate in calculating the adjusted gross estate.

Marital Deduction. As the estate tax was enacted in 1916, it imposed an unfair burden on residents of common law states (i.e., those states that have not adopted the community property system of marital property ownership). If a couple lived in a community property state, the IRS, recognizing the effect of the community property laws, taxed only one-half of the property a married decedent had acquired with his or her earnings during marriage on the theory that the other one-half was the legal property of the surviving spouse under the community property law of the state. However, decedents from the common law states had all the property they had acquired with their earnings during marriage taxed to their estates. In other words, there was "estate splitting" for married decedents in community property states, but none in the common law states.

In 1942, Congress sought to remedy this situation in a fashion that should surprise no one who has watched the Congress carry out its concern for the American taxpayer's purse. The estate tax was amended to require all the community property to be included in the gross estate of the first spouse to die, except where it was attributable to the services or property of the surviving spouse. Thus decedents' estates in community property states were placed on a par with decedents' estates in common law states. As anyone could have foreseen, this approach satisfied no one: it was unpopular with couples in community property states (who had just lost a significant estate tax break), and it did nothing to improve the tax situation for couples in common law states.

Finally, in the Revenue Act of 1948, the Congress moved away from equalization of disadvantages and toward the equalization of advantages by extending the tax splitting opportunities available in the community property states (in income, gift, and estate tax law) to the residents of common law states. This change was known as the marital deduction and, with respect to the estate tax law, provided that one-half of the decedent's adjusted gross estate could pass to the surviving spouse free of the estate tax.

Over the years from 1948 to 1981, the limit on the size of the estate that could pass tax free to the surviving spouse was varied and different approaches were taken to calculate the deduction. Finally, in the Economic Recovery Tax Act of 1981 (referred to by its acronym ERTA), all quantative limits were taken off the marital deduction and, as a result, *all* property that passes from a decedent to his or her surviving spouse now passes free of the estate tax. (Since the estate and gift taxes are unified into one tax structure, lifetime gifts from one spouse to another also pass free of the gift tax. We will take a closer look at this later.)

The idea behind the marital deduction is that the assets that pass from the one spouse to the other will ultimately be taxed in full, either by the gift tax if the surviving spouse gives the assets away or by the estate tax if the surviving spouse dies owning the assets. The tax is not really avoided, it is merely postponed.

ERTA also expanded the marital deduction by introducing the concept of *qualified terminal interest property* (which is known by its acronym QTIP). The concept of QTIP property is important because it allows one spouse to give property to the other under conditions that amount to less than full ownership and still have the gift qualify for the marital deduction. Here is how it works. Remember that we said that the central idea behind the marital deduction is that the assets that pass from the decedent spouse to the surviving spouse will ultimately be taxed to the surviving spouse, either by the gift tax or the estate tax. This presupposes, however, that the assets that are not taxed on the death of the decedent spouse are actually passed to the surviving spouse in such a fashion that they will be subject to tax when the surviving spouse gives them away (when the gift tax will be levied) or when the surviving spouse dies (and the estate tax will come into play).

But, suppose you are a woman executive with an estate of $1,000,000. Your husband is considerably older than you and you are not confident of his ability to manage the assets in your estate. If you leave your estate to a trust and provide that your husband is to have the income from that trust for his life and that when he dies the trust is to terminate and the $1,000,000 will pass to your daughter, you can avoid the possibility that he may "run through" your assets, and you can still assure that your husband will have the benefit of your estate until he dies. However, since you have merely given your husband a life estate in the $1,000,000 and your daughter has the remainder interest, there will be nothing of this $1,000,000 in your husband's estate to be subject to the estate tax when he dies, since his life estate in this property will terminate the moment he dies. Under the traditional estate tax rules, such a gift would not qualify for the marital deduction and you were faced with a difficult choice. You could leave the property outright to your husband and qualify for the marital deduction (and also run the risk that nothing will be left on his death to pass on to your daughter), or you could leave the property in a protective trust as outlined and have your estate pay a whopping estate tax bill, which will substantially reduce what is passed on to your husband.

The QTIP provisions permit a decedent spouse to leave assets to a surviving spouse under conditions that amount to less than absolute ownership and still qualify for the marital deduction. To be considered QTIP property, a donee spouse must be given what is known as a "qualifying income interest for life." That is,

(1) the donee spouse must be entitled to all the income from the property for life,
(2) the income from the property must be payable to the donee spouse annually or at more frequent intervals,
(3) no person can have the power to appoint any of the property to any person other than the surviving spouse during his or her lifetime (Code 2056; 2523).

In effect, what the QTIP changes do is allow a marital deduction for a simple life income interest, provided that no one can divert any of the property to another person during the surviving spouse's lifetime. If the surviving spouse should give away this income interest during his or her lifetime, the assets would then be taxable by means of the gift tax. If the surviving spouse dies without having conveyed away this interest, the estate tax is then due on the assets. (In essence, the QTIP rules "pretend" that the surviving spouse still has an interest in the property at his or her death and the estate tax is assessed then, rather than on the earlier death of the decedent spouse.)

Another important aspect to the QTIP provisions is that the donor (if the transfer is made during lifetime) or the decedent's executor (if the transfer is made at death) may elect whether to claim a marital deduction with respect to QTIP property. And an election can be made with respect to all the property or merely with respect to a portion of the property [Sec. 2056(b)(7)(B)(iv)]. This elective feature makes it possible for a decedent to leave property to a spouse in such a fashion that it qualifies for the marital deduction under QTIP rules, and then permits the executor to decide how much of the property to qualify for the deduction and how much of it to have subject to taxation now, in order to maximize (to use a dreadful but very efficient word) the tax savings. We will look more carefully at the type of planning that goes into consideration of the marital deduction and the use of the QTIP election in Chapter 11.

THE UNIFIED CREDIT

To protect smaller estates, the federal estate tax is not actually imposed until the size of a decedent's estate reaches a certain level. For the estates of decedents who die on January 1, 1987, or thereafter, the exemption will be $600,000.

The exemption of estates below a certain level from the estate tax is complicated by the fact that the exemption is not done directly by including in the Internal Revenue Code language such as "any estate under the amount of $XXX,XXX is not subject to the estate tax." Instead, the entire adjusted gross estate is determined and the tax is calculated on this figure. Then a dollar-for-dollar credit is deducted from the tax previously calculated to arrive at the tax payable. (Under the prior law the exemption of estates below $60,000 was accomplished simply by reducing the size of the estate before the tax was assessed.)

For example, assume that you die in 1987 with an estate of $750,000. You do not deduct $600,000 from your estate and calculate the estate tax on the remaining $150,000 (in which case the tax would be $38,800). Instead, you calculate a "tentative" estate tax on the entire estate of $750,000, which comes to $248,300. Then you deduct the *exemption equivalent* to arrive at the tax.

Since $192,800 is the tax that would be due on an estate of $600,000, you deduct $192,800 from the $248,300 tentative tax and arrive at a tax of $55,500, which is $16,700 more than if the $600,000 exemption had been deducted first and the tax computed only on the $150,000 remaining. (This occurs because, by utilizing the unified credit approach, you compute the tax initially at a higher level on the tax table than you would have had you first deducted the $600,000 exempt estate and merely calculated the tax on the $150,000 estate remaining.)

The amount of the taxable estate that is sheltered from taxation by the unified credit (i.e., the $500,000 in 1986, and the $600,000 in 1987 and thereafter) is known as the *exemption equivalent*, since it represents the size of the estate that would produce the amount of tax represented by the particular credit (see Table 8.1).

TABLE 8.1   Estate Tax Unified Credit

Year	Amount of Credit	Amount of Credit Equivalent
1987, and thereafter	192,800	600,000

Code 2010.

CREDIT FOR STATE DEATH TAXES

A further credit against the estate tax due is permitted for any state death taxes actually paid, up to certain limits. The credit is equal to the lesser of

(1) the total state death taxes actually paid, or

(2) the amount determined by using Table 8.2 (which is taken from Sec. 2011 of the code).

For purposes of calculating the credit for state death taxes, it is important to understand that the adjusted taxable estate referred to in Table 8.2 is the taxable estate less $60,000. Why do we start with this adjusted taxable estate and not simply the taxable estate? And why is the adjusted taxable estate the "taxable estate less $60,000" instead of some other figure? If you can accept the answer, "BECAUSE THAT'S WHAT THE CODE SAYS," you will make things much easier for yourself. Just remember that it is that way and always make this little "taxable estate less $60,000" calculation at the beginning and you will do quite well.

If you cannot accept this answer, it might help to understand that for many years the first $60,000 of an estate was exempt from taxation. When the law was changed to exempt larger amounts for taxation (up to $600,000 by 1987, remember), the $60,000 exemption concept was left unchanged in this one area of the estate tax computation. It remains there, ready to trip the unwary. So bear in mind this one simple, and to some degree irrational, calculation that must be made at the beginning of the calculation of the credit for state death taxes.

TABLE 8.2   Credit for State Death Taxes

Adjusted Taxable Estate Exceeding (1)	Adjusted Taxable Estate Not Exceeding (2)	Credit on Amount in Column (1) (3)	Rate of Credit on Excess over Amount in Column (1) (4)
$ 40,000	$ 90,000	—	0.8%
90,000	140,000	$ 400	1.6
140,000	240,000	1,200	2.4
240,000	440,000	3,600	3.2
440,000	640,000	10,000	4.0
640,000	840,000	18,000	4.8
840,000	1,040,000	27,600	5.6
1,040,000	1,540,000	38,800	6.4
1,540,000	2,040,000	70,800	7.2
2,040,000	2,540,000	106,800	8.0
2,540,000	3,040,000	146,800	8.8
3,040,000	3,540,000	190,800	9.6
3,540,000	4,040,000	238,800	10.4
4,040,000	5,040,000	290,800	11.2
5,040,000	6,040,000	402,800	12.0
6,040,000	7,040,000	522,800	12.8
7,040,000	8,040,000	650,800	13.6
8,040,000	9,040,000	786,800	14.4
9,040,000	10,040,000	930,800	15.2
10,040,000	—	1,082,800	16.0

CREDIT FOR FEDERAL ESTATE TAX PREVIOUSLY PAID

Occasionally, a decedent's estate will contain property that was previously taxed in the estate of another decedent. When this happens and when the property was included in the previous decedent's taxable estate within two years before or two years after the current decedent's death, Section 2013 allows a credit for the federal estate tax previously paid. The full amount of the credit is allowable if the present decedent died within two years of the time the property was transferred from the estate of the previous decedent. Thereafter, the amount of the credit diminishes by 20 percent every two years, so no credit is allowable if the previous decedent died more than ten years before the death of the present decedent.

For example, assume that George Mason died in 1983, leaving everything to his son Richard, and $200,000 federal estate tax was paid. If Richard dies within two years of George's death (and the assets he inherited from his father are still in Richard's estate), Richard's estate can claim $200,000 credit for the federal estate tax previously paid. If Richard dies three years after George, the credit will be 80 percent of $200,000 or $160,000 (see Table 8.3)

TABLE 8.3   Credit for Federal Estate Tax Previously Paid

Period of Time (years) Exceeding	Not Exceeding (years)	Percent Allowable
—	2	100
2	4	80
4	6	60
6	8	40
8	10	20
10	—	None

Code 2013.

CREDIT FOR GIFT TAXES PAID

When a decedent's estate contains property that was previously taxed by the gift tax prior to January 1, 1977, a credit is allowed under Section 2012. (This could occur if a decedent made transfers during his or her lifetime, and prior to 1977, but the property was still includable in his or her gross estate for one reason or another.) Gift tax paid on post-1976 gifts is deducted in computing the amount of the estate tax itself under Section 2001(b).

CREDIT FOR FOREIGN DEATH TAXES

On occasion a citizen or resident of the United States may have property in another country that is subject to the death tax of the foreign country. When that property is also included in the decedent's gross estate in the United States, a credit is allowed by Section 2014 for the amount of tax paid to the foreign government, with certain limitations. The amount of the credit may be affected by the terms of a gift and estate tax treaty between the United States and the foreign country imposing the tax.

CALCULATING THE FEDERAL ESTATE TAX

The federal estate tax is calculated in the following manner:

1. List and place a value on the property included in the gross estate (see pages 113-116).

2. Subtract the allowable deductions (i.e., funeral and administration expenses, mortgages and liens, debts of the decedent, etc.) from the gross estate to arrive at what Code 2051 defines as the taxable estate (see pages 103-108).

3. Add to the taxable estate the value of any taxable gifts that were made by the decedent after December 31, 1976. (We will discuss this step in detail later.) The figure that results is known as the *tax base*.

4. Compute the tentative tax on the tax base using the unified rate schedule from Code 2001 (Table 8.4).

TABLE 8.4   Unified Transfer Tax Rate Schedule

If the Amount Is:		The Tentative Tax Is		
Over	But not over	Tax +	%	On excess Over
$ 0	$ 10,000	$ 0	18	$ 0
10,000	20,000	1,800	20	10,000
20,000	40,000	3,800	22	20,000
40,000	60,000	8,200	24	40,000
60,000	80,000	13,000	26	60,000
80,000	100,000	18,200	28	80,000
100,000	150,000	23,800	30	100,000
150,000	250,000	38,800	32	150,000
250,000	500,000	70,800	34	250,000
500,000	750,000	155,800	37	500,000
750,000	1,000,000	248,300	39	750,000
1,000,000	1,250,000	345,800	41	1,000,000
1,250,000	1,500,000	448,300	43	1,250,000
1,500,000	1,750,000	555,800	45	1,500,000
2,000,000	2,500,000	780,800	49	2,000,000
2,500,000		1,025,800	5	2,500,000

5. Subtract from the net tax arrived at in step 4, the following credits, if applicable:

a. Unified credit (see Table 8.1)
b. Credit for state death taxes (see pages 109-110)
c. Credit for gift taxes paid
d. Credit for federal estate tax previously paid (see pages 110-111)
e. Credit for foreign death taxes (see page 111)
f. The figure that remains will be the federal estate tax due.

FILING THE RETURN AND PAYING THE TAXES

A federal estate tax return (Form 706) must be filed for every estate where the gross estate exceeds the amount of the exemption equivalent for the year in which the decedent died (see Table 8.1). The return is due within nine months of the estate owner's death and the tax is due and payable at that time, although an extension of time for payment of the tax may be granted for reasonable cause (Code 6161[a]).

VALUATION OF ASSETS

Section 2031 provides that assets in the estate are to be valued for estate tax purposes at their value on the date of the decedent's death. On the other hand, Section 2032 permits the personal representative of the estate to elect to value assets as of six months after the decedent's death (a time known as the *alternate valuation date*). In either event, all the assets in the estate are valued on one or the other of these dates, so you cannot value some assets at death and others six months after death.

The reason for the alternate valuation date is that the assets in an estate may undergo a sudden decline in value shortly after the decedent dies and, since the estate tax is a tax on transfers, it would be unfair to tax the assets at their date-of-death value when there will actually be fewer assets to transfer to the beneficiaries. For example, an estate that consists mostly of corporate stocks traded on the major exchanges may suffer a serious decline in value because of a bear market that begins shortly after the decedent's death. In such an event, the date exactly six months after the decedent's death may be used as the alternate valuation date.

But stating, as the code does, that assets are to be "valued" as of a certain date tells us nothing about how value is determined, a process both complicated and simple, depending on the nature of the asset being valued. The term *value* means the concept of fair market value, an always debatable concept. The Regulations [Secs. 20.2031-1(b) and 25.2512-1] define fair market value as "the price at which the property would change hands between a willing buyer and a willing seller, neither being under any compulsion to buy or sell and both having reasonable knowledge of relevant facts."

Real Estate

The value of income-producing real estate is established by one or more of the following methods:
1. Appraisal by a real estate professional

2. Replacement cost
3. Assessed value
4. Income produced by the property
5. Comparison with similar property that has sold recently

Real estate that is not used for the production of income is valued almost exclusively by appraisal by a qualified real estate appraiser who utilizes a comparison with similar property sold recently, assessed valuation, and replacement cost.

Special use valuation. The general rule for valuing real estate is to value it on the basis of its "highest and best use." The idea is that a buyer wishing to make the "highest and best use" of the property will be willing to pay more for the property than someone who wished to use the land for some less profitable purpose. Thus, land that is not in its most profitable use may be taxed at a higher value than its actual use would justify.

A common example of this is a family farm located on the edge of an expanding metropolitan area. The land may have a higher value as subdivided building lots than as a farm. Under the concept of the "highest and best use," then, the land would be taxed at its value as building lots and not as farmland, despite the fact that the family may prefer to continue to farm the land.

Concerned that the concept of the "highest and best use" may discourage the continued use of property for farming and other small business enterprises, the Congress provided in the Tax Reform Act of 1976 that the executor may elect to have what is defined in Code 2032A(b) as "qualified real property" valued in its current use. Thus, if a family wishes to continue using valuable real estate situated near an expanding city as farmland rather than to subdivide it into city lots, the land will be valued at its worth as a farm and not as city lots.

The reduction in value that results from the use of this concept (which is known as *special use valuation*) may not exceed $750,000 [Sec. 2032A(a)(2)]. If the property is disposed of or ceases to be used for its qualified purpose within ten years of the decedent's death, part of all of the reduction in estate tax that resulted from the lower valuation may be recaptured [Sec. 2032A(c)].

"Qualified real property" is defined in Section 2032(b), a fairly complicated subsection. Essentially, however, it is property

(1) located in the United States and owned by the decedent, who was a citizen or resident of the United States;
(2) used for farming or in a closely held business, the value of which is at least 50 percent of the decedent's gross estate;
(3) where at least 25% of the value of the decedent's gross estate consists of the qualified real property;

(4) in which there was material participation by the decedent or a member of the decedent's family in the operation of the farm or other business for five of the eight years immediately preceding the decedent's death; and

(5) where the real property passed to a qualified heir of the decedent.

If real property meets the requirements for special use valuation, the land is then valued under the detailed rules set forth in Section 2032A(e)(7) and (8).

There is no counterpart to the concept of special use valuation in the gift tax law. Thus a lifetime transfer of property that might qualify for special use valuation under the estate tax law may be subject to a substantially higher tax than would have been the case if the property had been retained by the donor until death.

Stocks and Bonds

If there is a market for stocks and bonds, on a stock exchange, over the counter, or otherwise, the value is the mean between the highest and lowest quoted selling prices on the valuation date (i.e., date of death or six months thereafter). If there were no sales on the valuation date but there were sales on dates within a reasonable period before and after the valuation date, the fair market value is determined by taking a weighted average of the means between the highest and lowest sales on the nearest date before and the nearest date after the valuation date [Regs. 20.2031-2(b)(1)].

If there were no sales within a reasonable period before and after the valuation date, fair market value may be determined by taking the mean between bona fide bid and asked prices on the valuation date. If there were none, value is determined by taking a weighted average of the means between the bona fide bid and asked prices on the nearest trading date before and the nearest trading date after the valuation date [Regs. 20.2031-2(c)].

The value of mutual funds is determined by their redemption price on the valuation date, although Regs. 20.2031-8(b) provides otherwise. [The Supreme Court made the change in *U.S.* v. *Cartwright*, 411 U.S. 546 (1973).]

Code 2031(b) and the Regulations provide special rules for unlisted and closely held stock. Among the factors considered are the risk factor, the economic situation and labor conditions, balance sheet indications of book value and significant financial changes, profits and losses and earnings potential, capacity to pay dividends, good will or other intangible value, and prior sales of the corporation's stock. In determining the value of bonds, the IRS will look to soundness of the security, interest yield, and maturity date.

Partnership or Proprietorship

The fair market value of a partnership or a proprietorship is determined by (1) appraising the tangible and intangible assets of the business, including good will, as of the valuation date, (2) considering the demonstrated earning capacity of the business, and (3) utilizing all the factors set forth in Regs. 20.2031-2 relating to the valuation of corporate stock that apply to nonstock ownership (Regs. 20.2031-3).

Notes

Secured or unsecured notes are valued at the amount of the unpaid principal, plus interest accrued to the date of death, unless the executor can establish that the value is lower or that the notes are worthless (Regs. 20.2031-4).

Cash on Hand or Deposit

Cash on hand or on deposit with a bank is included in the decedent's gross estate. Amounts included in bank checks outstanding at the decedent's death and subsequently honored by the bank and charged to the decedent's account are not included in the gross estate as long as they are not also claimed as deductions from the gross estate (Regs. 20.2031-5).

Household Goods and Effects

Household and personal effects are included at fair market value, and the Regulations suggest a room by room itemization of such items. However, when nothing in the room has a value in excess of $100, the total value of items in the room may be grouped [Regs. 20.2031-6(a)]. Special rules provide that items of "marked artistic or intrinsic value of a total value in excess of $3,000" must be accompanied by a sworn appraisal of an expert [Regs. 20.2031-6(b)].

Annuities, Life Estates, Terms for Years, Remainders, and Reversions

If the decedent's estate's interest in an annuity, life estate, term interest, remainder, or reversion is circumscribed by the lifetime of another, the value of the interest to the estate is computed by the use of actuarial tables in Regs. 20.2031-7.

FREEZING THE VALUE OF THE ESTATE

Occasionally, wealthy clients with assets that have considerable growth potential will seek to prevent any further growth in value of their estates through what is known as an *estate freeze*. Typically, the estate owner will exchange the assets with growth potential for assets with fixed dollar value, such as preferred stock or a promissory note. When the assets involved consist of stock in a family corporation, the technique used is the preferred stock recapitalization under Code 368(a)(1)(E). There the controlling shareholder will exchange all of his or her common stock for preferred stock that has a fixed value. The recapitalization typically leaves the company's equity interest, representing the growth potential of the corporation, in the hands of the younger family stockholders. The freeze in the estate owner's value is possible because the preferred stock will not increase in value even though the corporation prospers in the future. Instead, all the future growth will be reflected in the value of the common stock.

Other methods used to freeze the value of the estate include the installment sale, the private annuity, and the sale and leaseback. The installment sale, which is perhaps the least controversial and the most widely used of the three methods, freezes the value of the asset sold because, when the property has been sold for full and adequate consideration, only the value of the installment obligation is included in the seller's estate; any further appreciation in value of the property is excluded (Code 453).

The typical private annuity involves the transfer by a senior family member of appreciated property to a junior family member in return for the latter's unsecured promise to pay the transferor a specified annual amount for life. But the tax and nontax risks of using a private annuity are formidable enough to deter most planners and clients. The risk is that the IRS and the courts will treat the annuity transaction as a trust in which the grantor has retained a life interest and not as an annuity. If the transaction is treated as a trust,

(1) the income is taxable to the grantor under Code 677(a),

(2) the transfer of the remainder in the trust is taxable as a gift, and

(3) the trust principal is includable in the grantor's estate under Code 2036.

The sale and leaseback involves the sale of an office or equipment by a professional to family members (or to a trust for the family members), from whom the property is then leased back. Although there are some estate freezing characteristics, the sale and leaseback is primarily designed to redistribute income within the family.

"FLOWER BONDS": PAYING THE ESTATE TAX WITH BONDS BOUGHT AT A DISCOUNT

Some issues of U.S. Treasury bonds issued before March 31, 1971, are redeemable at par, plus accrued interest in payment of the federal estate tax on their owner's death [Reg. 20.6151-1(c)]. Because of the low interest rates that these bonds carry, when compared with interest rates that have prevailed since they were issued, bonds in this category with several years until maturity typically sell at substantial discounts. For example, the 3 percent bonds due in 1995 have sold for as little as 70% of par value. Redeemable bonds of this sort are called "flower bonds" because they "blossom" or "flower" into full value upon the owner's death. However, the bonds are redeemable only to the extent they are included in the decedent's gross estate. Therefore, the purchase of a $1,000 bond at discount for, say, $600 has the effect of increasing the value of the estate by $1,000, not $600. Thus, the purchase of these bonds, to the extent of the amount eligible for redemption, can have the effect of increasing the taxable estate, and hence the estate tax, by the difference between the purchase price and the par value of the bonds. But the total effect of the purchase may still be a substantial savings in estate tax, since the additional tax due on the difference between the purchase price of the bonds and their redemption value would be less than the additional savings that will result in the dollar-for-dollar reduction of the tax bill by the difference between the purchase price and the redemption price of the bonds.

While no more bonds eligible for redemption for this purpose may be issued, a number of issues are still outstanding. (The eligible issues are listed at 2 CCH Estate and Gift Tax, paragraph 9764.45.)

APPLYING THIS CHAPTER TO *YOUR* SITUATION

The unification of the federal estate and gift taxes into one system of *transfer* tax has severely limited the passage of property between generations without the payment of tax. And the gross estate, which is the starting point for determination of the estate tax, will usually include assets that one does not ordinarily think of as being owned.

But the opportunity to deduct debts and expenses of an estate, as well as the protection from taxation afforded by the marital deduction and the unified credit, afford a rich ground for reducing one's tax liability. With the addition of the concept of QTIP, one can provide a flexible estate plan that will avoid *all* estate tax on the death of the first spouse and, especially if the gift tax annual exclusion is utilized, also reduce or eliminate the tax on the death of the surviving spouse.

CASE PROBLEM

8.1 Calculating the Gross Estate, the Taxable Estate, and the Estate Tax.
Louise Stull, who died in 1985, owned the following property in her name alone:

Description	Value
Coin collection	$ 45,000
Real estate	550,000
Stocks and bonds	350,000
Automobile	27,000

Louise and her husband owned the following property as joint tenants with right of survivorship:

Description	Value
Home	$ 275,000
Bank Accounts	85,000
Vacation Home	200,000

In 1983, Louise gave her daughter, Anne Marie, a life insurance policy valued at $10,000, with a death benefit of $50,000. Louise's father had created a trust that was valued at $250,000 at Louise's death. Louise had a special power to appoint the assets in this trust among her children.

Life insurance of $100,000 was paid to Louise's estate and her husband received another $250,000 from a policy on her life that Louise owned at her death.

Louise's will left $500,000 to her husband, $100,000 to charity, and the remainder to her children. Debts and expenses will amount to $75,000.

Questions
What is the amount of:
1. Louise's gross estate?
2. Louise's taxable estate?
3. The estate tax due on Louise's estate?

SELECTED READINGS

BOWMAN, FOREST J., *The Complete Retirement Handbook.* New York: Putnam Publishing Co., 1983, pp. 118–125.

EISENSTEIN, LOUIS, "The Rise and Decline of the Estate Tax," 11 *Tax Law Review* 223 (1956).

FARR, JAMES F., and WRIGHT, JACKSON W., Jr., *An Estate Planner's Handbook.* Boston: Little, Brown and Company, 1979, pp. 231–258.

JOHNSON, DAVID C., "Cumulation of Lifetime Gifts in the Federal Estate Tax Computation," 1984 *Southern Illinois University Law Journal*, 283.

KURTZ, SHELDON F., *Family Estate Planning.* St. Paul, Minn.: West Publishing Company, 1982, pp. 4–20.

WEINSTOCK, HAROLD, *Planning an Estate.* Colorado Springs, Colo.: Shepard's/McGraw-Hill, 1982, pp. 18–29.

WESTFALL, DAVID, *Estate Planning.* Mineola, N.Y.: Foundation Press, Inc., 1982, pp. 48–50.

9

The Federal Gift Tax

Giving requires good sense.

Ovid, *Amores* I.viii

WHAT IS A GIFT?

Code 2501 imposes a tax on "the transfer of property by gift" by any individual. But, unlike the estate tax provisions, which explicitly define the "estate" to be taxed (Code 2031, 2051), the gift tax sections contain no definition of gift. Code 2511 clarifies the matter somewhat by explaining that the tax imposed by Code 2501 applies "whether the transfer is in trust or otherwise, whether the gift is direct or indirect, and whether the property is real or personal, tangible or intangible." Code 2512(b) makes it clear that the tax reaches only gratuitous transfers. Code sections 2514 through 2517 categorize a limited number of transactions for gift tax purposes. And in Reg. 25.2511-1(h), the commissioner provides "examples of transactions resulting in taxable gifts." But gift remains undefined.

At common law, the elements of a valid gift are:

(1) a competent donor's irrevocable present intention to give an interest in the property to the donee,

(2) delivery of either the subject matter of the gift, an instrument of gift, or some type of constructive delivery, and

(3) acceptance of the gift by the donee (Solomon, 1981, p. 243).

However, the common law concepts of a gift are not controlling. Regulations 25.2511-1(g)(1) provides "Donative intent on the part of the transferor is not an essential element in the application of the gift tax to the transfer." Rather than deal with what the Regulations call "the subjective motives of the donor," a transfer is a gift for purposes of the federal gift tax if it is made for less than an equivalent consideration in money or money's worth (*Commissioner* v. *Wemyss*, 324 U.S. 303, 306, 1945). There are certain exceptions for arm's-length business transactions and certain property settlements in connection with divorces.

Nonetheless, except for this special requirement of inadequate consideration, the courts have insisted that the common law concepts of a gift be present before a transfer can be taxed as a gift. In *Estate of Robert W. Hite*, 49 T.C. 580, 594 (1968), the Tax Court said that a lifetime gift for federal gift tax purposes involved these elements:

(1) a donor competent to make a gift;

(2) a donee capable of accepting the gift;

(3) a clear and unmistakable intention on the part of the donor to absolutely and irrevocably divest himself of the title, dominion, and control of the subject matter of the gift in praesenti;

(4) the irrevocable transfer of the present legal title and of the dominion and control of the entire gift to the donee, so that the donor can exercise no further act of dominion or control over it;

(5) a delivery to the donee of the subject of the gift or of the most effective means of commanding the dominion of it; and

(6) acceptance of the gift by the donee.

From all this we can conclude, then, that if a transfer is made for inadequate consideration and if it meets the common law standard of a gift, it is a gift for purposes of the federal gift tax.

For the gift tax to attach, however, the gift must be completed. According to Regs. 25.2511-2(b), a gift is complete as to any property "of which the donor has so parted with dominion and control as to leave him no power to change its disposition, whether for his own benefit or for the benefit of another." Where, then, the donor reserves any power over the disposition of the property, the gift is incomplete. Under this reasoning, a gift is not consummated by the *delivery* of the donor's check or note, but only when the check is paid, certified, accepted by the drawee, or negotiated for value to a third person, or when the note is paid or transferred for value (Rev. Rul. 67-396, 1967-2 C.B. 351).

THE GIFT TAX

Unlike the income tax, the gift tax is cumulative throughout the life of the taxpayer. Since 1982 there has been an annual exclusion of $10,000 per donee for gifts of present interests [Code 2053(b)]. (Before the Economic Recovery Act of 1981, the exclusion was $3,000 per year per donee.) There is also, as with the estate tax, an unlimited marital deduction for qualifying transfers to the spouse of the donor (Code 2523) and a deduction for certain transfers to charity (Code 2522). Finally, the unified credit that applied against the estate tax also applies against the gift tax.

Calculating the Tax

The federal gift tax is calculated in the following manner:

1. List and total all gifts made by the donor during lifetime through the current calendar year, with the following adjustments:
   a. Exclude the portion of any gift that qualifies for the annual exclusion.
   b. Subtract all the gift tax deductions.
   c. Subtract from the total gifts made before 1977 the amount of the lifetime exemption applicable to such gifts that the donor elected to use.
2. Compute the tentative gift tax on the aggregate total adjusted gifts for all years, through the current calendar year, by using the unified estate and gift tax rate schedule (Table 8.4).
3. Compute the tentative gift tax on the aggregate total adjusted gifts for all prior years by using the unified estate and gift tax rate schedule.
4. Subtract item 3 from item 2, which gives the tentative tax on the gifts made during the current year.
5. Subtract from item 4 the unused portion of the unified credit against the gift tax, which gives the net gift tax payable.

   Table 9.1 provides an example.

TABLE 9.1 Calculation of the Gift Tax

Assume that a donor made the following gifts before 1977 and during the calendar years 1978, 1982, and 1987. The gift tax for 1987 would be calculated in the following manner:

Pre-1977 gifts (after annual exclusions and deductions)		$280,000
Less: lifetime exemption used by the donor		30,000
Net taxable pre-1977 gifts		$250,000
1978 gifts (after annual exclusions and deductions)		$75,000
1982 gifts (after annual exclusions and deductions)		175,000
1987 gifts (after annual exclusions and deductions)		250,000
Total gifts		$750,000
Tentative gift tax on total gifts		$248,300
Less tentative gift tax on pre-1987 gifts		155,800
Tentative tax on 1987 gifts		$92,500
Less unified credit	$192,800	
Less unified credit allowed		
on gifts in 1978–1986 ($16,900 in 1978 and $46,800 in1982	$ 63,700	$129,100
Gift tax payable		—0—

Note that the donor of the gifts has only $36,600 remaining in the unified credit ($129,100 minus $92,500). If any lifetime gifts are made in the future in amounts that total $142,667, or if the donor dies with an estate in excess of $142,667, there will be estate or gift tax payable since $36,600 is the unified estate and gift tax on $142,667.

You should also have noted from Table 9.1 that the way the gift tax is calculated the prior gifts push the current gifts into higher brackets. While the 1978 and 1982 gifts are not taxed in 1987, they are added to the 1987 gifts to push the calculation of the 1987 gifts into higher brackets. If the pre-1987 gifts had not been added to the 1987 gifts, the tax on the 1987 gifts would have been $70,800 instead of $92,500.

AVOIDING THE GIFT TAX

The gift tax is the easiest tax of all to avoid. First, gifts are by their nature voluntary transfers of property, and a taxpayer who makes no such transfers incurs no gift taxes. Moreover, the gift tax is structured so that substantial sums of money can pass into the hands of donees without "triggering" the gift tax.

Annual Exclusion

Code 2503(b) excludes from the gift tax the first $10,000 of gifts per year to each of an unlimited number of beneficiaries. Thus, if you have five children, you can give each child $10,000 per year free of the gift tax. After ten years of such gifts, you will have transferred a half million dollars out of your estate and into the possession of your children, neatly avoiding both the gift tax and the estate tax.

Split gifts.   Moreover, a husband and wife may elect to treat all gifts made by either as having been made one-half by each of them [Code 2513(a)]. By utilizing this opportunity, then, you and your spouse may give up to $20,000 per year to each of an unlimited number of donees without incurring the gift tax. It is not necessary that your spouse actually give $10,000. Under the rules, one spouse can make the entire $20,000 gift. It is only necessary that both spouses consent to treat all gifts made to third parties during the calendar year as split gifts. In our earlier example, then, you and your spouse (assuming your spouse consents to having your gifts to your children treated as joint gifts from you and your spouse) can make tax-free gifts of $20,000 per year to each of your five children, for a total annual tax-free transfer of $100,000. If the children's marriages are sound and you and your spouse are so inclined, you can give each year $20,000 to each of your children and $20,000 to each of your children's spouses, for a total annual tax-free transfer of $200,000. In ten years you will have transferred two million dollars out of your estate to your children without incurring any transfer tax. Gifts, properly made, can be a significant planning tool.

The present interest rule.   The annual exclusion is available only for gifts of a present interest. Gifts of a future interest do not qualify for the exclusion [Regs.

25.2503-3(a)]. If a gift gives an unrestricted right to the immediate use, possession, or enjoyment of property or the income from property, it is a present interest [Regs. 25.2503-3(b)]. Outright gifts, then, clearly qualify as present interests and the first $10,000 ($20,000 in the case of a split gift by a husband and wife) thereof may be excluded from the gift tax. If, on the other hand, the gift is one to begin in the future, such as a remainder interest in property, the gift does not qualify for the annual exclusion. And it is not uncommon for a gift to include both a present and a future interest. For example, if a gift is made in trust and the trust provides that the income is to be paid to the income beneficiary on a current basis, the gift of the income is a present interest, but the gift of the principal is a future interest. The value of the income interest is calculated by using the tables set out in Regs. 25-2512-9(f) (see Appendix G).

Transfers for the benefit of persons under 21 years of age.   Since only a gift of a present interest will qualify for the annual exclusion, when the trustee has discretionary powers over the payment of income or the trust requires that the income be accumulated, there has been no gift of a present interest and the value of the income interest does not qualify for the annual exclusion. There is, however, one exception to this rule to permit gifts to be made to trusts for the benefit of minors without having to give the minor the right to present possession of the income from the trust. Code 2503(c) provides that no part of a gift made to a person under age 21 (not 18 but 21) will be considered a gift of a future interest if the principal and income may be expended for the benefit of such minor, and if any amounts not so expended will be distributed to the donee upon reaching the age of 21.

Medical or educational expenses.   A gift need not be a direct transfer to another person. When one pays the bills or debts of another, for example, the payor has made a gift to the person, who was otherwise obligated to pay these bills or debts. Within the family setting, this can have special application to adult children and their offspring. A parent has the duty to support his or her minor children, but not adult children or grandchildren, minor or otherwise. Thus, if a father pays the graduate school tuition for his 24-year-old son, he has made a gift to the son, even though the payment went directly to the university and not to the son. So, also, if a grandmother paid the medical expenses of a granddaughter, a gift has been made to the granddaughter's parents, who have the obligation to support the granddaughter. To avoid adding the burden of taxation to the already substantial burden of parents and others who provide for the education and health care support of their children and others, the Economic Recovery Tax Act of 1981 provides for an unlimited exclusion from the gift tax for amounts paid on behalf of any individual for medical payments or tuition. To be excluded, the payments must be paid by the donor directly to the medical care provider or educational institution. Moreover, only medical payments and tuition are exempt, not other educational or support expenses [Code 2503(e)].

The Marital Deduction

As with the estate tax, a donor spouse is allowed an unlimited deduction for lifetime gifts made to his or her spouse [Code 2523(a)]. As we saw in Chapter 8, the idea behind the marital deduction is that any assets passed from one spouse to another will later be taxed to the donee spouse, either by the gift tax if the donee spouse gives the assets away or by the estate tax if the donee spouse dies owning the assets.

The marital deduction is not allowable for a gift that will not be in the donee spouse's estate at his or her death. Thus, under traditional gift tax rules, a gift of a life estate or other interest that will terminate on the donee spouse's death would not qualify for the marital deduction. However, if the gift of a terminable interest is qualifying terminable interest property (QTIP) under Code 2523, it will qualify for the gift tax marital deduction. The rules for qualified terminal interest property for the gift tax are the same as those set forth in Chapter 8 for QTIP property for the estate tax.

The Gift Tax Charitable Deduction

Code 2522 allows an unlimited deduction for the value of gifts made to charities described in that section. However, the average client will usually want to make the bulk of his or her wealth available for noncharitable (and usually family) beneficiaries. This factor would seem to eliminate the charitable deduction as gift tax avoidance device. However, it is possible to make gifts that are not *solely* for charitable purposes and still gain some of the benefits of the charitable deduction.

In such an event, as we saw earlier with respect to the estate tax, a gift is usually made for the benefit of a noncharitable beneficiary for life or a term of years, with the gift then going to the charitable beneficiary upon the death of the noncharitable beneficiary or after the passage of the term of years. Such a gift is known as a *charitable remainder trust*, since the remainder (what remains of the gift after the noncharitable beneficiary has enjoyed it for life or the term of years) passes to charity. If the amount of money is quite large, the gift is often made to the charity first, for a term of years, after which the remainder passes to a noncharitable beneficiary. This device is known as a *charitable lead trust* and is used only when the donor or the beneficiaries are quite wealthy so that they will not be adversely affected by giving up a substantial amount of income until some time in the future.

For gifts to charity to qualify for the gift tax charitable deduction, the charitable interest *must* take one of three forms:

1. A remainder interest in a trust that is a charitable remainder annuity trust or a charitable remainder unitrust, described in Code 664, or a pooled income fund, described in Code 642(c)(5) [Code 2522(c)(2)(A)].
2. An income or lead interest in a trust in the form of a guaranteed annuity or fixed percentage of the fair market value of the property, which is to be determined and distributed yearly [Code 2522(c)(2)(B)].

3. An interest described in Code 170(f)(3)(B), which allows a remainder interest in a personal residence or farm, an undivided portion of the taxpayer's entire interest in property, or a qualified conservation contribution to qualify for an income tax deduction.

As paragraph 3 suggests, a major purpose of charitable trusts is as a vehicle for income tax savings. The gift tax charitable deduction is certainly a tax advantage of such trusts, but, because the income tax is much more savage in its assault on personal wealth than the gift tax, gift tax deductions always take a back seat to income tax deductions in importance.

The Absence of a "Tax-on-a-Tax"

You may have noted, when we discussed the calculation of the estate tax, that this tax is a tax-on-a-tax. For example, if you die with a taxable estate of $1,000,000 (after all deductions and exclusions), the estate tax will be calculated on the entire $1,000,000 estate, which will include $345,800 that will be used to pay the estate tax. So the estate tax is actually computed on a figure that includes the estate tax itself. If you had paid tax only on the $654,200 that passed to your beneficiaries after deduction of the $345,800 estate tax, your tax would have been $127,854.

The gift tax, on the other hand, is not a tax-on-a-tax. A gift of $1,000,000 on which a gift tax of $345,800 is paid is a gift of only $1,000,000, not a gift of $1,345,800. And the $345,800 that is used to pay the gift tax is never itself subjected to the gift tax.

Thus, while the estate and gift taxes have been unified into one system, it is still less expensive to make a lifetime gift and pay the gift tax than to die owning the asset and pay the estate tax on both the asset and the tax on the asset.

GIFT TAX RETURNS

The federal gift tax return (Form 709) is due annually on or before April 15 following the year the taxable gift is made. However, a return for the year that includes the death of the donor must be filed no later than the time for filing the donor's estate tax return (i.e., nine months after death) [Code 6075(b)(3)]. A return is considered timely filed if it is mailed within the time allowed, although cautious (and perhaps justifiably suspicious) taxpayers and personal representatives of estates usually send all documents to the IRS by registered mail, return receipt requested. (Just because you're paranoid doesn't mean they're really not out to get you! In the tax business, a healthy dose of paranoia can be a great help occasionally.)

STATE GIFT TAXES

Nine states impose a gift tax (Delaware, Louisiana, New York, North Carolina, Oregon, South Carolina, Tennessee, Vermont, and Wisconsin). There are two general types of state gift taxes, with their operation roughly akin to the difference between estate and inheritance taxes. The first is a tax imposed on the total taxable gifts as a whole, similar to the federal gift tax. The other is a tax imposed separately on transfers to each beneficiary. As with the inheritance tax, beneficiaries of gifts are divided into different classes depending on the degree of relationship to the donor, with lower tax rates and larger exemptions for close relatives.

APPLYING THIS CHAPTER TO *YOUR* SITUATION

While the gift tax was designed to prevent avoidance of the estate tax by lifetime giving, and the most recent major change in the tax was the unification of the gift tax with the estate tax into one transfer tax system, the gift tax remains the easiest tax to avoid. The annual exclusion and the gift-splitting opportunities that can be used in connection therewith afford the careful donor the opportunity to make tax-free transfers of substantial sums of money over a relatively short period of time.

However, in all the planning regarding the gift tax, as with all taxes, taxpayers must be certain that the evil sought to be avoided, taxes, is in fact greater than the means of avoiding it. Giving away one's assets during lifetime in such a manner as to avoid transfer taxes is a sound policy only if the taxpayer has sufficient assets that she or he will not miss these gifts and if the giving is consistent with other aspects of the taxpayer's estate plan. Gift tax considerations, as with all other tax considerations, must take a hind seat to more important non-tax considerations.

CASE PROBLEM

9.1 Gift Tax Liability.   In 1987, Stanley Wagner made the following gifts.

To his daughter Alice, $50,000.
To his daughter Barbara and her husband Carl, $50,000.
To his son David and his wife Elizabeth, $75,000.
To his son Frank and his wife Geraldine, $30,000.
To his grandson Harold (Alice's son), $25,000.
To his granddaughter Irene (Frank's daughter) and her husband John, $20,000.
To his wife Eleanor, $250,000.
To the Prince of Peace Military Academy, $150,000.
Stanley and Eleanor agree to split Stanley's gifts to third persons.

Questions
1. On what amount of taxable gifts will Stanley and Eleanor be subject to the gift tax?

2. Assuming that Stanley made taxable gifts of $250,000 in 1985 and that Eleanor made taxable gifts of $125,000 in 1984, what is their 1987 gift tax liability?

SELECTED READINGS

LLOYD, JAMES W., "Gift Valuation: Strategies and Developments." New York University, 43rd Annual Institute on Federal Taxation, pp. 49-1–49-31, 1985.

KURTZ, SHELDON F., *Family Estate Planning*. St. Paul, Minn.: West Publishing Company, 1982, pp. 7–12.

PRICE, JOHN R., *Contemporary Estate Planning*. Boston: Little, Brown and Company, 1983, pp. 58–67.

SOLOMON, LEWIS D., *Trusts and Estates: A Basic Course*. Charlottesville, Va.: Michie Bobbs-Merrill Company, 1981, pp. 251–257.

WEINSTOCK, HAROLD, *Planning an Estate*. Mineola, N.Y.: Foundation Press, Inc., 1982, pp. 30–35.

10

The Generation-
Skipping
Transfer Tax

Three generations of imbeciles are enough.

Justice Oliver Wendell Holmes, Jr.
Buck v. *Bell*, 274 U.S. 200, 207 (1927)

The purpose of the federal estate and gift taxes is not merely to raise revenue, but also to achieve the sociological goal of "evening up" or redistributing the wealth in this country to some degree. While it is questionable whether the transfer taxes have much effect on the distribution of wealth (the income tax appears to be much more effective in this regard), the effect of these taxes is certainly reduced if transfer taxes can be routinely avoided by the wealthy and not by those who are not so wealthy.

The federal transfer taxes are imposed on every generation where the property passes directly from parent to child, and then from child to grandchild. However, it is possible to shelter assets from this tax for several generations through the use of generation-skipping trusts.

For example, assume that John Jones has a son, Tom Jones, and a granddaughter, Mary Jones. If John conveys his estate to a trust with the Strong National Bank as trustee and provides in the trust that his son Tom is to have the income from the trust for his lifetime and, on Tom's death, the trust is to terminate and the principal pass to his granddaughter Mary, there will be no federal estate tax due on Tom's death. The reason is that there will be nothing in Tom's estate to be taxed since he had only a life interest in his father's estate. John Jones has achieved estate tax savings for Tom's generation by avoiding giving Tom ownership of John's wealth or any power over its disposition. Since John has managed to have the estate tax skip one generation, the trust he established with the Strong National Bank is known as a generation-skipping trust.

John could have skipped two generations by giving his granddaughter Mary merely an income interest in the property (as he had done for Tom) and providing that the trust terminate on her death and the principal be distributed among her heirs at that time. Moreover, John could have given Tom (and Mary, if he decided to skip another generation) substantial powers with respect to the use, management, and disposition of the trust assets that would amount to virtual outright ownership, but would still not require inclusion of the trust assets in their estates on their deaths.

As Congress viewed the problem, the evils of the generation-skipping trust were emphasized by the fact that, while the advantages of such trusts are theoretically available to all, in actual practice only the wealthier families have sufficient assets to be able to take advantage of the device. In families with limited wealth, the assets of one generation are generally passed outright to the next generation (because the next generation needs to have total use of the assets), while in wealthier families a wealthy child can do without the complete ownership of his or her parent's estate since the child will have sufficient wealth of his or her own. Thus, wealthier families would be subject to the transfer tax only once every several generations because they would shelter their estates behind generation-skipping trusts, while less wealthy families who cannot afford to use generation-skipping trusts must pay these taxes every generation. This fact has the effect of reducing the progressive effect of the transfer tax, since families with moderate levels of wealth may pay as much or more in transfer taxes over several generations as wealthier families who are able to utilize the generation-skipping trust.

Until the Tax Reform Act of 1976, the only limitation on the use of generation-skipping trusts was the common law *rule against perpetuities*. This rule of law, which comes to us from the sixteenth century but is still in effect in most American states in substantially its common law form, provides that an interest in property cannot last longer than 21 years beyond the death of the last survivor of named or ascertained individuals who were living when the interest was created (Kurtz, 1983, p. 355). However, an elderly person could select great-grandchildren or other young persons as the "measuring lives" under the rule and virtually ensure that the interest created would continue for 80 or 100 years, or perhaps longer. So the rule against perpetuities was not very effective against use of the generation-skipping trust as an estate tax avoidance device.

GENERATION-SKIPPING TRANSFER TAX

For this reason, when the Congress revamped the estate and gift tax system in the Tax Reform Act of 1976, it imposed a tax on generation-skipping transfers (Code 2601). Generally, everytime property passes from one generation to successive generations in trust form, the transfer is treated as an outright transfer from one generation to another. For purposes of this special tax, the term trust also includes nontrust arrangements that have substantially the same effect of splitting the beneficial enjoyment of assets between generations (Code 2611).

For example, if John Jones creates a trust for his son Tom, for Tom's life, and on Tom's death the trust assets are to go to Tom's daughter, Mary, the assets in the trust on Tom's death will be subject to the generation-skipping transfer tax, since Tom has no interest in the trust that would subject them to the estate tax on his death.

All generation-skipping transfers are taxed at a flat 55 percent rate, which is equal to the present maximum estate and gift tax rate and is scheduled to drop to 50 percent in 1988.

Imposition of the Tax

The generation-skipping transfer tax is imposed under the following three conditions:

1. When there is a taxable distribution (i.e., a distribution to a transferee who is a member of a generation at least two generations younger than the transferor), the amount received by the transferee is subject to the tax. The transferee also pays the tax [Code 2603(a)(1)].

2. When there is a taxable termination (by death, lapse of time, release of power, etc.) of an interest held in trust that passes to a transferee who is a member of a generation at least two generations younger than the transferor, the value of the property in which the interest terminates is subject to the tax. The tax is paid by the trustee [Code 2603(a)(2)].

3. When there is a direct skip (i.e., a transfer of property to, or for the benefit of, persons two or more generations below the transferor without the payment of estate or gift tax in the skipped generation), the value of the property received by the transferee is the amount subject to the tax. The transferor pays the tax [Code 2602(a)(3)].

Generation-skipping Tax Exclusions

Every individual is allowed a generation-skipping transfer tax exemption of $1,000,000; that is, a transferor is permitted to make generation-skipping transfers aggregating up to $1,000,000 during his or her lifetime and which at death will be completely exempt from the generation-skipping transfer tax. A married couple who elect to treat generation-skipping transfers as made one-half by each can effectively exclude up to $2,000,000 of generation-skipping transfers from the tax [Code 2632, 2652(a)(2)].

Determination of Generations

Since the generation-skipping transfer tax applies only to those transfers that skip generations, what constitutes a generation becomes important.

Family members.   Generally, generations are determined along family lines. The grantor's spouse and siblings are considered to be in the same generation as the grantor, without regard to their actual ages. The grantor's children (including adopted children) are the first younger generation, and the grandchildren constitute the second younger generation. Husbands and wives of family members are assigned to the same generation as their spouses (Code 2651).

Nonfamily members. When generation-skipping transfers are made outside the family, generations are measured from the grantor.

1. Individuals not more than 12 1/2 years younger than the grantor are considered members of his or her generation.
2. Individuals more than 12 1/2 years younger than the grantor, but not more than 37 1/2 years younger, are treated as members of his or her children's generation.
3. Each subsequent generation is measured in intervals of 25 years (Code 2651).

Grandfather Clause

The generation-skipping transfer tax applies to transfers under trusts and instruments made after September 25, 1985, unless

(1) the trust was irrevocable on that date and the generation-skipping transfer was not made out of corpus added to the trust after September 25, 1985, or
(2) the decedent was incompetent on September 25, 1985, and at all times thereafter until his or her death.

WHAT IS A GENERATION-SKIPPING TRANSFER

The tax is imposed, as we have seen, in the case of a generation-skipping transfer. The code defines this term to mean either a *taxable termination* or a *taxable distribution*.

Taxable Termination

A taxable termination means the termination of an interest or power of a younger generation beneficiary who is a member of a generation that is older than that of any other younger generation beneficiary [Code 2603(a)(2)]. You will be forgiven if this is not immediately clear to you. Perhaps this example will help.

> Assume that John made a gift in trust for his wife, Jane, for life, then for his son, Tom, for life, and then for his granddaughter, Mary, for life. On the death of Mary, the trust is to terminate and the principal to be distributed to Mary's then-living heirs. Assuming that the order of deaths is Jane, Tom, and then Mary, the tax consequences would be as follows:
>
> 1. There would be no taxable termination on Jane's death because she is not a younger generation member.
> 2. There would be taxable terminations for purposes of the generation-skipping transfer tax on the deaths of Tom and Mary, since they are members of generations that
>   a. are younger than John's generation, and

          b. are older than members of other generations who will take an interest in the trust after Tom and Mary's interests have terminated.

Taxable Distribution

A taxable distribution occurs when there is a distribution from a generation-skipping trust, other than a distribution out of trust income, to a younger generation beneficiary of the trust if there is at least one other younger generation beneficiary in a generation above that of the distributee [Code 2603(a)(1)]. This statement, too, is hardly a model of clarity. Perhaps this example will help.

> Using the family situation from the previous example, if the trustee had discretion to distribute principal to Mary during the life of Tom, such a distribution would be a taxable distribution.

AVOIDING THE GENERATION-SKIPPING TRANSFER

Some of the major ways to reduce the impact of the generation-skipping transfer tax include the following.

Generation-skipping tax exemption.   As noted earlier, every transferor is allowed a generation-skipping tax exemption of $1,000,000. Spouses who elect to split the gifts can exclude $2,000,000.

Income exclusion.   A distribution of current income from a trust to a grandchild is not a deemed transfer by a child and is not subject to the tax. (It also does not exhaust any available exclusion.) To utilize this technique, then, the trustee should be given discretion to pay income or principal to the grantor's descendants from time to time. The distributions of income will not be subject to the tax and will reduce the amount in the trust that will be subject to the generation-skipping transfer tax if the income were accumulated.

Exemption for future interests and powers.   Future interests are not subject to the tax. Thus a mother could provide an outright gift to a son on the mother's death and also create a trust that is to pay income to the son if he should ever become totally disabled or if, in the absolute discretion of the trustee, the son should need the money. If the son never requires the use of the income from the trust, it remains a future interest so far as the son is concerned and is not subject to the generation-skipping transfer tax.

APPLYING THIS CHAPTER TO *YOUR* SITUATION

The generation-skipping transfer tax does not apply to all situations, only those where the family's wealth is sufficient to avoid passing title to assets in a particular generation. But where the tax does apply, care should be taken to assure that this tax does not cause a significant reduction in the amount of the trust. Utilizing the exemption along with outright gifts to various generations, combined with gifts of future interests, can often result in partial or complete avoidance of the tax.

CASE PROBLEMS

10.1 Analyzing Trust Arrangements.　Determine in each of the following trust arrangements whether the trust is a generation-skipping trust.

1. David James transfers property to the Strong National Bank, in trust, to pay the income to David's wife for her life and, on his wife's death, to pay the corpus of the trust to David's brother, Ralph.
2. Mary transfers property in trust to pay the income to her granddaughter, Ellen, until she reaches 25 and then to pay over the corpus to her. Nothing is left to David's son, the father of Ellen.
3. David transfers property in trust to pay the income to his granddaughter, Ellen, for life, and on her death to pay the corpus to her then-living children.

10.2 Avoiding the Generation-Skipping Transfer Tax.　Edward Westfall is a 68-year-old businessman with an estate of approximately $3,000,000. He has two daughters, Ann and Amy, and each of them has two children. Edward is not confident that either daughter will be able to manage a substantial inheritance and so he wishes to leave each daughter a life interest in her share of his estate, with the property passing to each daughter's children on the death of the daughter. He proposes to establish a trust at the Strong National Bank and have the trustee pay the income from his estate to his daughters for their lives. On the deaths of each daughter, one-half of the trust assets will pass to that daughter's then-living children in equal shares.

Assuming that there will be approximately $2,000,000 left in Edward's estate after paying death taxes and that one daughter's estate at death will be approximately $500,000 and the other daughter's estate at death will be approximately $1,000,000, answer the following questions.

Questions
1. How much generation-skipping transfer tax will be payable out of the trust on the deaths of each daughter?
2. How could Edward structure his estate plan to reduce these taxes?

10.3 Tax Avoidance Techniques.　Assume that Edward creates a trust for each daughter and a separate trust for each grandchild, with all trusts to terminate on the deaths of the income beneficiary and the principal passing at that time to Edward's then-living great-grandchildren. Would this estate plan assist Edward in reducing the generation-skipping transfer tax? How?

SELECTED READINGS

BRUSH, LOUIS F., "The Generation-Skipping Transfer Tax: An Explanation and Analysis," 58 *Taxes* 451 (1980).

KURTZ, SHELDON F., *Family Estate Planning*. St. Paul, Minn.: West Publishing Co., 1983, pp. 442–490.

PRICE, JOHN R., *Contemporary Estate Planning*. Boston: Little, Brown and Company, 1983, pp. 80–97.

STRENG, WILLIAM P., *Estate Planning*. Washington, D.C.: Tax Management, Inc., 1981, pp. 561–588.

11

Marital Deduction Planning

Choose not alone a proper mate,
But proper time to marry.

William Cowper

We have already examined the marital deduction in a limited sense in Chapter 8. Now we need to understand how to utilize this device to save taxes, for the estate and gift tax marital deduction provisions are among the most important (and at times the most complicated) provisions of the federal transfer tax laws.

As we saw earlier, since the Economic Recovery Tax Act of 1981, the IRS has treated a married couple as a unit for purposes of the transfer taxes, with the result that any assets transferred from one spouse to another, during lifetime or on the death of one spouse, are exempt from the transfer taxes. This is an enormous improvement over prior law and opens up a highly attractive vista for tax planning.

HOW TO QUALIFY FOR THE MARITAL DEDUCTION

From a nontax viewpoint (which is always where the client and the estate planner should start) one of the client's major considerations will usually be how to provide for the surviving spouse. (If this is not a major consideration, assuming that the spouse does not have separate wealth, this may suggest deep-seated problems that the estate planner must address at once, lest the estate plan be one designed for one spouse only to be upset by the surviving spouse on death.)

The Necessity for a Spouse

Code 2056 (the estate tax marital deduction) and Code 2523 (the gift tax marital deduction) both speak of transfers to the spouse. But spouse is not defined. The courts have consistently held that the marital status of a decedent will be determined under the law of the state of the decedent's domicile (*Estate of Goldwater* v. *Commissioner*, 539 F.2d 878, 2d Cir., 1976).

Moreover, the Supreme Court of the United States has held that the marital deduction provisions are "to be strictly construed and applied" (*Commissioner* v. *Bosch*, 387 U.S. 456, 1967). Moreover, the numerous conditions, restrictions, and limitations incorporated within Codes 2056 and 2523 clearly indicate that Congress did not intend for the deduction to be loosely granted. Clearly, then, there is no justification for construing the term "surviving spouse" to include an alleged or claimed spouse. A common law spouse, however, may well be a perfectly legal spouse, depending on whether the requirements for a common law marriage in the state where the couple was domiciled were met.

Thus, the surviving spouse of a common law marriage must prove that all elements required of a common law marriage in the state where the marriage was celebrated were in fact present. In Revenue Ruling 76-155, 957 C.B. 286, for example, the survivor of an alleged common law marriage was found not to be a "surviving spouse" for purposes of Code 2056 because of what was described as "considerable doubt whether the understanding of [the couple in question] was a 'present assent' to be married, one of the critical elements of a common law marriage." If, on the other hand, the present assent to be married, along with the other elements of a common law marriage, had been present, the survivor of that marriage would clearly have qualified for the marital deduction.

The problem of determining if there has been a "surviving spouse" when there has been a Mexican or Nevada divorce can be difficult. American courts will not generally recognize a judgment of divorce granted by a court of another country unless, by the standards of the jurisdiction in which recognition is sought, at least one of the spouses was a good-faith domiciliary in the foreign nation at the time of the decree (*Bruneau* v. *Bruneau*, 3 Conn. App. 453, 489 A.2d 1049, 1985). And where a state court has held that a foreign divorce was of no effect and that the alleged "second wife" of the decedent was not his wife under state law, the alleged wife was not the surviving spouse for purposes of the federal estate tax marital deduction (*Estate of Steffke* v. *Commissioner*, 538 F.2d 730, CA7 1976).

However, occasionally, in trying to establish equity in a particular case, a court has held to the contrary. Thus, in *Estate of Spalding*, 537 F.2d 666 (CA2 1976), the court held that a declaration by the Supreme Court of New York that an ex parte Nevada divorce obtained by a husband prior to marriage to a second spouse in California was invalid did not "disentitle" (the court's word, not mine) the decedent second spouse's estate to the marital deduction on the theory that the husband was not the surviving spouse. So, be certain you have a surviving "spouse."

Assuming there is a spouse who will qualify for the marital deduction, the client must first consider what provisions he or she wishes to make for the surviving spouse, a question that is usually devoid of tax considerations. In the typical case of the husband doing estate planning for the protection of the wife and children, the age and nature of the marriage will bear heavily on the question. If the marriage is only beginning or if it is not thriving, the husband may not wish to provide generously for his wife. If the marriage is doing well but it is a second or third marriage, there may be prenuptial agreements or other arrangements (such as alimony and support for former spouses) that will limit the husband's generosity. Moreover, the husband may have children by a former marriage to whom he feels a greater obligation than to his current spouse. All these practical considerations and the state law that oversees them (which, among other things, will provide what minimal amount *must* be left to the wife) must be carefully taken into account.

If the husband decides he wants the wife to inherit everything he has, three additional questions must be asked and answered:

1. Can the wife manage all this property (or, if she can, does she *want* to)?
2. Will all the gifts to the wife qualify for the marital deduction?
3. Is this a tax-wise decision?

Determining if the Marital Deduction Is Tax-wise

By treating a married couple as a unit for purposes of the transfer taxes, the Congress has ensured that there will be no estate tax payable on the death of the first spouse for those assets left to the surviving spouse. This is laudable. However, since the assets that passed untaxed to the surviving spouse will be subject to the estate tax on the death of the surviving spouse, care must be taken that the estate of the surviving spouse (i.e., the combination of her separate estate and the estate that she inherited from her husband) is not so large at her death as to cause the estate tax to be higher on her death alone than would have been the case with separate tax bills on her death and the earlier death of her husband.

Put another way, assume that Jerome has an estate at his death of $1,000,000 (after all deductions). His wife, Edna, has an estate valued at $750,000 at her death. If Jerome died after 1986 and left nothing to Edna (and she does not claim a share of his estate, as she has a right to do), the federal estate tax will be $119,800 ($345,800 minus $192,800 unified credit and $33,200 credit for state death taxes). On Edna's later death, the federal estate tax will be $35,100 ($248,300 minus $192,800 and $20,400 credit for state death taxes). Thus the couple will have paid a total of $154,900 in federal estate taxes on their separate estates.

If, on the other hand, Jerome leaves his entire estate to Edna, there will be no estate tax payable at that time due to the marital deduction. On his wife's death, however, she will have an estate of $1,750,000 (her separate assets of $750,000 plus the $1,000,000 she inherited tax free from her husband). The federal estate tax due on an estate of $1,750,000 will be $281,400 (tax of $555,800 less $192,800 unified credit and $81,600 credit for state death taxes), a whopping $126,500 *more*. The reason, of course, is that Jerome, by leaving everything to Edna and avoiding the tax on his death, caused Edna's estate to be dramatically increased at her death. (In estate planning parlance, this is known as *estate stacking*. Since the estate tax rates are progressive, the tax on one estate of $1,750,000 is more than the combined taxes on separate estates of $1,000,000 and $750,000.

Moreover, by leaving everything to Edna, Jerome failed to take advantage of the fact that the law gives every decedent an exemption from the estate tax of $192,800, the equivalent of the tax on an estate of $600,000. In such event, he is said to have "wasted the unified credit."

On the other hand, Jerome did avoid having any estate tax payable on his death. And, considering the time value of money, this meant that Edna had the use, for her lifetime, of the $119,800 that would have otherwise been used to pay Jerome's estate tax. If we assume that she could earn 10 percent on this money annually, this means that she would have an additional $11,980 in income per year for life. If she should survive Jerome by ten and a half years, the additional income earned from the money not paid in taxes will exceed the extra taxes paid by reason of the estate stacking. And, if the money is placed in an account and allowed to accumulate at compound interest at, say, 10 percent interest, it will take just over eight years for the income on the tax savings to exceed the extra tax paid on Edna's death. This is a factor that is often overlooked by those who consider merely the taxes paid by the two estates and not the entire picture of the value of the use of money over time.

Not Wasting the Unified Credit

Still, had he planned carefully, Jerome could have had the best of both worlds. He could have completely avoided the estate tax on his death and reduced the effect of estate stacking in Edna's estate considerably. And he could have done all this by careful *marital deduction planning*.

Consider. If Jerome had left $600,000 of his estate in such a way that it would not qualify for the marital deduction, it would have been subject to the estate tax on Jerome's death. But, since the tax on a $600,000 estate is $192,800 and since the unified credit is $192,800, there would have been no estate tax payable on this $600,000. "Subject to the estate tax" is not the same as "paying the estate tax." So, for purposes of illustration, let's assume that Jerome leaves $600,000 of his $1,000,000 estate to his children. No tax is due on this $600,000 because of the unified credit. As to the remaining $400,000 in Jerome's estate, it would not be sheltered from tax by the unified credit. So Jerome leaves this to Edna and shelters it from tax by means of the marital deduction. Thus, on Jerome's death there will be no federal estate tax payable due to the combination of the unified credit and the marital deduction.

On Edna's death, her estate would be valued at $1,150,000 (her original $750,000 plus the $400,000 left her by Jerome). The federal estate tax payable on her death would be $172,500 ($407,300 tax minus $192,800 unified credit and $42,000 credit for state death taxes). So Jerome's estate paid no tax on his death and Edna's estate tax amounted to only $172,500. This is $108,900 less than would have been paid in estate tax on behalf of the couple had Jerome wasted his unified credit and only $17,600 more than the $154,900 tax on the combined estates if Jerome had left nothing to Edna. And, by paying no estate tax on Jerome's death, Edna and her children have had the use of the $119,800 that would have been used to pay taxes at that time.

Note that the secret of not wasting the unified credit on the death of the first spouse by leaving everything to the surviving spouse and sheltering it under the marital deduction is that $1,200,000 passes free of the transfer tax in the couple's generation because both used the unified credit to the maximum. Indeed, the difference between the $241,800 tax due if Jerome wastes his unified credit and the $172,500 tax due if Jerome does not waste his unified credit is solely due to the extra $600,000 being subject to tax at the highest marginal rates. So, utilizing the unified credit is an important part of the estate planning process when tax savings are of any concern to the estate owner.

Note also that, by using the unified credit in our example, we did *not* use some of the marital deduction available to Jerome. It is this combination of marital deduction and unified credit planning that can result in the maximum tax savings. Careful and effective marital deduction planning is negative as well as positive.

QUALIFYING FOR THE MARITAL DEDUCTION

Now, assume that Jerome says, "I don't care about taxes. I want to leave my entire estate to Edna. She helped me put it together and I want her to enjoy it after I'm gone. The kids can worry about taxes when they take the estate." This is not an unusual (or necessarily unwise) reaction. Is there any way that we can satisfy Jerome's desire to "leave his entire estate to Edna" but *not* have some of it qualify for the marital deduction (and thus waste the unified credit)? The answer is yes, and it is here that we enter the real world of marital deduction tax planning.

To qualify for the estate tax marital deduction, a gift from a decedent spouse to the surviving spouse must meet the following requirements:

1. The decedent must be survived by a spouse.
2. The decedent must have been a citizen or resident of the United States.
3. The property for which the marital deduction is claimed must have been included in the decedent spouse's estate.
4. The interest must pass from the decedent spouse to the surviving spouse.
5. The interest must not be a terminable interest.

The first three requirements do not ordinarily pose any difficult problems. As we have seen, the question of a surviving spouse is a question of law and seldom comes up, with the exception of problems involving common law marriages, questionable divorces, and questionable marriages (problems foreign to the typical estate owner). Citizenship and residency are also usually cut-and-dried matters.

The requirement that marital deduction property must have been included in the decedent spouse's estate is simply another way of saying that, if you wish to deduct something from the gross estate of a decedent, it must have been included in the estate in the first place. For example, if Jerome from our earlier example were the donee of a special power of appointment that gave him the right to say who among a certain group of people will receive some assets from the estate of Jerome's father, these assets are not includable in Jerome's estate. If, then, Jerome were to designate his wife Edna to receive these assets, this gift to Edna would not qualify for the marital deduction since the assets in question were not a part of Jerome's estate in the first instance. It could not be taken out of Jerome's estate because it had not been included in his estate in the first place.

The remaining two requirements for the marital deduction are, however, often the subject of considerable dispute over whether a deduction is allowable.

Interests That Pass to the Surviving Spouse

The marital deduction is only allowed for interests that pass to the surviving spouse. Code 2056(c) defines property as passing from the decedent to the surviving spouse if the spouse receives it:

1. By request or devise
2. By inheritance
3. As dower or curtesy (or statutory substitute therefor)
4. By lifetime transfer (in such fashion that it is still in the decedent spouse's estate for estate tax purposes)
5. By joint tenancy or right of survivorship
6. By the exercise or nonexercise of a general power of appointment
7. As the proceeds of a life insurance policy on the decedent's life

When a surviving spouse elects to take against the decedent's will, any property received is considered to have passed from the decedent to the surviving spouse. However, if the surviving spouse had to give up certain property as a result of the election to take against the will, the value of the property given up is not considered to have passed to the surviving spouse [Reg. 20.2056(e)-2(c)].

If there is a controversy involving the surviving spouse's right to certain property and the controversy is settled in a court action (either by decree of the court or as a genuine settlement), the property received by the surviving spouse is considered as having passed to the surviving spouse [Reg. 20.2056(e)-2(d)].

Terminable Interests

The central idea behind the marital deduction is that the property that passes tax free to the surviving spouse will be in the estate of the surviving spouse to be taxed when that spouse dies, unless the property has been given away (in which case the gift will have been taxed by the gift tax) or consumed (in which case it will have avoided the transfer tax, but not, perhaps, the sales tax).

Thus the property left to the surviving spouse on the death of the first spouse must not be of a nature that the surviving spouse's interest will necessarily terminate on the happening of some contingency or on the mere lapse of time. For example, if Jerome should leave Blackacre to Edna for five years, it is a certainty that Edna's title in Blackacre will terminate after five years and the property will not be in Edna's estate to be subject to the transfer tax on her death. Similarly, if Jerome leaves Blackacre to Edna for her life and then provides that it is to pass to their children on Edna's death, Edna's interest in Blackacre terminates at her death and there will be nothing of this asset to tax in her estate. Gifts of this nature are known as *terminable interests* and do not, as we saw earlier, qualify for the marital deduction, except under a special rule we will discuss in a moment [Code 2056(b)].

Dangers of joint and mutual wills. Terminable interests can turn up in some fairly unexpected places. For example, if a husband and wife execute a joint will or mutual wills under which the surviving spouse is obligated to dispose of the inherited property upon his or her death to specific individuals, the surviving spouse really has only a life estate in the property he or she received from the decedent spouse, and this property will not qualify for the marital deduction. For this reason, as for others outlined earlier in this book, joint wills should *never* be executed, and care should be taken with mutual wills that they are not held to contain a contractual agreement that will limit the surviving spouse's right to do as he or she pleases with his or her estate on death.

Six-month survivorship condition. Under the definition of a terminable interest, which we discussed earlier, a bequest conditioned upon the surviving spouse's outliving the decedent for a period of time will be a nondeductible terminable interest, because it terminates on the happening of some contingency. However, there are sound reasons why one spouse may wish his or her property not to pass to the surviving spouse if that spouse will not be able to enjoy it for very long. For example, a wife may not wish to have her assets pass to her husband (after going through the expense of probate) and then have him die a few months later and have the assets pass through probate again. In fact, the probate process is so slow that the surviving spouse would probably not have received anything from the decedent spouse after a few months anyway. Thus, many wills provide that nothing is to go to the surviving spouse (and others, for that matter) unless they survive for at least a certain period of time. Others provide that nothing shall go to the surviving spouse if both spouses die as a result of a common disaster. Code 2056(b)(3) provides an exception to the terminable interest rule for bequests conditioned solely on survivorship, as long as the period of survivorship does not exceed six months after the decedent's death.

Therefore, if a will leaves a bequest to the surviving spouse but provides that the bequest will fail if the surviving spouse does not survive the decedent spouse by at least sixty days, the bequest will qualify for the marital deduction, unless the surviving spouse does in fact die within sixty days of the decedent spouse, in which case nothing will have passed to the surviving spouse.

Power of appointment trust. Code 2056(b)(5) provides another exception to the terminable interest rule for a bequest known as a power of appointment trust. With a power of appointment trust, the surviving spouse (1) is entitled to all of the income from the trust for life, payable at least annually, and (2) has the power to appoint the entire principal of the trust either to himself or his estate, or to both (in other words, a general power of appointment).

Life estate with power of appointment. The transfer to the surviving spouse need not be in trust in order to qualify for the marital deduction. The decedent spouse could have left the property to the surviving spouse for life with a general power of appointment [Code 2056(b)(5)]. The general power of appointment is tantamount to ownership so that the property will be in the surviving spouse's estate at his or her death. Thus it qualifies for the marital deduction.

Estate trust. The reason that most interests that are less than outright bequests to the surviving spouse fail as terminable interests is that, when the surviving spouse's interest comes to an end, the property passes to someone else. If, however, a decedent transfers property to a trust under which all beneficial interest is in the surviving spouse or in the surviving spouse's estate, this trust will qualify for the marital deduction.

The estate trust differs from the power of appointment trust in that (1) income need not be paid annually to the surviving spouse, but may be accumulated for the surviving spouse or her or his estate, and (2) the principal and any accumulated income *must* be distributed to the surviving spouse's estate and on her or his death [Reg. 20.2056(e)-2(b)].

The QTIP Trust

The Economic Recovery Tax Act of 1981 (ERTA) added another method of avoiding the terminable interest rule, one that adds a great deal of flexibility to estate planning. This is a bequest to what is designated as a qualified terminable interest property trust, known by its acronym QTIP [Code 2056(b)(7)]. To qualify for the marital deduction under the QTIP trust rules, the following requirements must be met.

Income to the surviving spouse. The surviving spouse must be entitled to receive all the income from the trust, payable at least annually, for life [Code 2056(b)(7)(B)(ii].

Power of appointment. No person (including the surviving spouse) can have any power to appoint the trust property to any third person during the surviving spouse's lifetime [Code 2056(b)(7)(B)(ii)]. The surviving spouse can have the right to assign his or her income interest in the trust to a third party, but the property itself (as opposed to the income interest in the property) must remain in the trust.

Operation of the QTIP exclusion. On the death of the surviving spouse, the property subject to the QTIP trust is considered to be in the estate of the surviving spouse and is subject to the estate tax at that time. This is central to the QTIP trust concept. One problem with leaving terminable interest property to the surviving spouse, remember, is that there is nothing left in the surviving spouse's estate to tax on his or her death (since the interest has "terminated"), and so the property must be taxed on the death of the first spouse. With the QTIP concept, although the interest may in fact be terminable, we pretend that it is not and subject it to tax on the death of the surviving spouse. Since it can be taxed on the death of the surviving spouse, there is no need to subject it to tax on the death of the first spouse, and so we can qualify it for the marital deduction at that time if it actually passes to the surviving spouse.

Note, however, that the use of the QTIP trust does not mean that everything that is placed in the trust is *automatically* deductible under the marital deduction. To qualify for the marital deduction, the executor must elect to take it on the federal estate tax return, and once this election is made it is irrevocable [Code 2056(b)(7)(B)(v)]. This ability of the executor to calculate the size of the estate and the tax payable by the decedent's estate, to estimate the tax that may be payable out of the surviving spouse's estate, and to elect to leave only so much as will result in the maximum tax savings to the couple's combined estates is a valuable aspect of the QTIP concept.

Consider this example of the QTIP trust in action. Assume that Jerome has an estate of $1,000,000 to $1,500,000 and his wife Edna has an estate valued at $750,000 to $1,000,000. Jerome wants Edna to have everything, but he would also like to minimize his and Edna's estate tax. Like most persons undergoing estate planning, he has only an idea of what his estate will be worth. He is therefore reluctant to leave any set amount to Edna so that it will qualify for the marital deduction and allow the remainder of his estate to pass in some fashion that will not waste the unified credit. In short, he wants (1) maximum flexibility, (2) maximum protection for Edna, and (3) maximum protection from the estate tax on his death.

The QTIP trust is custom-designed for this situation. Jerome can leave his property to such a trust with the income going to Edna for her life and giving her the right on her death to appoint the principal in the trust among their three children in such shares as she shall determine. The trust can further provide that the trustee may dip into the principal on Edna's behalf if she should need additional funds for certain purposes. On Jerome's death, after the estate values have been established and after Jerome's executor determines the expenses of the estate (including the prospective estate tax), the executor can qualify so much of Jerome's property that Jerome has left in the QTIP trust for the marital deduction as will result in the reduction of Jerome's estate tax to zero and the passage of as much of his estate to Edna as possible. And, since she has (1) an income interest in all the property placed in the trust, (2) the right to say who gets this property after her death, and (3) the right to use part of the principal if necessary, Edna has rights in the property that are very close to outright ownership, thus satisfying Jerome's desire that she receive everything on his death.

If, as it develops, Jerome's estate is actually valued at $1,250,000, the executor can qualify $650,000 of the assets in the trust for the marital deduction and leave the remaining $600,000 to be subjected to the estate tax (where, because of the unified credit, there will be no tax due). When Edna dies, the only part of Jerome's former estate to be taxed will be the $650,000 that was qualified for the marital deduction in the QTIP trust.

Expressing the Marital Deduction Gift

Establishing how much to leave the surviving spouse so no tax is paid on the death of the first spouse, while keeping the amount of assets that will be "stacked" onto the surviving spouse's estate to a minimum, will depend on many variables not likely to be answerable until the first spouse dies. (Actually, they will not be answerable until *after* the first spouse dies, by which time it will clearly be too late for that spouse to make any changes in his or her estate plan.)

One solution to this problem is to utilize a formula marital deduction clause that leaves to the surviving spouse an amount equal to the maximum marital deduction allowable under the federal estate tax, reduced by the value of all other assets that have passed to the surviving spouse from the decedent spouse outside the will.

If, then, Jerome leaves an estate of $1,000,000, which includes his interest in a $200,000 home that he and Edna own in joint tenancy, and the remainder of the estate is left to Edna in Jerome's will, the amount of the marital deduction gift will be calculated as follows:

Total net estate	$1,000,000
Less:	
Amount passing to Edna outside will (one-half of the house)	−100,000
Amount of marital deduction gift	$ 900,000

Edna, of course, will "get" all of Jerome's estate and it will all qualify for the marital deduction, but only $900,000 will pass under the marital deduction clause in Jerome's will.

Taking this a step further, a couple desiring to (1) reduce the estate tax to zero on the death of the first spouse and (2) not waste the unified credit on the death of the first spouse will make use of what is known as an A-B trust plan. On the death of the first spouse (which, for purposes of our example, we will assume to be the husband), the husband's estate will be divided into two trusts. The A trust (or *marital* trust) will be the repository of the marital deduction gift, and the residue of the estate will pass into the B trust (or *residuary* trust). In making the marital deduction calculation, the amount of the unified credit will also be deducted from the sum passing to the wife, since to pass this amount to the surviving spouse and qualify it for the marital deduction would be to waste the unified credit.

If, then, the husband dies after December 31, 1986, with an estate of $2,000,000, of which $300,000 is held in joint tenancy, the marital deduction gift will be calculated as follows.

Total net estate		$2,000,000
Less:		
Amount passing to Edna outside will	$300,000	
Unified credit	600,000	
Total		−900,000
Amount of marital deduction gift		$1,100,000

The total marital deduction gift will be $1,400,000, but only $1,100,000 will pass to the wife under the formula marital deduction clause of the will.

The use of a formula clause has the following advantages:

1. It does not leave any more to Edna under the marital deduction than is absolutely necessary, thus keeping the increase in her estate by reason of Jerome's death to a minimum.
2. It automatically calculates the maximum marital deduction gift regardless of what the actual value of the estate may be on the owner's death.

Among the major disadvantages are the facts that the language used in the typical formula clause is, by necessity, complicated. Most testators (and many lawyers) will simply not understand it and will have to take it on faith that the clause does what the lawyer says it does. In an age when the "plain language" will has finally arrived, this can be a bit unsettling. Moreover, since the formula clause calculation is dependent on the amount and extent of deductions and the determination of the value of the decedent's estate, the use of a formula clause could cause a delay in the settlement of the estate until the federal estate tax due is finally calculated and accepted by the IRS.

Forms of Marital Deduction Formula Clauses

Strict pecuniary clause. The two most common marital deduction formula clauses are the strict pecuniary clause and the fractional share clause. With the strict pecuniary clause, the marital deduction gift is reducible to a fixed dollar amount. The example we used previously which resulted in a marital deduction gift of $1,100,000, is a strict pecuniary marital deduction clause, since by utilizing it the marital deduction gift is reduced to the fixed dollar amount of $1,100,000.

If, then, Jerome leaves an estate of $1,000,000, which includes a $200,000 home that he and Edna own in joint tenancy, and the remainder of the estate is left to Edna in Jerome's will, the amount of the marital deduction gift will be calculated as follows if we use a strict pecuniary marital deduction clause.

Total net estate		$1,000,000
Less:		
Amount passing to Edna outside will		
(one-half of the house)	$100,000	
Unified credit	600,000	
Total		−700,000
Amount of marital deduction gift		$300,000

This means that only $300,000 of the property that passes under Jerome's will is going to be qualified for the marital deduction and passed into the marital trust. Another $100,000 (Jerome's half of their $200,000 home) will qualify for the marital deduction. The remaining $600,000 will pass to the residuary trust, where it will be sheltered from taxation by the unified credit. Edna will have the income from this $600,000, but her interest will be a strictly terminable one and this $600,000 will not be in her estate to be taxed on her death.

An example of a strict pecuniary marital deduction clause is as follows:

If my wife survives me, I direct that my residuary estate be divided into two separate trusts, the marital trust and the residuary trust. The marital trust shall consist of the smallest amount, which if allowable as a marital deduction for federal estate tax purposes in the matter of my estate will result in no federal estate tax being due from my estate, taking into account all other deductions allowed to my estate for federal estate tax purposes and the amount of the unified credit, and the state death tax credit. However, the state death tax credit shall only be taken into account to the extent that it does not increase the amount of the tax payable to any state. The residuary trust shall consist of the remainder of my estate.

Fractional share clause. The fractional share of the residue marital deduction clause is even more complex than the pecuniary clause and leaves to the beneficiary the specified fractional interest in each asset that is included in the pool against which the fraction is applied.

A typical formula fractional share gift is as follows:

If my wife survives me, I give to a trust for her benefit a fraction of my residuary estate, determined after payment of all pecuniary gifts, expenses of administration, debts, and death taxes that are properly chargeable against my residuary estate. The numerator of the fraction shall be the smallest amount which, if allowable as a marital deduction for federal estate tax purposes in the matter of my estate, will result in no federal estate tax being due from my estate, taking into account all other deductions allowed for federal estate tax purposes, the unified credit, and the credit for state death taxes (but only to the extent that the latter does not increase the state death tax payable by my estate). The denominator of the fraction shall be the federal estate tax value of my residuary estate so determined.

The fractional share gift has a slight edge when it comes to fairness and security against manipulation. But the fiduciary of a will that utilizes the pecuniary share gift has much broader power in the selection and allocation of assets to the marital share. Moreover, the administration and accounting of a fractional share gift (like the language of the gift itself) is much more complicated than in the pecuniary share gift.

Pecuniary formula clause versus fractional share formula clause. Over the years a great deal has been written regarding the various advantages and disadvantages of the pecuniary share formula clause versus the fractional share formula clause. While the comparison is akin to an "apples versus oranges" debate, some advantages and disadvantages of each type of clause have emerged.

As noted earlier, a fractional share gift is much more complex to administer than a pecuniary share gift. Moreover, the fractional share formula makes it more difficult to exclude certain property from the marital share without "undershooting" the maximum marital deduction, when the fund against which the fraction is to be applied is less than the amount of the marital deduction as a result of the exclusions. Also, the fractional share formula may provide the surviving spouse with a greater dollar amount of property than was deducted because of appreciation in the value of the estate during the period of administration.

The use of the pecuniary share formula, on the other hand, may result in a taxable gain when assets are transferred to the marital share in satisfaction thereof.

The Tax Reform Act of 1976 had the effect of making the fractional share clause less desirable than under prior law in many estates. The reason is that, to the extent that the fractional share clause requires that a fractional share of *every asset* in the fund against which the fraction is to be applied must be transferred to the marital share, this substantially limits postmortem planning opportunities.

APPLYING THIS CHAPTER TO *YOUR* SITUATION

Determining the extent to which the marital deduction should be used in planning a particular estate requires an analysis of both spouse's estates. Avoiding the estate tax entirely on the death of the first spouse is easy: leave everything to the surviving spouse and everything in the decedent spouse's estate is sheltered by the marital deduction. But all assets that are sheltered from the tax in the decedent's estate and pass to the surviving spouse will increase the taxable estate of the surviving spouse. From a tax viewpoint, then, it is advisable to take full advantage of the unified credit and then determine how much of the residue of the estate should pass to the surviving spouse under the marital deduction.

The A-B trust concept permits the decedent spouse to leave his or her estate in such a fashion that the surviving spouse can have the benefit of the income from the entire estate. Part of the income will come from the A or marital trust, which contains assets to be taxed in the surviving spouse's estate, and the remainder from the B or residuary trust, which will be composed of assets not in the surviving spouse's estate.

Since equalization of the two spouse's estates will reduce the combined estate taxes to a minimum, it would appear at first glance that the first spouse to die should leave the surviving spouse only so much as to achieve optimum equalization of estates. In most cases, this will require the payment of some estate tax in the first estate, but will result in overall reduction of the estate tax burden in both estates.

However, avoiding tax completely in the first estate and deferring any estate tax payments until the death of the surviving spouse is usually the better course of action for the following reasons:

1. The surviving spouse will have the use of the money that would otherwise have been used to pay the decedent spouse's estate tax. Considering the time value of money, the income earned on the deferred tax money will usually more than offset the cost of deferral unless the surviving spouse dies very soon after the decedent spouse.

2. Liquidity problems on the death of the first spouse are eliminated. Any liquidity problems in the second spouse's estate are properly the problem of that spouse's heirs, usually the children, and not the parent who helped earn the estate. (Parents should never shortchange themselves in an effort to reduce taxes for their children.)

3. Potential problems caused by the possibility of the increased size of the estate of the second spouse can be eliminated or reduced by the surviving spouse through a program of making annual exclusion gifts.

The marital deduction, then, is an enormously effective tax saving device that affords flexibility in the estate planning process. But it requires careful planning and forethought.

CASE PROBLEMS

11.1 Marital Deduction Planning. Gene Rogers died in 1987 leaving a gross estate of $1,500,000. He left expenses of $250,000, a bequest of $100,000 to his church, a bequest of $50,000 to an invalid sister, and a home valued at $200,000, which he owned in joint tenancy with his wife, Shirley.

Questions
1. What is the *maximum* amount Gene can leave to Shirley that will be sheltered by the marital deduction?
2. What is the *least* he can leave to her in his estate and still incur no federal estate tax?

3. Assuming she has an estate of $800,000, what is the optimum he can leave to her so as to achieve complete equalization of their two estates for federal estate tax purposes?

4. Do the following bequests from Gene to Shirley qualify for the marital deduction? Why or why not?

    a. My farm, Blackacre, to my wife Shirely for her lifetime, remainder to my son, Joseph.

    b. My farm, Blackacre, to my wife Shirley for her lifetime, remainder to whomever my wife shall appoint in her will.

    c. My farm, Blackacre, to my wife Shirley for her lifetime, remainder to her estate.

    d. My farm, Blackacre, to my companion Shirley, with whom I have lived for the past fourteen years and by whom I have had two children. (The state of Gene's domicile does not recognize common law marriages.)

    e. The farm, Blackacre, over which I have a Special Power of Appointment under my father's will, to my wife Shirley.

SELECTED READINGS

FRIEDMAN, ELLIOTT M., "Choosing the Proper Formula Marital Bequest," 58 *Taxes* 632 (1980).

KASNER, JERRY A., "The 'Optimum' Marital Deduction—Pay Now or Pay Later," New York University 43rd Annual Institute on Federal Taxation, pp. 54-1–54-18, 1985.

PRICE, JOHN R., *Estate Planning*. Boston: Little, Brown and Co., 1983, pp. 225–296.

STRENG, WILLIAM P., *Estate Planning*. Washington, D.C.: Bureau of National Affairs, 1981, pp. 417–442.

WEINSTOCK, HAROLD, *Planning an Estate*. Colorado Springs, Colo.: McGraw-Hill Book Co., 1982, pp. 49–74.

12

The Revocable Living Trust

Form ever follows function.

Louis Henry Sullivan

While estate planning involves what often appears to be an undue concern with the saving of taxes, ironically, one of the most important estate planning devices in use today has virtually no impact on what income taxes an estate owner will pay during life or what estate tax will be assessed against his or her estate at death. The device is known as the *revocable living trust*. (Actually, the term is redundant and either "revocable" trust or "living" trust ought to be sufficient, since a trust that is revocable must have been created while the creator of the trust is still alive, and thus able to revoke it. But the term revocable living trust has gained such widespread acceptance that we will adhere to it here.)

All trusts share in common the central purpose of separating the responsibility of ownership of property from the benefits of ownership. If, for example, you own a portfolio of stocks and wish your daughter to enjoy the income from the stock but not have the burden of managing the property, you could transfer the title to the stock to the Strong National Bank as trustee and direct the trustee to pay the income from the stock to your daughter. Under these circumstances, the bank would have the responsibilities of ownership of the stock, and your daughter (known as the *beneficiary* of the trust) would have the benefits of ownership. The trustee's ownership of the stock consists of the legal title to the stock, while your daughter is said to own the *equitable* title. (You, incidentally, are known as the *grantor* of the trust or, for reasons that have to do with an imperfect translation of a Latin phrase into English, as the *settlor*. The terms are used interchangeably.)

ADVANTAGES OF THE REVOCABLE LIVING TRUST

Avoiding Probate

If you have conveyed the stock irrevocably to the trustee, retaining no rights in yourself, when you die the stock will not be included in your estate for probate and estate tax purposes. To obtain these advantages, you have given the stock away and, no matter how much you may later regret this act, the stock is no longer yours. However, if the trust is revocable, you have merely to revoke it and the title to the stock will revert to you. However, if you have conveyed the stock to a revocable trust, it will be included in your estate for tax purposes (under the theory that you have not really given it away but have retained substantial powers of ownership over it). But it will be excluded from your *probate* estate despite the fact that the trust is revocable. And, as we have seen earlier, this can be an important advantage, often resulting in significant savings in time and money.

There are, however, a number of other advantages to the revocable living trust that serve to make it highly attractive, although many of them are in themselves side effects of the larger advantage of avoiding probate.

Privacy

Probate records are public. When an estate is settled, the details of the settlement are recorded for all to see (on the theory that the rightful heirs and others have the right to check the settlement to be certain that the estate went to those who are entitled to it). However laudable this concept may be, it is also a boon to confidence men and women who prey on the elderly and recently bereaved, salespeople of all sorts of products, and the merely nosy. The probate records afford these people the details of "who got what" from the estate of the decedent. The bank robber, Willie Sutton, once said that he robbed banks because "that's where the money is." Probate records provide the same sort of information regarding a decedent's estate; they tell anyone who may be interested "where the money is."

But a revocable living trust is a private document, a contractual arrangement between the grantor of the trust and the trustee. The trustee may not reveal the details of the trust to anyone except the beneficiaries and the appropriate tax authorities. And the trust is not part of the probate records.

So, then, if you have placed most of your assets in a revocable living trust and wish to assure that anything else that you own at death and that you have not conveyed to the trust will pass outside the inquiring eye of the public, you merely draft a simple will that leaves the remainder of your estate "to my trust with the Strong National Bank dated such-and-so." After your death, your will is recorded in the probate records for all to see, but it tells them nothing—only that the assets that passed under your will were left to a trust with the Strong National Bank. (This will is known as a *pour-over* will, since it pours your assets over from your estate to your trust.)

If you are not concerned about avoiding probate on your assets, you can create a revocable living trust and place only a minimal amount of money, often only $5 or $10, in the trust to "fund" it, with the balance to be added on your death as assets are "poured over" from your will. You can even "fund" the trust by merely transferring your life insurance policies to the trust and making the trustee the beneficiary of the policies. You continue to pay the premiums on the policies during your lifetime (and retain all the incidents of ownership over the policies), but when you die your trustee collects the proceeds from the life insurance policies, and these assets, along with others that are poured into the trust by means of your will, make up the corpus of the trust. During your lifetime your trustee, having no duties to perform with respect to the trust, will not charge you a fee and the trust is merely waiting there to spring into service on your death. And when the trust is "brought to life" by your death and the "pouring" of assets into it, the disposition of those assets is a private matter that is not reflected on the probate records. You can alter or amend the trust anytime before your death and can even move assets into and out of the trust without the necessity of amending your will. This means, in effect, that you can make significant changes in your estate plan without the necessity of going through a formal change in your will. This is possible because of the Uniform Testamentary Additions to Trusts Act (8 U.L.A. 629, 1972), which has been adopted in 26 states, or local acts similar to this Uniform Act, or because state court decisions have permitted the adding to a trust after the execution of the will.[*]

Perhaps it is a small matter, but in a society that values privacy, this advantage of the revocable living trust should not be lightly regarded.

One note of caution: If real estate is conveyed to the trust, it may be necessary (depending on the law of your state) to record the trust agreement in order to have a

---

[*]American jurisdictions having statutes or decisions validating the pour-over to an inter vivos trust are as follows:

Ala. Code tit. 61, Sec. 4(1); Alaska Stat. Sec. 13.11.200; Ariz. Rev. Stat. Secs. 14-2511 to 2513; Ark. Stat. Ann. Secs. 60-601 to 604; Cal. Prob. Code Sec. 170; Colo. Rev. Stat. Sec. 15-11-511; Conn. Gen. Stat. Ann. Sec. 45-173a; Del. Code Ann. tit. 12, Sec. 111; D.C. Code Sec. 18-306; Fla. Stat. Ann. Sec. 732.513; Ga. Code Ann. Sec. 53-14-12; Haw. Rev. Stat. Secs. 560.2-510 and 511; Idaho Code Sec. 15-2-510, 511; Ill. Rev. Stat. ch. 3, Sec. 4-4; Ind. Code Sec. 29-1-6-1(j); Iowa Code Ann. Sec. 633.275; Ky. Rev. Stat. Sec. 394.075; La. Rev. Stat. Ann. Sec. 9:1754; Me. Rev. Stat. Ann. Sec. 7; Md. Est. & Trusts Code Ann. Secs. 4-411 and 412; Mass. Gen. Laws Ann. ch. 203, Sec. 3B; Mich. Comp. Laws Ann. Secs. 555.461-.464; Minn. Stat. Ann. Sec. 525.223; Miss. Code Ann. Sec. 91-5-11; *St. Louis Union Trust Co.* v. *Blue*, 353, S.W.3d 770 (Mo. 1962); Mont. Rev. Codes Ann. Sec. 91-321; Neb. Rev. Stat. Secs. 30-2335 to 2337; Nev. Rev. Stat. Secs. 163.220 to 163.250; N.H. Rev. Stat. Ann. Sec. 563-A; N.J. Rev. Stat. Secs. 3A:3-16 to 3A:3-16.5; N.M. Stat. Ann. Secs. 33-71-1 to 33-7-3; N.Y. Est., Powers & Trusts Law Sec. 3-3.7; N.C. Gen. Stat. Sec. 31-47; N.D. Cent. Code Secs. 30.1-08-10 to 12; Ohio Rev.Code Ann. Sec. 21107.63; Okla. Stat. Ann. tit. 84, Secs. 301 to 304; Or. Rev. Stat. Sec. 112.265; Pa. Stat. Ann. tit. 20, Secs. 2514-2515; R.I. Gen Laws Secs. 33-6-33; S.C. Code Sec. 21-33-20; S.D. Comp. Laws Ann. Secs. 29-2-18 to 29-2-23; Tenn. Code Ann. Sec. 32-307; Tex. Prob. Code Ann. Sec. 58A; Utah Code Ann. Sec. 75-2-510 to 512; Vt. Stat. Ann. tit. 14, Sec. 2329; Va. Code Sec. 64.1-73; Wash. Rev. Code Sec. 11.12.250; W.Va. Code Secs. 41-3-8 to 11; Wis. Stat. Ann. Sec. 701.08; Wyo. Stat. Sec. 2-4-107.

clear record of title to the property. In such a case, it may be advisable either to dispose of the real estate directly in the will or to have a separate trust that disposes of it.

Avoiding Interruptions and Delays in Asset Management

If you have conveyed assets to the revocable living trust and if these assets require some management (and any income producing assets will require occasional oversight and review at the very minimum), the trust can provide continued and uninterrupted management of the assets, even in the event of the grantor's death. If, on the other hand, the assets had not been placed in the trust, there will be some delay and confusion on the owner's death while the personal representative qualifies as manager of the postmortem estate. The amount of delay and confusion will depend on how complex the estate is and how streamlined the state's probate process may be. But there will be, inevitably, *some* delay and confusion.

And, once the personal representative is qualified and in place, the law places limits on his or her actions that may be inconsistent with how you wish your assets to be managed. The role of the personal representative is to conserve and liquidate the assets in the estate, rather than to invest aggressively. The trust instrument can, however, grant such powers of management to the trustee as the grantor wishes. The fact that the management of the assets in the trust need not be interrupted by the grantor's death means that the management style chosen by the grantor for his or her assets can continue uninterrupted by his or her death.

Anticipating and Avoiding Problems Relating to the Grantor's Incapacity

One of the saddest sights that occurs in dealing with the elderly is occasioned by a decline in physical and mental faculties that leaves them increasingly unable to manage their affairs or to make the necessary arrangements to have others provide this management. In some states (the author's home state of West Virginia is a notable example), the statutes that provide for court intervention in the event of incapacity are located in the Mentally Ill Persons section of the state code. Thus, not only must the family endure a public proceeding to have an elderly relative declared mentally incompetent and to have a guardian appointed, but the proceeding takes place under the law that relates to mental incompetents.

There ought to be a way that a person who has lived a long and useful life, with many contributions to the world around him, and who now cannot recall whether he has had breakfast, can be removed from the management of his assets without being declared mentally incompetent. But, no doubt, persons with declining mental capacity do not make up a sufficient group of votes to justify the attention of the legislature to this problem.

Nonetheless, one highly effective way to avoid this problem is through the use of the revocable living trust. For example, Mary Stein might convey her assets to herself and the Strong National Bank as cotrustees and provide that the income from the trust assets is to be paid to herself (or for her benefit) for her life. After her death, the income from the trust is to be paid to Mary's husband for his life and on his death the trust is to terminate and the principal be paid over to their two children in equal shares. The trust instrument could also provide that, while she is competent and wishes to manage the assets in the trust, Mary is to be the active trustee and the Strong National Bank will have no active duties as cotrustee. This relieves Mary of the responsibility of having to clear every act of management with the bank and avoids the necessity of having to pay trustee fees to the bank while Mary is actually managing the property. Finally, the trust will provide that Mary is to be removed as trustee if she should ever become incompetent. Proof of incompetency is to consist of a letter from her physician, to be delivered by certified mail to Mary, her lawyer, her husband and two children, and the Strong National Bank, stating that Mary is incompetent and should no longer manage her property.

By using this device Mary can provide a swift, private, and extremely simple means of protecting her property against mismanagement in the event of her incapacity. Relatives and friends of one who has become incompetent are understandably uncomfortable about enduring a public proceeding to have a loved one declared incompetent. When the formal incompetency proceeding must be used, it tends to be postponed or avoided as long as possible, while the problem usually continues to worsen. Since the process designed in Mary's trust is so simple and totally private, it is likely to be utilized in the early stages of Mary's incapacity, rather than later.

Finally, while we have used the Strong National Bank as cotrustee in Mary Stein's trust, Mary may prefer that one or both of her children manage her property in the event of her incapacity. Some states' laws require that only residents may serve as guardians or committees for an incompetent, eliminating nonresident children from the management of their parent's assets, even though the nonresident child may live just across the river in another state or the property may well lend itself to management by mail or telephone. The trust device, however, will permit Mary to select cotrustees without regard to where they reside.

Choosing the Governing State Law for the Trust

Mary may wish to have some state other than the state where she is domiciled at death manage the assets in her estate on her death. This may be especially true if she is planning to move to a warmer climate at some future date or if she now spends part of the year in one state and part in another and there is some question regarding which state is the state of her domicile for tax and other purposes. She can select the individual or institution she wishes to handle her property after she dies, and the fact that this individual or institution could not qualify as her executor or testamentary trustee when she dies (because she is domiciled in another state) will have no effect on the trust.

Avoiding Claims of Surviving Spouse

Revocable living trusts are also used on occasion to avoid the claims of a surviving spouse in a decedent's estate. As we have seen earlier, every state gives the surviving spouse some rights in the decedent spouse's property, either through the concept of community property or through a spouse's forced share. States vary greatly in the degree of protection accorded a surviving spouse and in the recognition given to such claims. While Mary Stein may live in a state that affords the surviving spouse substantial rights in her testamentary estate, she can establish and fund a trust in another state that provides lesser rights to the surviving spouse and perhaps avoid certain claims on her husband's behalf. This is, however, an extremely unsettled area of the law and, in the author's opinion, not likely to be very successful. It is not clear that transferring assets to a revocable living trust, while it places the assets beyond the reach of the probate process, places them outside the reach of the surviving spouse. Certainly, it can be argued that, as to the assets that have come into the wife's estate during the marriage, the husband should have his claim undiminished. Trying to avoid a spouse's claim in a decedent's estate may result in destroying the entire fabric of the wife's estate plan to no avail.

DISADVANTAGES OF THE REVOCABLE LIVING TRUST

Expenses

While a revocable living trust is generally much less expensive to create than an irrevocable trust, the cost of preparing a revocable trust with a suitable pour-over will is higher than merely preparing a simple will. Trustee fees can also be an additional cost, at least when there is an institutional trustee and the grantor is not serving as cotrustee and doing all the work.

Record Keeping

A trust is a separate taxpayer, and the trustee must obtain a taxpayer identification number for the trust (Code Sec. 6109; Rev. Rul. 63-178, 1963-2 C.B. 609) and prepare a statement of income, deductions, and credits of the trust, even though the income of the trust is taxable to the grantor. Moreover, the separate nature of the trust (i.e., the fact that it exists separate and apart from the grantor) requires that the trustee keep the assets in the trust segregated from the grantor's other property and carefully account for this property.

No Tax Savings

The creation of a revocable living trust has no immediate tax consequences and is for the most part neutral as to taxes. The income from the trust is taxed to the grantor during his or her lifetime, and the assets in the trust are included in the grantor's estate for estate tax purposes.

APPLYING THIS CHAPTER TO *YOUR* SITUATION

The revocable living trust, while it offers virtually no tax saving advantages, is an enormously attractive estate planning device for meeting other (and often more significant) needs of the estate owner and his or her family. Any property that is transferrable may be placed in a revocable living trust. The creation of such a trust and an accompanying pour-over will is, when compared with the irrevocable trust and other tax saving devices, relatively inexpensive and decidedly simple. It affords maximum flexibility in the management of the grantor's assets, both before and after death, and offers, in addition, the advantages of privacy, protection against incompetency, and the opportunity to select the state law that is to govern the trust, and helps avoid the interruption and delays in the management of trust assets that almost always accompany the probate process.

CASE PROBLEMS

12.1 Planning with a Revocable Living Trust. Pat is a successful stockbroker with stock holdings valued at over $1,000,000. She also owns real estate in Florida and North Carolina (where she is domiciled). She is unmarried, her father is deceased, and her mother lives in a nursing home in New Jersey. Her mother's assets consist of $500,000 of stocks, bonds, and bank accounts held in an investment management account at the Strong National Bank in Philadelphia. Pat's other assets are:

1. Her condominium valued at $120,000
2. Automobile valued at $12,000
3. Other tangible personal property valued at $35,000
4. Bank accounts with balance of $16,000
5. $100,000 of paid-up whole life insurance

Pat is concerned about probate costs, worries that Florida and North Carolina may both want to tax her estate (she spends the winters, October through March, in Florida), and wants to assure that her mother is adequately cared for if she survives Pat. Pat has no brothers or sisters. Other than her mother, her closest relative is a first cousin in Oregon with whom Pat has absolutely no contact. Pat would like to leave her estate to her church, her alma mater, and the Salvation Army (after making adequate provision for her mother's needs until her death).

Questions
1. Does Pat have any use for a revocable living trust?

2. If so, what should she transfer to the trust during her lifetime?

3. How can Pat utilize a revocable living trust and still provide for her mother?

4. Of the various reasons for a revocable living trust, which ones represent her most pressing needs?

SELECTED READINGS

BOWMAN, FOREST J., *The Complete Retirement Handbook*. New York: Putnam Publishing Co., 1983, pp. 108–116.

CASNER, A. JAMES, *The Revocable Trust, an Essential Tool for the Practicing Lawyer*. Philadelphia, Pa.: American Law Institute, 1965.

FARR, JAMES F., and WRIGHT, JACKSON W., JR., *An Estate Planner's Handbook*. Boston: Little, Brown and Co., 1979, pp. 75–127.

HALBACH, EDWARD C., JR., "Trusts in Estate Planning," 2 *Probate Lawyer* 1 (1975).

KURTZ, SHELDON, *Family Estate Planning*. St. Paul, Minn.: West Publishing Co., 1982, pp. 185–220.

PRICE, JOHN R., *Contemporary Estate Planning*. Boston: Little, Brown and Co., 1983, pp. 583–597.

STRENG, WILLIAM P., *Estate Planning*. Washington, D.C.: Tax Management, Inc., 1981, pp. 342–344.

WEINSTOCK, HAROLD, *Planning an Estate*. Colorado Springs, Colo.: McGraw-Hill Book Co., 1982, pp. 119–144.

WESTFALL, DAVID, *Estate Planning*. Mineola, N.Y.: Foundation Press, Inc., 1982, pp. 42–47.

13

Irrevocable Trusts

The manner of giving is worth more than the gift.

Pierre Corneille

For all its advantages, the revocable trust affords no tax relief to the creator of the trust since the property conveyed to the trust could be reacquired by the grantor simply by revoking the trust. Therefore, the IRS concludes that the grantor of the revocable trust has not really given the property away. All the income from the trust will be taxed to the grantor and, on the grantor's death, the trust property will be taxed to the grantor's estate.

The irrevocable trust, on the other hand, can be used to move the income from the trust property out of the grantor's tax return and to keep the trust property out of the grantor's taxable estate at death. Thus, paradoxically, the irrevocable trust can provide the tax advantages that are missing with a revocable trust, but since irrevocably means "irrevocably," much of the flexibility of the revocable trust is lost. Because of this loss of flexibility, the use of the irrevocable trust is much more limited than that of the revocable trust.

CREATING AN IRREVOCABLE TRUST

Pitfalls of the Irrevocable Trust

One of the most common mistakes made in estate planning is the ill-advised absolute transfer of income producing property. Whether made for tax advantages or other reasons, the grantor often comes to regret having irrevocably transferred away assets which she or he now needs or wishes to still own. For this reason, a basic rule of estate planning ought to be: *persons of less than independent wealth ought not part with substantial property irrevocably.*

You will note that we have made no distinction between outright irrevocable gifts and gifts in trust. The reason is that, from the viewpoint of the grantor's continuing interest in the property, there is no distinction. Once the property is gone, it is gone.

A further disadvantage of the irrevocable trust (as with an outright transfer that is irrevocable) is that it is subject to the gift tax. Unless the gift is small enough to permit the grantor to take advantage of the gift tax annual exclusion, some tax must be paid or some of the unified credit must be used up.

Advantages of the Irrevocable Trust

Despite the dangers of absolute transfers, the irrevocable trust has its special place in estate planning, particularly when used by persons of substantial wealth. As we have seen, the transfer of income producing assets to an irrevocable trust will result in the exclusion of the income on the property from the grantor's income tax return and will remove the assets from the grantor's estate on death. Because of this, the irrevocable trust can be used to transfer income from a high-bracket family member to a low-bracket family member, with substantial tax savings to the family as a whole. And it can be used to transfer wealth from one generation to another while avoiding the unified estate and gift taxes.

LONG-TERM (NONREVERSIONARY) TRUSTS

As we saw earlier, unless a trust to which gifts are made is irrevocable, the gifts will be disregarded for tax purposes and the assets and the income therefrom will be deemed to belong to the donor. So, to make a completed gift to a trust, at least for tax purposes, the trust must be irrevocable. In addition to being irrevocable, however, the trust should be structured so as to take maximum advantage of other tax laws in making gifts. For example, the trust should be structured so as to qualify for the gift tax annual exclusion, and care should be taken to avoid the use of prohibited powers that may cause the assets to be included in the donor's estate or the income from the trust to be taxable to the donor.

Gift Tax

Annual exclusion. A donor is, as we have discussed many times, permitted to exclude from taxable gifts up to $10,000 per donee in each calendar year, or up to $20,000 per donee if the spouse joins in the making of the gift. This $10,000 to $20,000 excluded is never added back to the tax base in computing the estate tax. It is, then, a valuable exclusion.

To qualify for this exclusion, however, a gift must be of a present interest [Code 2503(b)]. If a gift is made in trust, however, the principal is not a gift of a present interest because the donee does not have the unrestricted right to its *immediate* use, possession, or enjoyment [Regs. 25.2503-3(b)]. However, if the trust provides that the income is to be paid currently to the income beneficiary, the income interest (not the corpus of the trust) is considered to be a present interest and qualifies for the $10,000 annual exclusion. The value of the income interest is computed by using the tables in Regs. 25.2512-9(f), which are found in Appendix G. For example, if $200,000 is given to a trust which provides that the income is to be paid to John for John's life, and on John's death the remainder is to go to Mary, and John is 55 years old, 0.61776 percent of the gift, or $123,552, will be the value of the income interest. Since this amount exceeds the $10,000 annual exclusion (as well as the $20,000 split gift annual exclusion), the full annual exclusion can be taken.

Crummey trust. If the trust provides that the beneficiary is allowed to withdraw each year the lesser of (1) the annual exclusion or (2) the value of the assets transferred to the trust during that year, the annual exclusion will be allowed, even if there is otherwise no gift of a present interest [*Crummey* v. *Commissioner*, 397 F.2d 82 (9th Cir 1968)]. Thus, when a donor transfers $200,000 to a discretionary trust that permits the beneficiary to withdraw in the year of the gift the lesser of the $200,000 gift or $10,000 (the amount of the annual exclusion), the annual exclusion will be allowed. Moreover, under the Crummey case, the gift will qualify as a gift of a present interest when the beneficiary has this right to withdraw, even if the beneficiary is a young minor who cannot practically exercise her or his right to withdraw and even though no legal guardian is appointed. An adult beneficiary, however, must be informed of her or his right to withdraw and must be given a reasonable time to make the withdrawal (Rev. Rul. 81-7, 1981-1 C.B. 474).

When the beneficiary is given the right to withdraw annually more than the greater of $5,000 or 5 percent of the value of the principal, as would be the case, for example, when she or he is given the right to withdraw the $10,000 annual exclusion amount, and the beneficiary does not exercise this right, this failure will be considered a lapse for gift and estate tax purposes. The result of such a lapse is that the income beneficiary will be deemed to have made a taxable gift to the remainder beneficiary of the trust. Moreover, the assets that could have been withdrawn may be taxable in the beneficiary's estate.

This problem can be avoided by limiting the beneficiary's right to withdraw to the lesser of (1) the amount of the annual exclusion or (2) the greater of $5,000 or 5 percent of the principal of the trust [Code 2041(b)(2) & 2514(b)].

Minor's trust. Another exception to the rule that no present interest is created by transfer to a trust when the beneficiary does not have the unrestricted right to the immediate use, possession, or enjoyment exists in the minor's trust. If the trust does not provide unrestricted right to the assets on the part of the minor, but provides that both the principal and the income may be expended by, or for the benefit of, the donee before she or he reaches 21, and, to the extent that the principal and income are not expended, it will pass to the donee on reaching age 21 and will qualify as a gift of a present interest [Code 2503(c)(2)(B)]. Such a trust is known, because of the code section creating it, as a "2503(c) trust." If the donee dies before reaching 21, the trust must provide that the accumulated income and principal are payable to the donee's estate or she or he may appoint under a general power of appointment.

Note, too, that the required pay-over occurs at age 21, not age 18, which is the age of majority in most states. This makes the "2503(c) trust" a bit more attractive for those who feel that age 18 is too young for substantial assets to be paid over to a donee.

Estate Tax

If assets that have been given to an irrevocable trust are included by the courts and the IRS in the donor's estate, there will be two adverse tax consequences:

1. The entire gift to the trust, including the $10,000 annual exclusion, will be included in the gross estate.
2. The asset will be valued at the time of death, rather than at the time the gift was made, with any appreciation in value after the time of the gift subject to the estate tax.

Therefore, care must be taken that assets conveyed to an irrevocable trust not be included in the donor's estate.

The reason assets previously conveyed to an irrevocable trust are included in the donor's estate, despite the conveyance to the trust, involves the retention of certain prohibited benefits, rights, or powers. These prohibited transfers fall into two categories. In the first category, the grantor retains a beneficial interest in the assets that have been given to the trust, such as a reversionary interest (Code 2037), a life estate (Code 2036), or a power to revoke the gift (Code 2038). In the second category of prohibited transfers, the donor retains the power to affect or rearrange the beneficial interest given under the trust [Code 2036(a)(2) & 2038].

Income Tax

Since a prime motive for giving assets to an irrevocable trust is to reduce the grantor's income taxes, care should be taken to structure the trust so that the income is taxable to the trust or to the beneficiary, but not to the grantor.

PRACTICAL CONSIDERATIONS IN THE USE OF TRUSTS

Selection and Removal of the Trustee

While the Restatement of Trusts (Second) provides, at Sections 89, 96–98, that any individual, association, partnership, or corporation may act as trustee, except where limited by law, the basic choice in the selection of a trustee generally falls between an individual (the grantor, a close family member, or friend) and a corporate trustee (a bank or trust officer). The choice is an intensely personal one that involves consideration of the purpose of the trust, size of the trust assets, the complexity and duration of the trust, the availability of reliable and experienced individual trustees, and the willingness of the grantor of the trust to accept the trustee's investment philosophy. (Corporate trustees usually follow a relatively conservative investment policy, designed with preservation of the trust assets as the first consideration, and this may not coincide with the grantor's goals and aspirations for the trust assets.)

The quality of services provided by a corporate trustee will be as varied as those provided by individual trustees. The grantor should be thoroughly familiar with the trustee and what can be expected of her or him. For various reasons, the grantor's lawyer should usually not agree to serve as trustee.

Judicial removal of a trustee is very difficult to obtain in the absence of a serious breach of trust. For this reason, some responsible person or persons should be given the power to remove and replace a trustee. Usually, this power will be given to the beneficiary, provided, however, that the beneficiary should not have the power to appoint herself or himself, unless the beneficiary could have acted as trustee from the creation of the trust without adverse tax consequences. The grantor should not be given the power to remove a trustee at will and appoint another, since this has been held to be the equivalent to a reservation of the trustee's powers (Rev. Rul. 79-353, 1979-2 C.B. 325).

Power to Allocate between Principal and Income

The trustee should generally have the discretion to allocate receipts and disbursements between principal and income, since the income and principal beneficiaries are not usually the same in the average trust. Most states have attempted to solve this problem with the adoption of the Uniform Principal and Income Act. Nonetheless, certain problems remain, and the trustee should have broad discretion for her or his own protection and for maximum efficiency in the management of the trust.

Trust Investments

The trustee should also give considerable authority to invest and reinvest trust property. Limiting the range of permissible investments can unduly restrict the trustee's ability to respond to changing economic circumstances and can impair the value of the trust. At the very least the trustee and beneficiary may have to undergo an expensive legal proceeding to acquire broadened investment authority for the trustee.

CHARITABLE TRUSTS WITH NONCHARITABLE INTERESTS

When the client is a person of substantial wealth, a trust in which both charitable and noncharitable beneficiaries have interests can be an attractive planning device. There are three varieties of such trusts:

1. Charitable remainder trusts
2. Charitable lead trusts
3. Pooled income funds

Charitable Remainder Trusts

The charitable remainder trust is one in which noncharitable beneficiaries receive periodic payments until the trust terminates, at which time the undistributed principal and income are paid to a charitable beneficiary. A charitable remainder trust may be either of the following:

1. An annuity trust, which requires annual payments to the noncharitable beneficiary of a fixed dollar amount or percentage of the *initial value of the trust principal*. The annual payments must not be less than 5 percent of the initial value of the trust principal. An annuity trust is, then, especially valuable to the noncharitable beneficiary in times of declining market values, since the amount of the annual payment remains the same even though the value of the trust principal may be declining [Code 664(d)(1)(A)].

2. A unitrust, which requires annual payments of at least 5 percent of the value of the trust principal *as determined each year*. The unitrust is most attractive in times of inflation, since the amount of the annual payment will increase along with the value of the trust principal {Code 664(d)(2)(A)].

The creation of a charitable remainder trust triggers the gift or estate tax to the extent of the interests of the noncharitable beneficiaries. However, for charitable remainder trusts created during the grantor's lifetime, the grantor is entitled to a gift tax charitable deduction for the value of the charitable remainder interest as determined by actuarial tables [Code 2522(c)(2)(A)]. Moreover, if the trust is created during the lifetime of the grantor, she or he is entitled to an income tax deduction for the value of the charitable remainder interest, which may largely offset the estate or gift tax incurred (Code 170; 664). This income tax deduction is available even though the charity will not be entitled to possession of any of the trust property until the noncharitable interests have terminated. For estate tax purposes, the estate tax charitable deduction is allowed for the value of the charity's remainder interest as of the grantor's death [Code 2055(e)(2)(A)].

Charitable Lead Trusts

Whereas the charitable remainder trust is for the most part an income tax avoidance device, the charitable lead trust is primarily useful to save estate and gift taxes on assets that will ultimately pass to noncharitable beneficiaries. The charitable lead trust differs from the remainder trust in that the charity receives the payment of a certain percentage of the principal for the life of the trust, after which the principal passes to the noncharitable beneficiary. The grantor is entitled to a gift tax charitable deduction for the value of the charitable lead interest [Code 2522(c)(2)(B)] as determined by actuarial tables. The gift of the noncharitable interests, on the other hand, will constitute a taxable gift.

Pooled Income Funds

A pooled income fund is essentially a charitable remainder trust to which more than one donor makes contributions and that qualifies under the definition of a pooled income fund as set forth in Code 642(c)(5). Generally, the pooled income fund allows gifts of two or more grantors to serve purposes comparable to those served by individually created charitable remainder trusts.

APPLYING THIS CHAPTER TO *YOUR* SITUATION

Despite certain dangers inherent in the absolute transfer of assets, irrevocable trusts offer great income and estate tax saving opportunities. And when care is taken to maximize the gift tax exclusion possibilities, the gift tax as well can be reduced or totally avoided. In all trusts, but especially in those that cannot be revoked or amended, the selection of the trustee and the granting of trustee powers is a matter of great significance and requires special care.

CASE PROBLEMS

13.1 Planning with the Irrevocable Trust. Ted Costello is a 53-year-old automobile dealer with an annual income in excess of $200,000. His daughter, Kate, is a senior in high school and his son, Tom, is a college sophomore. Both children plan to go to graduate school and Kate appears headed for a medical career. Ted's major assets include ownership of 80 percent of the stock in his auto dealership (valued at $600,000); stocks, bonds, and liquid savings valued at $150,000; a Keogh plan with a value of $75,000 to Ted; half-interest in his home, which is valued at $250,000; and tangible personal assets valued at $75,000. Ted wants to reduce his income tax, avoid having to pay any estate tax on his death, and avoid the gift tax while living. (In short, Ted is the "typical" estate planning client—all he wants is everything!)

Questions
1. Should Ted transfer assets to a short-term trust for the benefit of his children? If so, what assets should he consider transferring to the trust?
2. Assuming that he transfers $100,000 to a trust for ten years, providing that the income is to be paid to his children for the term of the trust, what will be the gift tax consequences? Can he avoid or further reduce the gift tax by taking any special steps?
3. What special steps should Ted take to assure that the income from the trust is not taxed to him?

4. Should Ted consider a nonreversionary irrevocable trust? Why or why not?

5. What would be the estate tax result of transferring $150,000 of corporate stock to a nonreversionary irrevocable trust for the benefit of Ted's children? The gift tax result?

SELECTED READINGS

HALBACH, EDWARD C., "Trusts in Estate Planning," 2 *Probate Lawyer* 1 (1975).

PRICE, JOHN R., *Contemporary Estate Planning*. Boston: Little, Brown and Company, 1983, pp. 597–616, 638–651.

WEINSTOCK, HAROLD, *Planning an Estate*. Colorado Springs, Colo.: Shepard's/McGraw-Hill, 1982, pp. 163–178.

WESTFALL, DAVID, *Estate Planning*. Mineola, N.Y.: Foundation Press, Inc., 1982, pp. 334–343.

14

Powers
of Appointment

*Very few men, properly speaking, live at present,
but are providing to live another time.*

Jonathan Swift

USE OF THE POWER OF APPOINTMENT

A major disadvantage of the irrevocable trust is the loss of flexibility that accompanies the permanent giving away of one's assets. Once the property is gone, circumstances may change that could warrant a different dispositive pattern than the one already "set in stone" in the irrevocable trust. Marriages may fail, injuries or loss of health may plague a family, a business may fail or propser, or an unforeseen sequence of deaths may cause a profound disruption in what would otherwise have been a "natural" dispositive plan. One son-in-law may prosper and become a respected pillar of the community, while another ends up a failure. All the uncertainties of life seemingly lie in wait for the person who gives away his or her assets irrevocably, and especially for the one who tries to plan for the future somewhat through the use of a trust.

It is common, for example, for a trust to provide that assets be held in trust for the lifetime of the donor's spouse, with the remainder to pass to their children on the spouse's death. The spouse may live for a long time after the creation of this trust, during which time the needs of the children may vary greatly. But if the trust is irrevocable, upon the death of the spouse the assets will pass to the children (or their estates) in fixed and immutable shares.

A power of appointment can provide some flexibility under these circumstances, while still complying with the donor's wishes that the trust assets not go to certain persons or institutions.

A power of appointment is a power of disposition over property that is given by the owner (the donor) to another person (the donee) to designate, by deed or by will, those persons (the appointees) who shall receive beneficial interests in the property.

(Until the power of appointment is exercised, the persons in whose favor the power may be exercised are known as the *objects* or *beneficiaries* of the power.) Finally, a well-drafted power designates who will take the property if the donee fails to exercise the power. These persons are known as the *takers in default*.

Assume, then, that Robert West establishes a trust that provides income to his wife, Helen, for her life and on her death the trust is to terminate and the assets are to go to their children, Jon, Linda, and Sarah, in such proportions as Helen shall appoint in her will. If Helen fails to appoint the assets in her will, the trust instrument provides that they shall pass to Robert's nephew, Edgar. The various roles of the family members in this power of appointment are as follows:

Robert	Donor
Helen	Donee
Jon	
Linda	Objects or beneficiaries until the power is exercised; then they are known as the *appointees*
Sarah	
Edgar	Taker in default

If we assume that Robert establishes this trust in his will, which was drafted in 1970, that he died in 1975 and the trust took effect then, and that Helen lived until 1995, look at what Robert was able to do.

He gave Helen the right to alter his estate plan 20 years after his death and a full quarter-century after he had first set it down on paper. Helen could watch how the children turn out, see what their needs are, and determine what they should receive from their father's irrevocable trust. Human nature being what it is, her right to dispose of Robert's assets no doubt will have some impact on the children's attitude toward her. They are far more likely to pay attention to her if they know she can shower some money on them than if she has no way to reward their attention. (I know. This is a harsh statement. But countless studies of human nature bear it out. Blood may be thicker than water, but it is not thicker than inherited money!) Finally, although Helen may distribute this money among the children as she alone sees fit or permit it to pass to Robert's nephew Edgar by her failure to exercise the power, she cannot give the money to anyone else. If, for example, she should remarry, she may not leave Robert's trust assets to her new husband or any of his clan. It can only pass to that carefully delineated group of people Robert has designated.

The availability of the limited power of appointment to Helen, combined with the trust, gives Helen the advantages of ownership of the property while protecting her from the duties of ownership. The trustee will manage the property and pay the income to Helen, while she has only to enjoy it and be prepared to decide which of her children should get what proportions of the assets on her death (or whether, in the alternative, the property should pass to Edgar by Helen's failure to appoint). If Helen is incapable of managing the trust assets, this is of no concern, since the management will be done by the trustee. So Helen cannot squander the assets of pass them on to someone who would be offensive to Robert, but she can still make changes in his estate plan that are necessitated by changed circumstances since Robert's death.

If Robert created the trust in an inter vivos instrument executed before his death, there will also be privacy regarding the disposition of the trust assets, and the community at large need not be aware of Helen's power of disposition over Robert's trust assets. Thus, the drama of "who gets what by reason of Mama's appointment" will not be played out before the inquiring eyes of the public. But Helen still has the opportunity to rewrite an estate plan that Robert established years before to take into account changed circumstances since that time. From the viewpoint of human nature, it is a most attractive arrangement.

CLASSIFICATION OF POWERS

General Power

A general power of appointment is one that enables the donee to appoint the property to himself, his creditors, his estate, or the creditors of his estate. Thus, a general power is virtually the same as outright ownership of the trust assets since all that stands in the way of outright ownership of the assets by the donee of the power is a letter saying "I appoint to myself." Not surprisingly, the IRS agrees and Code 2041(a)(2) includes in the decedent's gross estate the value of all property over which the decedent had, at the time of his or her death, a general power of appointment.

There are, however, some important exceptions to the inclusion of property in a decedent's estate under Code 2041.

1. Property subject to a general power of appointment created before October 22, 1942, is not includable in the decedent's gross estate unless the power is exercised [Code 2041(a)(1)].

2. A power is not considered a general power if the power is exercisable only with the consent or joinder of (a) the creator of the power or (b) a person having a substantial adverse interest [Code 2041(b)(1)(C)].

3. A power limited by an ascertainable standard relating to the health, education, support, or maintenance of the power holder is not a general power of appointment [Code 2041(b)(1)(A)].

Special (or Limited) Powers

Traditionally, a special or limited power is one that the donee can exercise only in favor of persons other than himself or his estate, "who constitute a group not unreasonably large" [Restatement of Property, Sec. 321, comment (d)]. For tax purposes, however, the definition of a special power is a bit broader. Since a general power is one that permits the donee to appoint the property to himself, his creditors, his estate, or the creditors of his estate, a special power includes all other powers. Thus, a power to appoint to anyone *other than* the donee or his or her estate would be a special power for tax purposes. For property law purposes, however, such a power is neither a general nor a special power, but a hybrid power [Restatement of Property, Sec. 320, comment (a)].

Tax Consequences

The major tax consequences of the possession or exercise of powers held by someone other than the donor are as follows:

1. For trust income tax purposes, the holder of a power that is exercisable at present solely by the holder and that enables the holder to vest income or principal in himself or herself is taxable as the owner of such income or principal [Code 678(a)(1)].

2. For estate and gift tax purposes, the possession, exercise, or release of a general power of appointment created after October 21, 1942, is ordinarily treated as if the holder had owned the property subject to the power and had transferred such property [Code 2041(a)(2), 2514(b)]. In the case of a general power created before October 21, 1942, only the exercise is taxable.

3. For purposes of the generation-skipping transfer tax, a limited or special power does not subject the holder to any adverse tax consequences, regardless of whether the power was exercised, unless the holder previously held (and partially released) a general power [Code 2041(a)(2), 678(a)(2)].

4. Although a lapse of a general power is ordinarily treated as a release, there is a limited exception for purposes of estate and gift taxes for lapses of powers of withdrawal during the life of the holder [Code 2041(b)(2); 2514(e)].

5. Joint powers exercisable in favor of one or more of the power holders may be treated as general powers for estate and gift tax purposes, but not for trust income tax purposes [Code 678(a)(1), 2041(b)(1)(C), 2514(c)(3)].

In addition to the nontax uses of the power of appointment as a means of permitting the donee to alter the donor's estate plan long after the plan has been created, the power of appointment has also played an important role in tax planning. Before the Economic Recovery Tax Act of 1981 introduced the concept of QTIP, a most important function of general powers of appointment was to qualify otherwise nonqualifying terminable interests for the marital deduction [Code 2056(b)(5) and (6)]. A spouse could be given a life estate in property coupled with a general testamentary power of appointment. Thus the surviving spouse would be entitled to the income from the property for her life and could on death appoint the property as she wished, including to her estate or creditors. The power to appoint to herself or her creditors was sufficient to cause the assets to be included in her estate, and so the property qualified for the marital deduction on the death of the first spouse. In the meantime, however, the surviving spouse did not have the power to convey the property away during her lifetime, so she was assured that the property would be there during her lifetime to provide a steady income.

The new QTIP rules eliminate the necessity of leaving a general power of appointment over property to qualify otherwise terminable property for the marital deduction. However, under state law it may still be necessary to give the surviving spouse either outright ownership of property or a general power of appointment over the property in order to qualify it for the state death tax marital deduction.

EXERCISING A POWER OF APPOINTMENT

Since donors may create powers of appointment in others, there will be donees who will hold the powers of appointments under estate plans created by others. In advising clients on the exercise or nonexercise of powers of appointment they hold, a number of factors must be considered:

1. Is the power general or limited? This question gets to the heart of whether the assets subject to the power, as well as the income from those assets, are to be included in the income, estate, and gift tax returns of the holder of the power.

2. If the power is limited, is it exclusive or nonexclusive? With exclusive power, the holder may exclude one or more persons in the class of potential beneficiaries. With nonexclusive power, the holder must appoint something to each member of the class. Suppose the donor created a limited power that permits the donee to appoint among the five children of the donor. If the donor may appoint to some of the children and exclude others, the power is said to be exclusive. If, on the other hand, the donor must appoint something to each of the five children who make up the class of potential appointees, the power is said to be nonexclusive.

3. Are takers in default provided for and are they persons whom the holder would like to benefit? A well-drafted power of appointment will always provide for takers in default. But not all powers are well drafted. The donee must consider, then, what will be the effect on the property (i.e., where will it go) if the power is not exercised. Often takers in default will be the same persons who make up the class of persons to whom appointment may be made, with the power existing merely to permit the donee to alter the respective shares of the potential appointees under the power. For example, a wife may give a limited power of appointment to her husband to appoint assets among their three children in such proportions as he may choose and provide, and in default of appointment, the assets are to pass to the three children in equal shares. Under these circumstances the question is not one of who shall take, but rather whether the father wants to divide the appointive assets unequally among the children by exercising the power of appointment he holds or to let the assets pass to the children in equal shares by default.

4. Is the power testamentary or may it be exercised during the donee's lifetime? Testamentary powers are, obviously, much more limited than inter vivos powers. Whatever the power, however, the donee must take care that the way the power is exercised is consistent with the instrument creating it.

5. What effect will the appointment of the assets have on the tax (and nontax) situation for the appointees? Just as the donee must carefully look at the prospective appointees' needs and any "rights" to the property they may have "earned" (as, for example, by taking care of the donee or some other loved one), so the donee must also consider what will be the tax effect on the appointees. If the prospective appointee already has a substantial estate or if he or she has considerable income, it may be a more tax-wise decision to forego exercising the power in this person's favor and instead exercise it in favor of another prospective appointee. The same consideration must be made with respect to nontax matters. If the prospective appointee is a profligate, or is undergoing bankruptcy, or has abandoned the donee or other members of the donee's family, the donee may wish to forego providing the prospective appointee with the benefits to be attained from an appointment of the property.

6. What will be the effect of a disclaimer of the power? A disclaimer is the refusal by a beneficiary to accept an interest in property. The advantage of disclaiming a power of appointment is that the disclaimer causes the tax in question to be applied as if the power had never been given to the client. Thus, where the existence of a general power of appointment created after October 21, 1942, may subject the holder to the estate or gift tax, regardless of whether he or she exercises the power [Code 2041(a)(2), 2514(b)], a disclaimer of the power may result in no transfer tax being payable.

7. If the time for a qualified disclaimer has passed, would it be to the donee's advantage to release the power in whole or in part? A release of a general power of appointment created after October 21, 1942, is treated, for estate and gift tax purposes, as if the holder of the power had owned the property subject to the power [Regs. 20.2041-3(d)(1), 25.2514-3(c)(1)]. The release of such a power, then, may constitute (1) a gift for purposes of the gift tax or (2) a transfer that will cause the property to be includable in the transferor's estate for estate tax purposes. For tax purposes, then, the decision to release a general power of appointment turns on the same factors that are involved in deciding to make a gift of assets that the holder of the power owns outright.

DRAFTING CONSIDERATIONS

Whether to create a power of appointment is a question that can be answered only after considering and answering a series of other questions. The questions include, in some semblance of order, the following:

1. Is the power to be general or limited? As we have already seen, this question involves consideration of the tax effect of the power on the holder. If the power is general, the holder will be treated as the owner of the assets subject to the power. Thus, if the holders other assets are significant, making the power general may only add to an already large estate, with a considerable portion of the assets subject to the power eaten up by the transfer taxes.

Moreover, since the donee of a special power of appointment has no beneficial interest in the appointive assets, property subject to a special power of appointment is not subject to the claims of creditors of the donee or to the expenses of administration of his or her estate. This is not to say, however, that the law with respect to general powers of appointment can be so simply stated. Suffice it to say that there is some question. A general power that the holder can exercise at present can be reached in bankruptcy and by statute in a few states. Under the common law, however, assets subject to a general power of appointment, whether exercisable by will or deed, cannot be reached by the donee's creditors as long as the power remains unexercised.

2. Is the donor to have the power to appoint during his or her lifetime or only at death? If the power is general, with the assets includable in the donee's estate at death, the right to appoint the assets inter vivos permits the donee to remove the property from his or her taxable estate should he or she choose to do so. While this would trigger the gift tax, the effect of the gift tax is slightly less destructive than the effect of the estate tax because of the grossing up principle.

On the other hand, an inter vivos general power might be used to squander the property, while an inter vivos special power may expose the holder to the pressures of importuning prospective appointees. Providing that the power may be exercised by will only at least insulates the holder of the power from pressures to appoint during lifetime and increases the likelihood that the holder will consult with a lawyer to make the appointment.

3. Who are the beneficiaries? The beneficiaries of a power should be established with clarity in order to avoid confusion as to whether the power is general or limited. For example, it may appear desirable to give a limited power of appointment to the donee, along with the widest possible latitude in the selection of beneficiaries, by providing that the donee may appoint "to such persons other than himself, his estate, his creditors, or the creditors of his estate, as he may appoint." The problem with such a description of beneficiaries, however, is that there is some authority for the proposition that the attempted restriction against creditors is inconsistent and of no effect. Thus, where a donee's estate is insolvent, the assets may be subject to the claims of the donee's creditors although this was clearly not the intention of the donor of the power.

Beneficiaries should be carefully described in terms that will permit the donor's intentions to be carried out. For example, inflexible terms such as "children" or "nieces and nephews" may be unsatisfactory to meet the desires of the donor if a child or niece or nephew should die unexpectedly leaving issue. In such cases, the donor may wish the assets to be available for appointment to the issue of the children or the nieces and nephews. Describing them as "my descendants" or as "descendants of my mother" would provide more flexibility than the terms "children" or "nieces and nephews." Consideration should be given to the donor's wishes with respect to appointment to the spouses and widows and widowers of the prospective objects of the power. A grandfather may wish to leave a power to his son to appoint among his grandchildren, wishing to benefit the grandchildren and their families. However, if a grandchild should die before the power is exercised, leaving a spouse of whom the grandfather was fond, and if the power was appointable only among "grandchildren," the assets subject to the power cannot be used to benefit the deceased grandchild's widow or widower. Thus, the grandfather should be advised to consider including the spouses of his grandchildren within the class of prospective appointees.

4. If the power is limited, is it to be exclusive or nonexclusive? The instrument creating the power should specify this matter explicitly. Where no such specification is stated, there is some authority to the effect that the power will be interpreted as non-exclusive (Estate of Sloan, 7 Cal. App. 2d 319, 46 P.2d 1007, 1935). If the power is intended to be nonexclusive, the instrument should state carefully what minimal appointment is to be considered a substantial share so as to avoid the problem of an illusory appointment.

5. In what form of estates may the property be appointed? The general rule is that the donee of a general power of appointment may appoint the property in any desired combination of present and future interests, outright or in trust, and subject to any conditions that are normally permissible under local property law. There is some question whether the donee of a general testamentary power of appointment may exercise the power to create new powers of appointment, but the prevailing view is that he or she can. A carefully drawn power should make it clear whether it may be exercised by the creation of new powers.

With respect to special powers of appointment, it is generally believed that the donee may appoint the property in successive estates or in trust. But where the right to create new powers in appointment of a special power is not expressly conferred by the terms of the original power, it is doubtful that the donee can create such new powers. To be safe, the grantor of the power should expressly state whether the donee is authorized to appoint by creating a new power of appointment.

6. What is required to exercise the power? The grantor should make it clear what method of exercising the power is required. Often a donee of a power will make no explicit reference to powers, but will provide a rather broad residuary clause in his or her will. The question that arises, then, is whether the general residuary clause of the donee's will is sufficient to exercise the power of appointment. Not surprisingly, the statutory and nonstatutory rules differ from state to state, although most states that have addressed the question have adopted the rule that a general disposition or residuary clause, without more, does not constitute the exercise of a power of appointment (French, 1979). It is impossible to say what most donees may intend in any given situation, but since it is within the power of the donor to specify what method of exercise will suffice, this should be done in the instrument creating the power. The most satisfactory solution to this problem is for the instrument creating the power to require express reference to the power to exercise it in order to prevent ill-considered exercise of the power by such devices as a general residuary clause of a will.

7. Avoiding the Rule against Perpetuities: The Rule against Perpetuities, as we have already seen, is a holdover from medieval times that is designed to prevent the control of one's assets from the grave. The rule works its purpose by invalidating interests that do not vest within a certain period of time. Suffice it to say that great care must be taken to assure that the rule in effect in the state where a power of appointment is created is not violated by this rule.

In a nutshell, in those states that still recognize the common law rule against perpetuities, a power of appointment is invalid at its creation unless it is absolutely certain that the power will become exercisable, if at all, within 21 years after some life in being at its creation. It is, then, especially important that the donor exercise great caution whenever he or she attempts to create a power of appointment in an unborn person or creates a power that will pass to successor trustees of a trust that might endure for longer than the period of the rule.

APPLYING THIS CHAPTER TO *YOUR* SITUATION

The proper use of powers of appointment can add enormous flexibility to an estate plan by permitting the donee of the power to alter the donor's estate plan long after the plan was first designed. The two major types of powers of appointment, the general power and the special power, differ essentially in that a general power of appointment conveys virtually outright ownership of the assets to the donee, and thus subjects these assets to taxation in the donee's estate. Assets subject to a special power, however, are not includable in the donee's estate since the donee cannot appoint them to himself or herself. Thus, the tax consequences to the donee, along with other questions raised in this chapter, will have considerable bearing on which type of power to use.

CASE PROBLEMS

14.1 Exercising a Power of Appointment. If Joan Dumire is given a power of appointment by her father's will, should she exercise it? What does Joan need to know in order to make an intelligent answer to this question?

14.2 Taxation and Power of Appointment. William Dumire dies in 1970 leaving a will that creates a trust under which his daughter, Joan Dumire, is income beneficiary and has a general power of appointment exercisable by deed or by will. What are the federal gift and estate tax consequences if:

1. Joan dies in 1985, never having exercised the power?
2. In 1980, Joan appoints the property outright to her daughter, Elizabeth. Joan dies in 1985.
3. In 1980, Joan appoints the remainder interest in the property to her daughter, Elizabeth. Joan dies in 1985.

SELECTED READINGS

FRENCH, SUSAN F., "Execution of Powers of Appointment," 1979 *Duke Law Journal* 747.

KURTZ, SHELDON F., *Family Estate Planning*. St. Paul, Minn.: West Publishing Company, 1983, pp. 279–302.

McGOVERN, WILLIAM M., JR., *Wills, Trusts, and Future Interests*. St. Paul, Minn.: West Publishing Company, 1983, pp. 444–463.

PRICE, JOHN R., *Contemporary Estate Planning*. Boston: Little, Brown and Company, 1983, pp. 78–80.

"Report of Subcommittee on Estate and Tax Planning, Use and Drafting of Powers of Appointment," 1 *Real Property, Probate and Trust Journal*, 307 (1966).

SOLOMON, LEWIS D., *Trusts and Estates: A Basic Course*. Indianapolis, Ind.: Bobbs-Merrill Company, Inc., 1981, pp. 393–408.

STRENG, WILLIAM P., *Estate Planning*. Washington, D.C.: Tax Management, Inc., 1981, pp. 391–416.

WESTFALL, DAVID, *Estate Planning*. Mineola, N.Y.: Foundation Press, Inc., 1982, pp. 363–390.

Life Insurance

It is thrifty to prepare today for the wants of tomorrow.

Aesop, *The Ant and the Grasshopper*

For most families, life insurance is the single most important asset the family owns, apart from the family residence. Certainly, it will be the largest single liquid asset available to the average family on the death of the family income earner.

WHAT IS LIFE INSURANCE?

Life insurance is an agreement between an insured and an insurance company under which the insured agrees to pay a certain amount of money (known as the *premium*) over a designated period of time, in return for which the company promises to pay, upon the death of the insured, a certain amount of money (known as the *death benefit* or *policy proceeds*) to whomever the insured has designated.

Life insurance companies do not like to admit it, but a life insurance policy is in a sense a bet. The insured is betting (albeit not hoping) that he or she will die before having paid much money to the life insurance company in premiums. The company, on the other hand, is betting that the insured will live a long life and will, consequently, pay premiums for many years before he or she dies. The company hopes that the premiums the insured pays over the years, together with the income that is made by investing these premiums, will be greater than the death benefit that the company must pay on the death of the insured.

And the company covers the possibility that any one insured will die (and the death benefit on that insured's policy will have to be paid) before very much has been collected from that insured in premiums by use of what is known as a *risk pool*. The risk pool consists of premium payments from a large number of designated persons, out of which any death benefit payments can be made on the death of any insured covered by the pool. By use of actuarial tables to calculate the expected rates of death of those in the risk pool, the insurance company can assure that there will always be sufficient funds to pay the death benefits on the death of those in the risk pool and also leave something for a profit.

In a pure sense, life insurance is really this simple. But, for reasons that can be understood only by one in the public relations and advertising business (and perhaps by an occasional alchemist), the insurance industry has taken this essentially simple concept and given us a product that is at times mind boggling in its complexity. Different terms are used for the same concept. ("Straight life" and "ordinary life" come to mind immediately.) The various basic forms of insurance have been amended in subtle (and not so subtle) ways to create "new" forms of insurance. And, until recently, it could be said that the art of legal obfuscation had reached its apex in the drafting of the life insurance policy. The average policy had become so abstruse and complicated that the "plain language" movement focused its early attention on life insurance policies. Now, thankfully, most life insurance policies and the correspondence regarding them can be read and understood by anyone possessing a working familiarity with the English language.*

BASIC PURPOSES OF LIFE INSURANCE

Life insurance is almost always purchased for one of three reasons:

1. To create an estate
2. To preserve an estate
3. To fund business and employment agreements

All the complicated, and often quite specialized, reasons given for a life insurance purchase can usually be broken down into one or more of these three reasons. Thus it can be fairly said that there are "only three reasons to buy life insurance." But, of course, these are three good and rather all-inclusive reasons.

Creating an Estate

For most wage earners, and especially younger ones who have not had time to accumulate much in the way of assets, life insurance provides the major source of funds or the protection of their families. Lacking an estate in the ordinary sense, they create one by purchasing a policy of life insurance that will pay the family a sum of money in the event of the untimely death of the wage earner. Thus, when an estate

---

*This is not meant so much as an indictment of the life insurance industry as it is a condemnation of what has come to pass for "legal writing" over the years. Lawyers, who, after all, wrote the insurance policies and the letters "explaining" them have finally begun to learn that clarity and simplicity have their virtues.

does not exist or is too small to support the family in the event of the insured's death, life insurance can provide the necessary support.

Preserving an Estate

In larger estates, where there may be assets of considerable value, a different problem is present, liquidity. Life insurance may be the only feasible or practical means of providing an estate with liquid assets with which to pay death taxes, immediate living expenses, and the costs of administration of the estate without having to undergo the forced sale of valuable illiquid assets. Life insurance for this purpose is especially valuable in estates that are sufficiently large to support the family, but not large enough to absorb the additional expenses attendant upon the death of the insured.

Funding Business and Employment Agreements

In business planning, life insurance policies frequently provide the funds necessary for the purchase of a decedent's interest in the business upon his or her death. Life insurance is also used to fund an employee's retirement. Such policies of insurance are often backed up by detailed buy–sell agreements or other employment agreements.

These three purposes of life insurance constitute the *only* reasons one should purchase a life insurance policy. All the other reasons frequently given (all perfectly sound ones, by the way) are, when carefully considered, actually one of these three or some combination thereof.

For example, if you purchase a home and buy mortgage insurance to protect your spouse from being saddled with a huge mortgage in the event of your untimely death, you are actually buying insurance to create the estate necessary to pay off the mortgage. If you have considerable assets but buy life insurance to assure that, if you should die unexpectedly, your spouse does not have to sell off the family home to educate your children, your purchase of life insurance was a combination of estate creation and estate preservation. The list is endless.

COMMON LIFE INSURANCE TERMS

As with any discipline, certain terminology has grown up around life insurance. The *insured* is the person whose life is insured. (In most cases the insured was the person who applied for the insurance coverage and, until the policy was issued, was known as the *applicant*.) The *insurer* is the company that issues the life insurance policy. The *beneficiary* is the person who is paid the *policy proceeds* (also known as the *death benefit*) on the death of the insured.

KINDS OF LIFE INSURANCE

The two major forms of life insurance are term and whole life.

Term Insurance

Term insurance is "pure" insurance. It insures against a risk (the death of the insured) during a specified period (the life of the policy). It has no loan value, no cash surrender value, no investment element. It is simply insurance on a risk, much the same as automobile accident insurance, fire insurance, or flood insurance.

Since the risk of dying increases with age for adults (no matter how we try not to think about it), the cost of a fixed amount of term life insurance increases with the age of the insured. For example, based on the Internal Revenue Service's one-year term insurance rates published in Revenue Ruling 55-747, 1955-2 CB 228 (the "P.S. 58" rates, which represent the amount of employer-provided, nongroup insurance that will be taxed to the employee), the annual premium on a $10,000 term insurance policy will be $32.10 for a 35-year-old-person, $34.10 for a 36-year-old, $36.30 for a 37-year-old, $38.70 for a 38-year-old, and $41.40 for a 39-year-old. By age 50 the annual premium will have risen to $92.20 and by age 60 it will be $207.30.

Decreasing term. One form of term insurance, known as decreasing term, has a premium that does not increase, but the face amount of the insurance policy decreases as the insured ages. The result, from an insurance viewpoint, is the same as with the typical term insurance policy. Decreasing term policies are often written to provide for the payment of the balance due on a home mortgage or automobile loan if the insured (usually the primary family income earner) dies. The policy is structured for coverage to decrease at approximately the same rate as the balance due on the mortgage or loan, and the premiums are structured accordingly.

Some term insurance policies establish *level* premium rates for a certain number of years, thus assuring that the premium will not automatically increase each year. For example, using the previous P.S. 58 rates, the policy may provide that a 35-year-old insured will pay a premium of $36.52 per year for a $10,000 term policy and that this premium will not increase for five years. What the company has done, of course, is to charge a slightly higher premium in the early years of the five-year period and a lesser amount in the latter years. For example, the actual cost to the insurance company of protecting against the risk of the insured's death during any particular year of the five-year period, versus the premium charged during that year, would be as follows, if the P.S. 58 rates were used:

Year	Age	Insurance Cost	Premium
1	35	$ 32.10	$ 36.52
2	36	34.10	36.52
3	37	36.30	36.52
4	38	38.70	36.52
5	39	41.40	36.52
Totals		$182.60	$182.60

For the next five-year period the annual premium will rise to $51.02, reflecting an actual cost of providing the insurance that will range from $44.20 in the first year to $58.50 in the fifth year. But the steady premium provided by the *level premium* term insurance policy merely masks the fact that, over the long run, the cost of the insurance policy will reflect mortality rates that increase with age. (Actually, the total premium collected over the five-year period will not add up to quite $182.60, since the insurance company will take the extra premium collected in the early years and invest it. The interest earned will reduce the premiums required in the later years somewhat.)

Term insurance will frequently provide for automatic renewal at the end of the term. That is, the company is required to renew the policy for another term no matter what the insured's health may be at the time of renewal. In such a case, the policy is said to be *guaranteed renewable*. The guaranteed renewability option carries an additional small premium, of course, since the insurance company's risk is increased. Nonetheless, when the term expires and the insurance is not renewed, the policy has no value.

A term insurance policy may also provide (again for an additional premium) that the insured may convert her or his term insurance into whole life without undergoing any medical examination and upon paying the going premium for the whole life policy at the age at which the insured converts. Both the guaranteed renewable option and the right of conversion are desirable: guaranteed renewability in order to be able to continue the insurance protection regardless of the state of the insured's health, and the conversion right because term insurance becomes quite expensive as the insured ages and she or he may wish to provide permanent coverage at a fixed-for-life premium rather than continue with the increasing premiums that accompany term insurance. Generally, term insurance that is renewable and convertible is often the best buy for a relatively young person seeking to obtain maximum life insurance protection at the lowest cost.

Whole Life

A whole life insurance policy differs from a term policy in that the insurance exists for the entire period of the insured's life (as long as the premium is paid) and not merely for a specified term. A level premium is charged, based on the insured's age at issue of the policy, and this premium continues unchanged throughout the insured's lifetime (as does the amount of the insurance). During the early years of coverage, the insured's premium payments will be greater than the actuarial risk of death (much the same as in the level premium term policy), and a reserve will develop. The insurer will invest this reserve and produce earnings that will build the cash value of the policy, that is, the amount for which the policy can be redeemed (or borrowed against) by the insured prior to death. If the insured dies while a loan is outstanding against the policy, the beneficiary receives the face amount of the policy less the unpaid loan balance and any interest due thereon. The reserve also serves to offset the increasing cost of insurance as the insured ages.

In the typical whole life policy, premiums are payable until the insured dies or the policy matures, which will be at a very advanced age, usually 99 or 100. In that case, when the insured has lived to maturity, the policy terminates and the face amount of insurance is paid to the policy owner (In a sense, I suppose, the insurance company is saying "O.K. You win. We give up. Here's your money." But, of course, they have had the use of the insured's premiums over the life of the policy, so the insurance company wins, too).

Limited-payment life is a variation of the typical whole life policy that involves payment of premiums for a limited period, usually a fixed amount of years or until the insured reaches a specified age. Common examples of limited-payment policies are those on which premiums are payable for 20 years ("twenty-pay-life") or until the insurer reaches age 65 ("paid up at sixty-five"). Naturally, since the premiums will be paid for a shorter period of time, the premium on a limited-payment policy is higher than on the typical whole life policy, but the cash value of the limited-payment policy will build up faster since there will be a greater reserve factor built into the premium.

Single-premium insurance, as the name implies, is insurance where the purchaser pays only one premium at the time of obtaining the policy. *Joint life* insurance covers more than one life, usually a husband and wife or business partners. Usually, the face amount of a joint life policy is paid on the death of the first of the two persons insured. With *joint and survivor life*, however, the face amount is payable on the death of the survivor of the joint insureds.

Another major form of whole life is the endowment policy, which provides for payment of the face amount of the policy to the policy owner when the insured reaches a specified age. Endowment policies are usually planned to pay off when the insured retires or when children are ready to begin college. Premiums are payable on an endowment policy until the insured dies or the policy endows. If the insured dies before the policy endows, the face amount of insurance is payable to the designated beneficiary. Thus the endowment policy combines the protection of insurance with the forced savings of the endowment.

Endowment policies are usually very expensive, since the premium will only be payable for what is usually a brief period of time, and a major purpose of the policy is to accumulate money for the endowment.

The distinguishing feature of all whole life insurance, then, is the existence of an investment element as well as an insurance element. The insurance element is the amount of each premium necessary to provide the pure insurance protection for the insured, while the investment element is the amount of each premium paid that exceeds what is required for pure insurance. As explained earlier, the insurer invests this excess premium (the *investment element*) to provide a cash surrender value for the policy, as well as to offset the increasing cost of providing pure insurance protection as the insured ages.

A controversy has raged for years over the relative attractiveness of term and whole life insurance. Those who insist that whole life insurance is a poor investment usually advance one (or more) of the following arguments:

1. Insurance companies usually pay relatively low rates of interest on the investment element of an insurance policy. The insured would be better advised to buy term insurance for pure insurance protection and invest the difference in investments that pay a higher rate of return than the insurance policy's rate of interest. Indeed, in times of inflation, a relatively youthful insured would be better off to place the investment portion of an insurance premium in growth-oriented investments.

2. While an insured can borrow from a whole life policy that has built up some loan or cash surrender value, the insured must pay interest to the insurance company for what is arguably the insured's money.

3. When the insured dies with a policy that has built up a substantial cash surrender value, the insured receives only the face amount of the policy, not the face amount plus the cash surrender value.

The "buy term and invest the difference" argument is, of course, perfectly sound except for one thing: human nature. The effectiveness of the whole life insurance policy as an investment device to accumulate a source of liquidity is that the premium *must* be paid. It is a regular debt of the insured that must be dealt with as routinely as the bills for heat, light, and food. If one would indeed buy the lower-costing term life and invest the difference on a regular basis, that would be fine. But most consumers buy term insurance and fail to invest the difference.

It also begs the question to argue that the investment element of a whole life policy "belongs" to the insured and that he or she should not have to pay interest to the insurance company to borrow it. The company's actuaries have calculated how much money the company must have in investment reserves at any one time for the company to meet its obligations and still earn a profit. If the investment element were to be available to the insured free of any interest obligation, this money would not be earning income for the company, and the premium would simply have to be higher.

It would be a futile act to attempt to resolve the term-versus-whole life controversy in these few pages. Suffice it to say that each form of insurance has its advantages. The prudent investor will select the type of insurance that is best for him or her based on a careful evaluation of such factors as his or her needs at the time and for the foreseeable future, age and state of health, and the purpose for which the insurance is being purchased.

PARTICIPATING VERSUS NONPARTICIPATING POLICIES

Insurance policies on which the insurer pays annual dividends are known as *participating* policies (the idea being that the policyholder participates in the company's earnings by receiving a dividend in a profitable year). For the most part, whole life policies issued by mutual insurance companies (and some policies offered by stock companies)* are participating. Some term policies are participating, but most are not.

*A mutual company is one of which each policyholder "owns" a piece of the company. A stock company is one that is owned by its stockholders.

A participating policy does not guarantee that a dividend will be paid annually, but in fact most participating policies do pay an annual dividend and it can be quite large.

The dividends from participating policies are not true dividends in the sense that one receives a dividend from a share of stock, but they are in effect a refund of excess premiums previously paid on the policy. For this reason, dividends on a participating life insurance policy are not currently considered taxable income until they reach the point where they exceed the premium paid.

Policy owners usually have four options with respect to the use of policy dividends:

1. Payment in cash
2. Application of the dividends against current premiums to reduce them
3. Leaving the dividends with the insurance company to earn interest
4. Purchase additional paid-up insurance

Of these choices, number three is often thought a poor choice, given the relatively low interest rates many insurance policies pay and the fact that such interest is taxable. Receiving cash or reducing the cost of the annual premium is tempting since it reduces current expenses for insurance. But using the premium to purchase additional paid-up insurance may be the wisest choice of all since it will provide additional insurance, which may help offset some of the reduction in value of the original policy caused by inflation.

HOW MUCH LIFE INSURANCE SHOULD YOU BUY?

A vastly more important question than whether to buy term or whole life is the question "How much insurance do I need?" To answer this, you must answer the following questions:

1. Why is the insurance being bought? That is, is the purpose of the policy estate creation or estate preservation or a purpose related to the insured's business?
2. What other assets are available to meet the needs of the insured for this purpose? For example, if the purpose of the life insurance is estate preservation, what other assets will be available to meet this need on the insured's death?
3. How much money does the insured have available to pay life insurance premiums?

For prospective purchasers of life insurance, the Consumer's Union has prepared a very helpful paperback book, *The Consumer's Union Report on Life Insurance: A Guide to Planning and Buying the Protection You Need*, revised edition (1977). This book, which can be ordered from the Consumer's Union of the United States, 256 Washington Square, New York, N.Y. 10553, is basically directed at helping the consumer determine how much life insurance to purchase for protection of the family (estate creation). In addition, most life insurance companies will provide personalized information of the same nature for prospective buyers of insurance. The prospective buyers need not worry that the company will "stack" the information in such a way that they will be encouraged to purchase unnecessary insurance. Since most Americans are underinsured, the companies can safely report the true facts and rest assured that most of us will be in need of additional insurance.

A helpful form for the calculation of life insurance needs can also be found in Appendix E. This form follows somewhat the approach of the Consumer's Union, but is also directed at helping to determine life insurance needs for purposes of other than merely estate creation.

The important thing to understand here is that, while much of life insurance is sold based on simple formulas such as "carry life insurance equal to five or six times annual earnings" or "spend x percent of gross or net income for whole life insurance," these formulas miss the point. They do not necessarily have any relationship to the actual financial needs or circumstances facing the insured and her or his family. The formulas are helpful in the sense that they permit this often complex question to be reduced to a simple rule and also serve as a useful sales technique. But the real reason they are used is that they permit the sale of life insurance without requiring the insured to face up squarely to the question of his or her own mortality. To accurately determine how much life insurance one needs, the prospective insured must face the difficult personal question of "what will happen to my family, my estate, or my business when I die?" This is not exactly the most upbeat way to spend one's time, so we tend to ignore questions of this sort. But an accurate assessment of one's life insurance needs requires just such a personal (and painful) evaluation. (Some things are never easy.) Once this point has been reached, however, and the insured has accepted the need to make this sort of evaluation, the actual determination of life insurance needs can be relatively easy, and certainly more accurate than the formula approaches commonly used. And, of course, circumstances and needs change, making it necessary to periodically reevaluate life insurance needs.

TWO COMMON POLICY RIDERS

Two additional options are typically available as *riders* to both term and whole life policies: accidental death coverage and waiver of premium.

Accidental Death

The accidental death rider pays an additional death benefit equal to the face amount of the policy in the event the insured dies as the result of an accident, as that term is defined in the rider. Since the policy payoff is doubled in the event of accidental death, it is often known (partly, perhaps, because of a movie by this title) as the *double indemnity* rider. Some policies go even further and offer a triple payoff if the accidental death is caused while riding a licensed public conveyance as a fare-paying passenger.

While the cost of the rider is minimal (usually around one dollar per year per thousand dollars of insurance), its value is questionable. Death following a lingering illness is usually far more debilitating to the family's bank account than a sudden accidental death. The accidental death rider is simply a gamble that looks far more attractive than it actually is.

Waiver of Premium

The waiver of premium rider provides that the insurer will waive the payment of premiums while the insured is totally and permanently disabled prior to a certain age, typically 65. Usually, there is a brief waiting period before the rider takes effect (six months is typical). In essence, the waiver of premium rider is a small disability policy that covers only the premiums on a specific life insurance policy. The cost and availability of the rider will vary with the age, health, occupation, and avocations of the insured. The cost of this provision is minor (partially because of the low incidence of total and permanent disability) and it is a valuable addition. Values of the underlying policy continue to build as if the premiums were being paid by the insured. But, note, however, that this rider only pays the life insurance premiums of the insured and is *not* a substitute for disability income insurance.

LIFE INSURANCE AND THE FEDERAL ESTATE TAX

The unique feature of life insurance as an instant estate makes it an attractive vehicle for tax planning. For purposes of the federal estate tax, there are several ways in which the proceeds of a life insurance policy could be included in the insured's gross estate (and, alternatively, a number of ways to keep life insurance out of the estate).

Avoiding the federal estate tax on life insurance proceeds is especially important when the insurance was acquired for estate preservation purposes. If, for example, the owner of a farm valued at $1,000,000 buys life insurance to avoid forcing his or her family to sell the farm to pay death taxes, he or she will need approximately $300,000 of insurance to provide the necessary liquidity to pay estate and inheritance taxes. If this $300,000 of life insurance is itself subject to death taxes, this will add another $125,000 to the estate's tax burden, which in return will require additional insurance (which itself will raise the taxable estate higher, requiring even more insurance; the formula never ends). Thus, avoiding death taxes on the life insurance proceeds can be an important step in the planning process.

Includability of Life Insurance Proceeds in an Insured's Estate

1. Policy proceeds receivable by or for the benefit of the deceased insured's estate are includable in the gross estate to the same extent as any other assets the decedent owned at death. This concept is quite clear and is consistent with the rules by which most other types of property are included in a decedent's estate.

2. Policy proceeds payable to other beneficiaries are includable if the decedent possessed, at the time of death, any *incidents of ownership* over the policies. (We will discuss this concept in greater detail later, but essentially it means that if the insured had the right to control who received the policy proceeds on his or her death or if the insured had the right to enjoy the economic benefits of the policy during his or her lifetime, for example, if he or she had the right to borrow against the policy or cash it in for its cash surrender value, it is considered an asset of value to the insured and should be included in the estate just like other assets of value.)

3. If the insured transferred the policy (along with the incidents of ownership over it) within three years of his or her death, it will be includable in the gross estate under a special provision of the Internal Revenue Code [Code 2035(d)(2)]. The idea here is that a gift of life insurance so close to the insured's death should not be taxed merely by the gift tax (which, you will recall, results in a lower overall tax than the estate tax), but should be subject to the estate tax.

Insurance Receivable by or for the Benefit of the Estate

Code 2042(1) requires inclusion in a decedent's gross estate of the proceeds of life insurance received by or for the benefit of the estate. Thus, a policy on the life of the decedent could be owned and controlled by a third party; but if the proceeds are payable to the decedent's personal representative for the benefit of the estate, these proceeds are includable in the decedent's estate for purposes of the federal estate tax [*Draper* v. *Commissioner*, 536 F.2d 944 (1st Cir. 1976)].

If you think about it, the treatment of life insurance that is payable to the estate as an asset of the decedent, even though the decedent did not own it during his or her lifetime (and, thus, could not enjoy any of the economic benefits of ownership during his or her lifetime) is very similar to the treatment of property subject to a general power of appointment. There the donee of the power may never have enjoyed the property during his or her lifetime, but it is includable in the estate on his or her death.

Moreover, Code 2042(1) also includes in the gross estate any proceeds receivable by other beneficiaries if they are under a legal obligation to apply the proceeds for the benefit of the estate. For example, if Frank Maxwell conveyed his life insurance policies irrevocably to a trust, along with sufficient monies to pay the premiums on these policies for his lifetime, and if he retained no interest in these policies whatsoever (that is, he gave up the right to change beneficiaries, borrow from the policies, and the like), and if the trust provided that the trustee *must* apply the policy proceeds to pay the debts, taxes, and other expenses of Frank's estate, the proceeds would be includable in the decedent's estate.

If, on the other hand, the trustee were merely *authorized* to expend the corpus of the trust to satisfy the estate's obligations, the insurance proceeds would not be includable in the decedent's estate.

Incidents of Ownership

Code 2042(2) includes in the gross estate of the insured the proceeds of any insurance policy, payable on the decedent's death, over which the decedent possessed any incidents of ownership at the time of his or her death. Perhaps the best definition of the term incidents of ownership is found in the Regulations, at Section 20.2042-1(c)(2):

> [T]he term "incidents of ownership" is not limited in its meaning to ownership of the policy in the technical legal sense. Generally speaking, the term has reference to the right of the insured to his estate to the economic benefits of the policy. Thus it includes the power to change the beneficiary, to surrender or cancel the policy, to assign the policy, to revoke an assignment, to pledge the policy for a loan, or to obtain from the insurer a loan against the surrender value of the policy.

Note that the right of the insured to obtain a loan against the surrender value of the policy is an incident of ownership and furnishes grounds for including the *entire policy proceeds* in the gross estate, even though the decedent's power to borrow is limited to the amount of the policy premiums [*Estate of Neuberger* v. *Hickey*, Civil No. 836 (N.D.N.Y. August 13 1942)].

The powers defined in the Regulations are not meant to be all-inclusive. For example, the code provides [at Sec. 2042(2)] that more than a 5 percent reversionary interest is an incident of ownership. Thus, if there is a possibility that the policy or its proceeds may return to the insured or become subject to a power of disposition by the insured, and if this possibility is valued at more than 5 percent of the value of the policy, this is an incident of ownership. (Whether the value of a reversionary interest exceeds 5 percent of the value of the policy is determined by reference to the actuarial tables and principles set forth in Reg. 20.2031-10.) Moreover, the right to change the time or manner of payment of proceeds to the beneficiary by electing, changing, or revoking settlement options has been held to be a taxable incident of ownership [*Estate of Lumpkin, Jr.*, v. *Commissioner*, 474 F.2d 1092 (5th Cir. 1973)].

Whether an individual possesses an incident of ownership in a life insurance policy is determined according to the terms of the policy and not the intention of the parties (*Commissioner* v. *Estate of Noel*, 380 U.S. 678, 1965). Regulations 20.2042-1(c)(4) require the inclusion of the proceeds of a policy over which the insured held an incident of ownership as trustee (Rev. Rul. 76-261, 1976-2 C.B. 276). However, where the incidents of ownership cannot be exercised for the economic benefit of the insured-fiduciary but only for the benefit of third parties, the proceeds of the policy need not be included in the estate of the insured-fiduciary. (An example would be when the insured transferred all incidents of ownership to his wife who died and whose will established a residuary trust for her child and named the insured trustee of the trust. The insured-fiduciary role of the trustee here does not subject the policy proceeds to inclusion in his estate [Rev. Rul. 84-179].)

Cross-owned life insurance. One of the simpler ways to avoid having life insurance included in the gross estate of the insured is, obviously, to have any insurance policies on the life of the insured owned by someone else. Thus, a husband may have his wife own all of his life insurance policies, which means that the wife, not the husband, will have the right to enjoy all the economic benefits of ownership of the policies that flow from possessing the incidents of ownership. At the time, the wife may wish to avoid having her life insurance policies included in her estate and may provide that her husband be the owner of her policies. In such a case, the policies are said to be *cross-owned*, and on the death of the first party, his or her life insurance policy proceeds will not be includable in his or her gross estate. Cross-owned insurance is relatively simple to set up, and it provides for avoidance of some estate tax on the death of the first party. But it does nothing to reduce estate tax on the death of the second party. For that, we will look to the irrevocable life insurance trust, to be discussed later in this chapter.

Transfer of a Policy within Three Years of Death

As we saw earlier, gifts made within three years of the death of the donor ae not generally includable in the donor's gross estate for purposes of the federal estate tax. However, this is true only of donors who die after December 31, 1981. Prior to that time, all gifts made within three years of the donor's death were brought back into the gross estate and subjected to the estate tax. But when the prior rule was changed by the Economic Recovery Act of 1981, it did not apply to gifts of life insurance [Code 2035(d)].

Thus, Code 2035 requires inclusion in the decedent's estate of the full proceeds of a life insurance policy that is transferred within three years of death, together with any gift tax paid. Moreover, the proceeds of a policy transferred by the insured within three years of death are includable, even though the value of the policy was within the allowable annual gift tax exclusion at the time of the transfer (i.e., it was valued at less than $10,000 to $20,000) and no gift tax return was required to be filed.

If, however, any part of the premiums were paid by a person other than the insured after the transfer, the portion of the proceeds of the policy that bears the same relation to the total proceeds as the premium payments made by the assignee bear to the total amount of premium payments may be excluded from the insured's estate (Estate of Morris R. Silverman, 61 T.C. 338, 1973). This is quite a mouthful and can perhaps be better understood from the following example.

> Frank Maxwell irrevocably assigned a $250,000 policy on his life to his wife, Charlotte, within three years of his death. Frank paid three $2,000 premiums on the policy before the assignment and Charlotte paid two premiums after the assignment. After Frank's death, the policy proceeds were paid to Charlotte. Only three-fifths of the $250,000 policy proceeds, or $150,000, are includable in Frank's gross estate. However, if Frank had continued to pay the premiums before his death, the entire proceeds of the policy would have been includable in his estate.

Note, however, that if Frank had survived three years after making the gift of the life insurance, no part of the policy proceeds would have been includable in his gross estate under Code 2035, even though he may have continued to pay the premiums after the transfer. The only way *any part* of the policy proceeds are includable in the insured's gross estate is for death to occur within three years of the transfer of the policy.

There is one final "wrinkle" on the three-year rule that deserves mention. As we saw earlier, Code 2042(2) requires that the proceeds of policies over which the insured possessed any incidents of ownership at her or his death be included in the insured's estate. And Code 2035(d) requires the inclusion of the proceeds of a policy that the insured transferred within three years of death. Read together, these two provisions seem to require the inclusion of the proceeds of a life insurance policy when the insured transferred the policy more than three years before death, but retained an incident of ownership that she or he gave up within three years of death.

LIFE INSURANCE AND THE FEDERAL GIFT TAX

A gift of an interest in a life insurance policy is subject to the same gift tax rules as a gift of any other asset. However, no gift occurs when the owner of the policy *revocably* designates a beneficiary (Rev. Rul. 81-166, 1981-1 C.B. 477). The gift tax annual exclusions are available for outright transfers of life insurance, except where the transfer is to an irrevocable trust [Regs. 25.2503-3(c), Examples (2), and (6)]. An absolute assignment of a life insurance policy may qualify for the gift tax marital deduction (Code 2523) or the gift tax charitable deduction.

Valuation of interest in life insurance is done under Regulations 25.2512-6(a). For the typical insured the value of a life insurance policy at any one time will depend on how long the insured is likely to live, which is, of course, the basis for the actuarial tables. However, if the insured is terminally ill, an insurance policy on his or her life will be likely to pay off the face amount in a shorter period of time than that calculated by the actuarial tables, and thus the policy is worth more than a similar policy on the life of an insured whose policy is not likely to pay off until much later. The gift tax regulations provide that "all relevant facts and elements of value at the time of the gift shall be considered." Thus, in a factual situation such as that outlined previously, this may require that the physical condition and insurability of the insured be taken into account (*U.S.* v. *Ryerson*, 312 U.S. 260, 262, 1941).

ESTATE AND GIFT TAX PLANNING WITH LIFE INSURANCE

Settlement Options

A major decision in any life insurance policy is what mode of settlement to elect for the payment of policy proceeds upon maturity. The election is usually made by the insured at the time the policy is purchased, although it may be left to the beneficiary to make the election at the time the policy matures. The five most common settlement options offered by most life insurance policies are as follows:

1. *Lump sum settlement*: This settlement option entitles the beneficiary to receive the proceeds of the policy, together with any dividend values, in a lump sum. Once the policy proceeds are paid in a lump sum, the insurance company is relieved

of any further obligations under the policy. The advantages to the lump sum settlement are that it provides the beneficiary with immediate funds to meet any obligations that may have arisen because of the death of the insured. And, if any money is left over after meeting these obligations, these funds can be invested at substantially higher rates of return than those typically provided by the life insurance company. The major disadvantage is that if significant amounts of cash are visited upon a beneficiary who is unable to manage the money, it may be dissipated in short order, and the intended protection sought by the life insurance policy will have been wasted. The beneficiary is not subject to the federal income tax for any amounts received under a life insurance lump sum settlement [Code 101(a) and (c)].

2. *Interest option*: Under this settlement option, the policy proceeds are held by the company for the benefit of the beneficiary, who receives interest on the proceeds. (In some cases, if the company has had a profitable year, it may even pay excess interest to the beneficiary. But this is solely within the company's discretion.) The interest option usually provides that the beneficiary may terminate the arrangement at any time and receive the settlement proceeds in a lump sum. For this reason, the interest option is generally considered a variation of the lump sum settlement option. Interest income received by the beneficiary under this option is subject to the federal income tax [Code 101(c)].

3. *Installment annuity option:* This settlement option provides for fixed amounts, actuarially determined, to be paid to the beneficiary for life. The older the beneficiary, the larger the benefit. To avoid having the insurance company come into a substantial windfall if the beneficiary dies prematurely, this option generally provides for a guarantee of annuity payments for a minimum period of time. (Five, ten, or twenty years are the typical guarantees.) Obviously, the longer the guaranteed payment period, the lower will be the annual benefits. Thus, if Frank Maxwell dies and leaves a life insurance policy under which he has selected an annuity option settlement for his wife Charlotte, with payments guaranteed for her life or a minimum of ten years, the company will pay Charlotte an annuity for as long as she lives. If she dies before ten years' annuity payments have been made, these payments will be paid to her estate or to whomever she has designated. If, however, she dies after ten years' payments have been made, nothing further is payable under the policy to a beneficiary. The major advantage of the installment annuity option is that the beneficiary is guaranteed an annuity for life.

4. *Installments for a fixed amount*: This option provides the beneficiary as much money as he or she decides to receive over a period of time. The company actuarially determines how long these payments can be made until the policy proceeds and any interest earned thereon are exhausted. If the beneficiary dies before the payments are completed, the payments remaining to be made are paid to another beneficiary, selected by the first beneficiary. If the payments are exhausted before the beneficiary dies, nothing further is forthcoming from the insurance company. The advantage of this method of settlement is that it permits the beneficiary to establish payments at a size that will meet his or her financial needs for the short range. The disadvantage is

disadvantage is that, once the payments are exhausted, the beneficiary must rely on other means of support.

5. *Installments for a fixed period*: Under this settlement option, the beneficiary determines how long he or she would like to receive benefits, and the amount of the annual benefit is determined by dividing the policy proceeds plus interest thereon by the number of years the beneficiary wishes to receive benefits. Obviously, the longer the period, the lower the payments. As with the installments for a fixed amount settlement option, if the beneficiary dies before the exhaustion of the fund, the remaining benefits are payable to another beneficiary selected by the first beneficiary or the insured–owner.

Life Insurance Trust

It may well be that the insured will not be totally satisfied with *any* of the settlment options offered by her or his life insurance company. The insured may wish to build into her or his estate plan a bit more flexibility than that offered by the company's options. The life insurance trust is an excellent device to achieve this purpose, along with several others.

Revocable life insurance trust. The simplest of the life insurance trusts consists of a revocable trust that contains no assets other than the insurance policies on the life of the insured. The insured continues to pay all premiums and continues to own the policies (and the incidents of ownership therein). The owner names the trustee beneficiary of the insurance policies and provides that the trustee is to collect the policy proceeds on the death of the insured. Finally, the trust provides for the disposition of the insurance proceeds (which now constitutes the corpus of the trust) in whatever fashion the insured may have determined upon establishing the trust.

There are several advantages to the life insurance trust over the selection of one of the policy settlement options. For example, the insured can select an option not available in the life insurance policy. As we have seen, the amounts that can be paid and the times when they can be paid are somewhat limited under the typical insurance company settlement option. For example, the insured may wish to have payments made to one child for a sufficient time to complete college, then to another child for a like period, and then to a third beneficiary for life, after which the funds are to pass to yet another beneficiary. No life insurance company settlement option is likely to provide this sort of arrangement. But the life insurance trust can be designed to pay out in any fashion the insured desires, assuming that other provisions of the law, such as the rule against perpetuities, are not violated.

Then, too, the insured may wish to avoid paying the policy proceeds to a particular beneficiary in a lump sum, but want to have the money invested at a higher rate of return than that provided by the typical life insurance company settlement option.

Also, as we have seen, the insured can execute a will that leaves his or her estate to a life insurance trust, which means that the assets that pass under his or her will will "pour over" from the insured's estate to the trust and, ultimately, pass as directed by the trust, thus providing the same privacy for the insured's other assets as it afforded to his or her insurance proceeds.

Irrevocable life insurance trust. If the insured wants to have all the advantages just discussed and also avoid inclusion of the policy proceeds in his or her gross estate, the insured can establish an irrevocable life insurance trust and transfer to this trust all of his or her rights under the policy (including all incidents of ownership). By doing this, the insured can have all the flexibility of the revocable trust, plus the tax advantage of having the policy proceeds avoid the estate tax on his or her death (assuming the insured does not die within three years of the transfer of the life insurance into the trust). At the time this transfer is made, some gift tax will be incurred, but since the value of the policy for gift tax purposes will be substantially less than the proceeds payable on the insured's death, the gift tax cost will be minimal in comparison to the estate tax savings.

The irrevocable life insurance trust also avoids the major shortcoming of cross-owned insurance. There, you will recall, the insurance of the first party to die is kept out of the estate of that party; but when the second party dies, his or her insurance is includable in the gross estate. With the irrevocable life insurance trust, both the husband and wife can convey their policies to the trust (a single trust will do), and the insurance will not be includable in the estate of either on death.

Of course, an irrevocable trust is irrevocable, and you have had plenty of warnings about making irrevocable transfers of assets during lifetime. The same warnings are applicable to gifts of life insurance.

SPLIT-DOLLAR LIFE INSURANCE

Split-dollar life insurance is primarily designed as an employee fringe benefit (although it could be used between family members, such as between a father and his son-in-law). It is a means of making a substantial amount of life insurance available to the employee (the insured) at little or no cost to him or her. Typically, the employer will pay the portion of the premium that is equal to the annual increase in the cash value, and the employee will pay the balance (if any) of the premium. On the death of the employee, the policy proceeds will be split between the employer and the employee's beneficiary. The employer will receive an amount equal to the cash value of the policy, and the employee's beneficiary will receive the balance. Since the cash value of a typical whole life insurance policy will increase over the years, the employee's premium cost will also decrease over the years. So, however, will the amount of insurance protection that belongs to the employee. Because of this, the dividend on participating policies is usually applied under the fifth dividend option to buy term insurance equal to the increase in the cash value. Thus, the employee will have insurance protection that costs her or him less every year while the amount of coverage is not reduced.

There are virtually unlimited ways that split-dollar insurance can be structured.

1. The employer might own the policy and be responsible for payment of the premiums. The employee could then be required to reimburse the employer for her or his share, if any, of the premiums. This is known as the *endorsement* system.

2. The employee might own the policy and pay the entire annual premium. The employer could make an annual loan to the employee (at low interest or no interest, although care should be taken if the employee is also an officer or stockholder of the company) equal to the annual increase in cash surrender value, but not to exceed the annual premium. The employee then assigns his or her policy to the employer as collateral for the loans, and the loans are paid from the policy proceeds on the death of the employee. This is known as the *collateral* system.

3. The employee might pay for only the cost of the "pure" insurance protection (the P.S. 58 cost), while the employer pays for the rest.

4. The employee might contribute nothing toward the policy and be taxed on the value of the term insurance protection he or she is receiving from the employer (the P.S. 58 cost). Then the employer will pay a bonus to the employee equal to the premium taxed to the employee.

There are, obviously, two major advantages to split-dollar life insurance. First, it offers the employer a means of providing a major fringe benefit, life insurance, to a key employee at a relatively low cost to the employer. Since the employer receives his or her share of the premium payments back at the time the employee dies, all it has cost the employer is the loss of interest on the premium payments over the years. Second, the employee receives life insurance protection at a much lower cost than if he or she purchased the life insurance on his or her own.

LIFE INSURANCE FOR THE HARD TO INSURE

Persons who suffer from physical problems (such as diabetes) or who have hazardous occupations (deep-sea divers come to mind), or who pursue risky hobbies such as mountain climbing often have a difficult time obtaining life insurance. Traditionally, such high-risk persons can obtain coverage from companies that sell the substandard policies, coverage that costs more or is less comprehensive than usual. Fortunately, there are some ways to reduce this cost for the high-risk individual.

Check the High-Risk Rating

If a life insurance company rejects an applicant or offers coverage only at an exorbitant premium, the applicant should make certain that the high-risk rating is justified. Most major life insurance companies provide information from insurance applications and doctor's reports to the Medical Information Bureau, a record-keeping organization funded by the insurance industry. Applicants who have been given a high-risk rating can write to the bureau at P.O. Box 105, Essex Station, Boston, Massachusetts 02112, and inquire about the reasons for the rating. The bureau will send the applicant occupational and avocational information and will forward the applicant's medical information to his or her physician. Together, the applicant and doctor can determine if there appears to be any rational basis for the high-risk rating. If the rating is based on outdated or erroneous information, the bureau's files can be corrected and the applicant can apply for coverage at ordinary rates. It is also possible that the experience with a particular hazard (health or otherwise) by companies differs and thus different ratings might be assessed among different companies.

Group Life Insurance

Perhaps the easiest way for a high-risk individual to get life insurance coverage is through some sort of group coverage plan. While small-group policies (usually covering fewer than ten lives) require medical information, they are generally far less picky about the risks involved in any one applicant because the group pool protects their risk. Employer sponsored group life plans also offer the possibility of conversion to individual coverage if the insured leaves her or his job, although the individual policies are generally less comprehensive and more costly than the group coverage they replace. Fraternal organizations, volunteer fire companies, professional associations, college alumni groups, and social clubs often offer group life insurance as a fringe benefit of membership, although such policies are usually not convertible if the insured drops her or his membership in the organization. These policies are usually not less expensive than substandard individual policies, but it is usually easier to qualify for them.

Substandard Risk Policies

Those who are not covered by group insurance can still obtain an individual policy by shopping around. The easiest way to find such a policy is by having an insurance agent refer the applicant to an insurance broker who specializes in high risks. If the applicant can get several brokers working on coverage, he or she can usually come up with the broadest coverage for the lowest cost, since there is plenty of room for negotiation in substandard risk policies (since such policies are not ordinarily underwritten according to the usual formulas). Applicants following this procedure might be wise to consider "locking in" their original (and higher premium) policy while shopping for a better offer to avoid withdrawal of the original offer by the company. A better offer might not be forthcoming.

Term Insurance

Since term insurance is less expensive than whole life, it follows that high-risk term insurance will be less expensive than high-risk whole life. This can be a relatively simple way for a high-risk applicant to obtain the necessary coverage at a premium he or she can afford. Most companies limit the issue of term insurance for some hazards in both the coverage amount and the types of extra risk that are acceptable.

Graded Death Benefit Policy

A special type of policy that exists for the high-risk individual is the graded death benefit policy. With this policy, the death benefit gradually increases over the years until it equals the face value of the policy. This type of policy is often used in pension preretirement death benefits to avoid the extra cost of ratings. As a form of lien-type rating, it is used by mail order insurance companies to avoid adverse selection by buyers of this type of insurance (since, generally, only extra-risk applicants apply for this type of insurance).

Lying about Special Risks

Of course, an applicant for life insurance can always seek to avoid all problems with respect to insurability by covering up any medical problems or especially hazardous jobs or hobbies. But it is a risk not worth taking. Should the insured die within the period when the insurance company can still contest the payment of the policy proceeds (usually within two years of the issuance of the policy), all the company would be obligated to pay to the survivors would be the amount of premiums that the insured paid. Insurance companies are, understandably, very careful about the accuracy of an application for insurance coverage.

VALUABLE LIFE INSURANCE INFORMATION

A major part of the portfolio of information that a person should keep to assist his or her loved ones with the settlement of his or her estate on death will consist of life insurance information. Generally, the insured should maintain a file containing the following information regarding life insurance:

1. Name, address, and phone number of life insurance agent.
2. List of life insurance policies, by company name and policy number, and additionally the following information might be helpful:
   a. Type of policy (i.e., term or whole life)
   b. Face amount
   c. Annual premium (and how paid)
   d. Any riders
   e. Dividend option selected if participating policy
   f. Who owns the policy
   g. Beneficiary
   h. Settlement option selected (if any)
   i. Policy loans, if any
   j. Any assignments to trust
   k. Where the policies are located

APPLYING THIS CHAPTER TO *YOUR* SITUATION

Life insurance can be an excellent way to create an estate where none exists or provide the necessary funds to preserve an estate from the ravages of taxation and other expenses on the death of the insured. If care is taken and family conditions warrant it, life insurance proceeds can be kept out of the insured's estate for federal estate tax purposes, thus permitting the insured to leave behind a substantial chunk of assets with no adverse tax effects. The questions of what kind of insurance to buy and how much coverage is necessary can only be answered after a careful calculation of the specific needs of the individual applicant and his or her family. And, as we have seen, with some planning, a part of the cost of whole life insurance can be made tax deductible, reducing the after-tax cost of whole life to very nearly the cost of term insurance.

CASE PROBLEMS

15.1 Determining Life Insurance Needs. Frank Maxwell is 53 years old and in moderately good health. He has assets of roughly $175,000 and debts of $75,000. He and his wife, Charlotte, have two children: Mark, age 21, and a college junior studying premedicine; and Lisa, age 19, who plans to attend college and become a stock broker. Charlotte is 51 and has completed three years of college work toward a degree in elementary education. Frank has only $10,000 life insurance, a term policy that he obtained through his local "Racoon" Lodge.

Questions
1. Assuming that the family will not qualify for any Social Security pension until Charlotte reaches 62, how much life insurance does Frank need and why?
2. How much life insurance does Charlotte need and why?
3. Should Frank buy any life insurance for Mark or Lisa? Why or why not?

SELECTED READINGS

CHAPMAN, PETER F., "Life Insurance as a Planning Tool: The Life Insurance Policy," 34 *NYU Institute on Federal Taxation* 723 (1976).

HILL, STANFIELD, and McKAY, T. JOSEPH, "CLU, The Flowering of Financed Life Insurance," 118 *Trusts and Estates* 59 (1979).

MORGAN, CHARLES C., "Split-Dollar Insurance—New Developments Suggest Planning Techniques That Save Taxes," 58 *Taxes* 269 (1980).

PRICE, JOHN R., *Estate Planning.* Boston: Little, Brown and Co., 1983, pp. 299–401.

SOLOMON, LEWIS D., *Trusts and Estates: A Basic Course.* Indianapolis, Ind.: Bobbs-Merrill Company, Inc., 1981, pp. 307–314.

WEINSTOCK, HAROLD, *Planning an Estate.* Colorado Springs, Colo.: McGraw-Hill Book Co., 1982, pp. 194–230.

WESTFALL, DAVID, *Estate Planning.* Mineola, N.Y.: Foundation Press,Inc., 1982, pp. 520–540.

16

The Six Basic
Estate Plans

A place for everything, and everything in its place.

Samuel Smiles

While there are an infinite variety of ways one can plan an estate, the various estate plans can actually be broken down into six fundamental plans. A look at these plans provides a simple review of the entire subject of estate planning.

SIMPLE WILL WITH GIFTS OUTRIGHT

The simplest, and most common, form of estate plan consists of a will in which the testator makes gifts to friends and loved ones, with the gifts to take place on the testator's death. The testator makes no attempt to control the use of these gifts after her or his death by means of a trust, power of appointment or other estate planning device. The gifts are made in the will, they become effective on the testator's death, and that is that.

Even when a testator requires a more complicated estate plan, the use of outright gifts is often made for certain types of assets. For example, a father with considerable stock holdings may leave the stock to a trust to provide an income for his children after his death. But, in the same will that creates or pours over to the trust, the father may dispose of certain nonincome producing assets by outright gifts. He may leave his books to one child, his stamp collection to another, and his automobile to yet another, all outright gifts that become final once the father's estate is settled.

The simple will has much to commend it. When the testator's assets are relatively uncomplicated, or when she or he leaves behind no one who requires the special protections of a trust or similar device, there is no reason to resort to a more complicated estate plan. Often, however, estate planning clients will request more complicated plans than they actually need because someone with limited knowledge of their needs has suggested it or because a certain device becomes popular (the revocable living trust comes to mind), or because they know of someone else who has utilized a particular device and it appeals to them. The estate planner must patiently and tactfully help the client to abandon these grandiose plans and understand the practicality of a simpler plan under the circumstances. If the estate planner doesn't do it, no one else will.

WILL WITH TRUST: NO TAX PROVISIONS

A will with a trust containing no tax provisions is most commonly used by the client who wishes to protect a loved one from the necessity of managing certain assets after the testator's death and who has no tax reasons for creating the trust. Since the federal estate tax does not apply to decedents who die after January 1, 1987, with estates of less than under $600,000, a testator with an estate of less than this amount has no need to plan to avoid the estate tax. Nonetheless, she or he may wish to protect certain loved ones from the necessity of managing the assets after her or his death and may wish to have continuing court oversight of the management of these assets. The testamentary trust with no tax provisions is an excellent device for this purpose.

Of course, by including the trust in the will, the testator gives up the privacy that accompanies an inter vivos trust, but the testator gains the continuing oversight of the probate court of the state where her or his will is probated. If this oversight is important, this may be a valuable trade-off.

WILL WITH TRUST: TAX PROVISIONS

When the testator's assets are valued at substantially more than $600,000, she or he may wish to utilize the testamentary trust with tax provisions. The most common device to use is a combination of a marital deduction trust and a credit shelter trust, which together can assure that all the estate of the first spouse to die passes free of the estate tax because of the marital deduction and the unified credit. Schematically, here is how this works:

Gross estate	$x,xxx,xxx
Amount passing free of estate tax because of unified credit	600,000
Amount passing free of estate tax because of marital deduction (all of the decedent's estate in excess of $600,000)	xxx,xxx
Amount subject to tax	–0–

Thus, if the gross estate is $1,000,000, this plan would work like this:

Gross estate	$1,000,000
Amount passing free of estate tax because of unified credit	600,000
Amount passing free of estate tax because of marital deduction	400,000
Amount subject to tax	–0–

On the other hand, an estate of $500,000 would look like this if this device is used:

Gross estate	$500,000
Amount passing free of estate tax because of unified credit	500,000
Amount passing free of estate tax because of marital deduction	–0–
Amount subject to tax	–0–

When there is no surviving spouse, the testator may utilize a charitable remainder trust, which will leave the estate assets for the use of the testator's loved one for his or her lifetime, and then pass those assets to a charity on the loved one's death. On the testator's death, as we have seen earlier, the estate can take a deduction based on the value at that time of the remainder interest to the charity.

As with any testamentary trust, the trust provisions will be a matter of public record on the probating of the decedent's will. But the trade-off will be that the probate court will exercise continuing oversight over the management of the assets in the trust.

REVOCABLE LIVING TRUST WITH POUR-OVER WILL: NO TAX PROVISIONS

The planning for this estate planning device is quite similar to the testamentary trust with no tax provisions. The major differences are that the trust is freely revocable and amendable during the testator's lifetime, and the provisions of the trust remain private following the testator's death, since the trust instrument is not admitted to probate. Thus the testator can make any changes she or he wishes up to the point of death. The trust as it is constituted at death is a private contract between the testator (known in the trust as the *trustor* or *settlor*) and the trustee. When the testator dies, the trust takes on permanence, but its provisions are never subject to public scrutiny; only the trustee and the beneficiaries have any right to know what is contained in the trust.

The testator must still write a will, but the will is usually a very simple document that merely leaves certain outright gifts to individuals or institutions and then pours over the remainder of the testator's estate (that which has not already been given away earlier in the will or conveyed to the revocable living trust during the testator's lifetime) to the revocable living trust the testator created earlier.

The advantages of this estate plan include:

1. Increased flexibility in planning, since the trust is freely revocable and alterable until the testator's death.
2. Complete privacy with respect to the provisions of the trust, since it is never admitted to probate.
3. Protection of the beneficiaries, since the trustee will manage the trust assets and pay out the income to the beneficiaries.

It is true that the oversight of the probate court is lost since the trust is never admitted to probate, but in most cases the substantial requirements that are placed on the average trustee by virtue of the fiduciary laws will be sufficient protection for the beneficiaries.

REVOCABLE LIVING TRUST WITH POUR-OVER WILL: TAX PROVISIONS

This estate plan seeks to combine the advantages of the revocable living trust with some tax saving devices. The most common combination is the use of the ordinary revocable living trust with the marital deduction and credit shelter trusts described earlier. If the testator's estate is not sufficiently large to require use of the marital deduction trust, as we saw earlier, it is simply not brought into operation, and the assets in the estate pass free of the estate tax by means of the unified credit as provided in the credit shelter trust. If, on the other hand, the assets in the estate exceed $600,000, both the credit shelter trust and the marital deduction trust will be called into play to shelter the entire estate from the estate tax.

The great advantage of this estate plan is that it permits a relatively young person with assets that are substantially below $600,000 to design an estate plan that will provide protection from the estate tax in the event that her or his estate should grow to over $600,000 by the time of death. This is especially attractive to young professionals, who may be burdened with debts now and facing relatively low "start-up" incomes, but whose incomes (along with the size of their estates) will likely soar as they establish themselves professionally.

IRREVOCABLE LIVING TRUST

With irrevocability comes rigidity and a certain loss of freedom on planning. But irrevocability also brings with it the opportunity to expand the tax planning extensively.

As we saw earlier, the estate tax is based on the size of the estate at the decedent's death. If, therefore, the decedent has given away substantial portions of her or his estate, the estate tax on those assets can be avoided. (And, as we saw earlier, if the decedent has taken careful advantage of the gift tax exclusions, the gift tax can also be avoided.)

Thus, the wealthy estate owner who has no need of certain of her or his assets can give them away irrevocably before death and avoid having these assets taxed in the estate. The trust device becomes useful here if the testator wishes to maintain some control over the assets after death. If the testator has a son, for example, in whom she or he does not have the utmost confidence, the testator can give the assets to an irrevocable living trust and provide that the income only is to pass to the son for his lifetime, with the trust to terminate on the son's death and the assets to pass then to the son's heirs. In this fashion, the testator has assured that the profligate son will have a lifetime income and that something will still be passed on to his heirs. Moreover, the assets given to this trust are not included in the testator's estate on her or his death, and thus the estate tax has been reduced (although the gift tax will be assessed on the irrevocable gift to the trust at the time the gift is made).

Perhaps more important, however, insofar as tax planning is concerned, is the fact that the income on the assets that have been placed in the trust will also not be taxed to the testator, once she or he has given them to the trust. Rather, the income will be taxed to the beneficiary of the trust, the testator's son. Since the son will likely be in a lower income tax bracket than the father, the family will save income tax as well as estate tax.

The irrevocable living trust thus has all the advantages of the various devices we have outlined earlier, plus the chance to avoid *both* the estate tax and the income tax with respect to the assets placed in the trust and to avoid the income tax on the income from those assets. But it has the enormous disadvantage that always accompanies irrevocability: should the testator wish to change her or his mind after transferring assets to the trust, it will be too late. Irrevocable means just what it says.

Still, the opportunity to trade a loss of flexibility for substantial estate tax and income tax savings may be a perfectly good trade-off for the testator who

(1) is absolutely certain she or he will never need the assets or their income again,

(2) wishes to avoid the income tax and estate tax,

(3) wants to use the protection of a trust for the assets left to her or his loved ones, and

(4) wants to have the privacy that accompanies not having the trust assets subject to probate.

Which of these estate plans is best for you or your client? It is a question (and not always an easy one) of individual needs, assets, aspirations, and concerns. Just because the task of an estate planner is well nigh impossible in some instances, doesn't mean we can't do our best.

APPENDIX A

Requirements for a Valid Will in the 50 States and the District of Columbia

Requirements for a Valid Will in the 50 States and the District of Columbia

State	Minimum Age	No. of Witnesses	Holographic Wills	Marriage Revoke Will?	Divorce Revoke Will?
Alabama	18	2	No	No	Yes
Alaska	18	2	Yes	No	Yes
Arizona	18	2	Yes	No	Yes
Arkansas	18	2	Yes	No	Yes
California	18	2	Yes	Yes	Yes
Colorado	18	2	Yes	No	Yes
Connecticut	18	2	No	Yes	Yes
Delaware	18	2	No	No	Yes
District of Columbia	18	2	No	Yes[a]	Sometimes
Florida	18	2	No	No	Yes
Georgia	14	2	No	Yes	Yes
Hawaii	18	2	No	No	Yes
Idaho	18[b]	2	Yes	No	Yes
Illinois	18	2	No	No	Yes
Indiana	18[c]	2	No	No	Yes
Iowa	18[d]	2	No	No	Yes
Kansas	18	2	No	Yes	Yes
Kentucky	18	2	Yes	Yes	Yes
Louisiana	16	3	Yes	No	No
Maine	18	2	Yes	No	Yes
Maryland	18	2	Yes[e]	Yes[a]	Yes

(continued)

State	Minimum Age	No. of Witnesses	Holographic Wills	Marriage Revoke Will?	Divorce Revoke Will?
Massachusetts	18	2	No	Yes	Yes
Michigan	18	2	Yes	No	Yes
Minnesota	18	2	No	No	Yes
Mississippi	18	2	Yes	No	No
Missouri	18	2	No	No	Yes
Montana	18	2	Yes	No	No
Nebraska	18	2	Yes	No	Yes
Nevada	18	2	Yes	Yes	No
New Hampshire	18[a]	3	No	Yes[a]	No
New Jersey	18	2	Yes	No	Yes
New Mexico	18	2	No	No	Yes
New York	18	2	Yes[e]	No	Yes[b]
North Carolina	18	2	Yes	No	Yes
North Dakota	18	2	Yes	No	Yes
Ohio	18	2	No	No	Yes
Oklahoma	18	2	Yes	Yes[a]	Yes
Oregon	18	2	No	Yes	Yes
Pennsylvania	18	2	Yes	No[b]	Yes
Rhode Island	18	2	Yes[e]	Yes	No
South Carolina	18	3	No	Yes	Yes
South Dakota	18	2	Yes	Yes	No
Tennessee	18	2	Yes	Yes[a]	Yes
Texas	18[b,c]	2	Yes	No	Yes
Utah	18	2	Yes	No	Yes
Vermont	18	3	No	No	No
Virginia	18	2	Yes	No	Yes
Washington	18	2	No	Yes	Yes
West Virginia	18	2	Yes	Yes	Yes
Wisconsin	18	2	No	Yes	Yes
Wyoming	19	2	Yes	No	Yes

In many cases where it is noted that divorce revokes a will, it revokes it only as to the former spouse.
[a] Only if a child is born or adopted during the marriage.
[b] Any emancipated minor may execute a will.
[c] Any person in the armed services or merchant marines may also execute a will, regardless of age.
[d] Any married minor may execute a will.
[e] Such wills are recognized for service members on active duty and mariners at sea under certain conditions.

APPENDIX B

Estate and Gift Tax Rates

Unified Transfer Tax Rate Schedule

| If the Amount Is: | | | Tentative Tax Is: | | |
Over	But not over	Tax	+	%	On excess over
$ 0	$ 10,000	$ 0	18		$ 0
10,000	20,000	1,800	20		10,000
20,000	40,000	3,800	22		20,000
40,000	60,000	8,200	24		40,000
60,000	80,000	13,000	26		60,000
80,000	100,000	18,200	28		80,000
100,000	150,000	23,800	30		100,000
150,000	250,000	38,800	32		150,000
250,000	500,000	70,800	34		250,000
500,000	750,000	155,800	37		500,000
750,000	1,000,000	248,300	39		750,000
1,000,000	1,250,000	345,800	41		1,000,000
1,250,000	1,500,000	448,300	43		1,250,000
1,500,000	2,000,000	555,800	45		1,500,000
2,000,000	2,500,000	780,800	49		2,000,000
2,500,000	3,000,000	1,025,800	53		2,500,000
3,000,000	—	1,290,800	55		3,000,000

SOURCE: Internal Revenue Code Sec. 2001.

This rate schedule applies to estates of decedents dying and gifts made in 1984, 1985, 1986, and 1987. After 1987, the top rate will fall to 50 percent to be applied to amounts in excess of $2,500,000.

Unified Credit

Year	Amount of Credit	Amount of Exemption Equivalent
1981	$47,000	$175,625
1982	62,800	225,000
1983	79,300	275,000
1984	96,300	325,000
1985	121,800	400,000
1986	155,800	500,000
1987 and thereafter	192,800	600,000

SOURCE: Internal Revenue Code Sec. 2010.

State Death Tax Credit for Estate Tax

Adjusted Taxable Estate At least	But less than	Credit =	+	%	Of Excess over
$ 0	$ 40,000	$ 0	0	$ 0
40,000	90,000	0	.8	40,000
90,000	140,000	400	1.6	90,000
140,000	240,000	1,200	2.4	140,000
240,000	440,000	3,600	3.2	240,000
440,000	640,000	10,000	4	440,000
640,000	840,000	18,000	4.8	640,000
840,000	1,040,000	27,600	5.6	840,000
1,040,000	1,540,000	38,800	6.4	1,040,000
1,540,000	2,040,000	70,800	7.2	1,540,000
2,040,000	2,540,000	106,800	8	2,040,000
2,540,000	3,040,000	146,800	8.8	2,540,000
3,040,000	3,540,000	190,800	9.6	3,040,000
3,540,000	4,040,000	238,800	10.4	3,540,000
4,040,000	5,040,000	290,800	11.2	4,040,000
5,040,000	6,040,000	402,800	12	5,040,000
6,040,000	7,040,000	522,800	12.8	6,040,000
7,040,000	8,040,000	650,800	13.6	7,040,000
8,040,000	9,040,000	786,800	14.4	8,040,000
9,040,000	10,040,000	930,800	15.2	9,040,000
10,040,000	—	1,082,800	16	10,040,000

SOURCE: Internal Revenue Code Sec. 2011.
The *adjusted taxable estate* is the taxable estate reduced by $60,000.

APPENDIX C

Inheritance and Estate Taxes in the 50 States and the District of Columbia

Inheritance and Estate Taxes in the 50 States and the District of Columbia

State	Type of Tax [a]	Surviving Spouse Exemption[b]	Surviving Spouse Rates[c]	Gift Tax?[d]
Alabama	Credit estate tax			No
Alaska	Credit estate tax			No
Arizona	Credit estate tax			No
Arkansas	Credit estate tax			No
California	Credit estate tax			No
Colorado	Credit estate tax			No
Connecticut	Succession and transfer tax	300,000	5%– 8%	No
	Credit estate tax			
Delaware	Inheritance	70,000	2%– 4%	Yes
	Credit estate tax			
District of Columbia	Inheritance	5,000	1%– 8%	No
	Credit estate tax			
Florida	Credit estate tax			No
Georgia	Credit estate tax			No
Hawaii	Inheritance		2%– 7%	No
Idaho	Inheritance	50,000	2%–15%	No
	Credit estate tax			
Illinois	Credit estate tax			No
Indiana	Inheritance	All		No

(continued)

State	Type of Tax [a]	Surviving Spouse Exemption [b]	Surviving Spouse Rates [c]	Gift Tax? [d]
Iowa	Inheritance	1/3 of tax due [e]	1%– 8%	No
	Credit estate tax			
Kansas	Inheritance	All		No
	Credit estate tax			
Kentucky	Inheritance	50,000		No
	Credit estate tax			
Louisiana	Inheritance	25,000	2%– 3%	Yes
	Credit estate tax			
Maine	Inheritance	50,000	5%–10%	No
	Credit estate tax			
Maryland	Inheritance	150	1%	No
	Credit estate tax			
Massachusetts	Estate	Up to 1/2 adjusted gross estate	5%–16%	No
	Credit estate tax			
Michigan	Inheritance	65,000	2%–10%	No
	Credit estate tax			
Minnesota	Credit estate tax			No
Mississippi	Estate	None	1%–16%	No
Missouri	Credit estate tax			No
Montana	Inheritance	All		No
Nebraska	Inheritance	All		No
	Credit estate tax			
Nevada	No state death tax			No
New Hampshire	Inheritance	All		No
	Credit estate tax			
New Jersey	Inheritance	15,000	2%–16%	No
	Credit estate tax			
New Mexico	Credit estate tax			No
New York	Estate	All		Yes
	Credit estate tax			
North Carolina	Inheritance	All		Yes
	Credit estate Tax			
North Dakota	Credit estate tax			No
Ohio	Estate	60,000	2%–7%	No
	Credit estate tax			
Oklahoma	Estate	All		Yes
	Credit estate tax			
Oregon	Inheritance [f]		12%	Yes
	Credit estate tax			

(continued)

State	Type of Tax [a]	Surviving Spouse Exemption [b]	Surviving Spouse Rates [c]	Gift Tax? [d]
Pennsylvania	Inheritance	Property owned in joint tenancy with spouse	6%	No
	Credit estate tax			
Rhode Island	Estate	175,000	2%–9%	No
	Credit estate tax			
South Carolina	Estate	All		Yes
	Credit estate tax			
South Dakota	Inheritance	All		No
	Credit estate tax			
Tennessee	Inheritance	600,000	5 1/2%–9 1/2%	Yes
	Credit estate tax			
Texas	Credit estate tax			No
Utah	Credit estate tax			No
Vermont	Credit estate tax			Yes
Virginia	Credit estate tax			No
Washington	Credit estate tax			No
West Virginia	Credit estate tax			No
Wisconsin	Inheritance	All		Yes
	Credit estate tax			
Wyoming	Credit estate tax			No

[a]Where the type of tax listed is credit estate tax, the tax levied is equal to the maximum federal credit for state death taxes. Where both an inheritance or estate tax are listed, the credit estate tax is payable only for any amount by which the state inheritance or estate tax is less than the maximum federal credit. For example, if the federal credit for an estate is $10,000 and the state inheritance tax is only $8,000, the credit estate tax is $2,000.

[b]The exemption listed is that of the surviving spouse. In some states, the surviving spouse has a separate exemption, and in others the spouse is lumped in with other beneficiaries.

[c]The rates listed are the minimum and the maximum rates for the estate passing to the surviving spouse after subtracting the spouse's exemption.

[d]Most state inheritance or estate taxes apply to any gift made within three years of death.

[e]Increases to two-thirds of tax due for death after 1/1/87, and tax is eliminated on surviving spouse's share for deaths after 1/1/88.

[f]Tax rates on all estates drop to zero for decedents dying on or after 1/1/87.

APPENDIX D

Glossary
of Legal Terms

Adjusted gross estate The amount upon which federal estate tax is levied after deductions are taken from the gross estate.

Administrator The individual or institution appointed by the court to administer the estate of a person who died without a will or whose will did not designate an executor or whose designated executor could not or would not serve.

Advancement Assets given by a parent to a child by way of anticipation of the share that the child will inherit in the parent's estate.

Agent One who acts for another.

Annual exclusion The $10,000 that the Internal Revenue Code permits to be given to each donee free of the federal gift tax each year. (The amount is $20,000 if the donor's spouse joins in the gift.)

Annuity The periodic payment of a specific sum of money for life or for a designated period of time.

At-risk rule The rule that prohibits an investor from taking a deduction for any amount that exceeds the amount of his or her investment.

Attorney-in-fact A legal agent appointed to act for another in a power of attorney.

Beneficiary One for whose benefit a trust is established or to whom a bequest is made in a will.

Bequest A gift made in a will.

Capacity Soundness of mind required to execute a will.

Capital gain Gain from the sale of a capital asset.

Cash value The cash reserve element of permanent life insurance that is created with the excess premium charged above the cost of pure protection or term insurance.

Charitable deduction A deduction from gross income or gross estate for contribution to charity.

Clifford trust A type of trust, recognized by the IRS, to which income producing property may be conveyed for a period of at least ten years, during which time the income from the trust is taxed to the beneficiary of the trust. Also known as a short-term trust, ten-year trust, or reversionary trust.

Codicil A formal amendment to a will.

Credits A dollar-for-dollar subtraction from tax liability. A $100 credit saves $100 in taxes, regardless of tax bracket.

Crummey trust A trust which provides that the beneficiary is allowed to withdraw each year at least the lesser of (1) the annual exclusion or (2) the value of the assets transferred to the trust during that year. The annual exclusion is allowed for a Crummey trust, even if there is otherwise no gift of a present interest.

Decedent A deceased person.

Deduction Amounts allowed to be subtracted from gross income or gross estate in order to arrive at taxable income or taxable estate.

Depreciation Charges permitted to be deducted against earnings from an asset to reflect the asset's decline in value as it "wears out." Depreciation is a bookkeeping entry only and does not represent any actual money payment or loss.

Discretionary trust A trust under which the trustee has absolute discretion as to how much (if any) income or principal shall be paid over to the beneficiary.

Donee The person who receives a gift; also, a person given authority under a power of appointment.

Donor The person who makes a gift.

Durable power of attorney A power of attorney that, by state law and in accordance with the terms of the instrument, is not revoked by the incompetence of the grantor of the power.

Estate tax A tax levied against the entire estate of a decedent at death.

Exclusion ratio The percentage of an annuity that escapes taxation because it represents the portion of the annuity the owner has purchased with after-tax dollars.

Executor An individual or institution designated in a will to administer the estate of a person who has died.

Exemption The deduction allowed from gross income for the taxpayer and persons cared for or supported by the taxpayer.

FICA Federal Insurance Contributions Act. These initials on a worker's paycheck identify the amount paid for Social Security.

Generation-skipping transfer tax A tax on the transfer of assets to members of a younger generation that would not otherwise be subject to transfer tax.

Gift tax A tax on lifetime transfers of assets.

Gross estate The entire estate of a decedent, before any deductions are made.

Gross income The entire income of a taxpayer, before any deductions are made.

Guardian An individual or institution charged with the duty of taking care of the person and property of another individual.

Holographic will A will written entirely in the handwriting of the person making the will; not valid in all states.

HR-10 plan See *Keogh retirement plan.*

Income averaging A method of calculating income tax that allows an individual to take a small tax break after a year of unusually high income following four years of substantially lower income.

Inheritance tax A tax imposed on the beneficiary of an inheritance, often with the rate increasing as the beneficiary is further from the deceased in relationship.

Individual retirement account A private pension plan, the contributions to which are tax deductible when invested and taxable when withdrawn after age $59^{1/2}$. Also known as an IRA.

In terrorem clause A clause in a will which provides that any person who contests the will shall not take any interest under the will.

Inter vivos trust Another name for a living trust.

Intestacy Dying without a will.

Intestate One who dies without a valid will.

Irrevocable trust A trust that cannot be altered or revoked by the person who established it.

Joint will A single will made by two or more persons and jointly executed by them.

Keogh retirement plan A pension plan used by self-employed persons, the contributions to which are tax deductible when they are invested and taxable when withdrawn after retirement. Also known as an HR-10 pension plan.

Life estate An interest in property that lasts only during the owner's lifetime.

Life insurance A contract between an individual and an insurance company under which the individual agrees to pay a certain amount of money annually, in return for which the insurance company agrees to pay the individual's beneficiaries a specific sum of money in the event of that person's death during the life of the contract.

Life insurance trust A trust to which an insured person conveys all the incidents of ownership in a policy of life insurance and that is made the beneficiary of the life insurance policy.

Lifetime exclusion The amount of assets that may be conveyed during lifetime by an individual without incurring federal gift tax liability. After 1986, this amount will be $600,000.

Limited-payment life insurance A variation on whole life insurance in which premiums are not payable during the insured's entire life but for a limited period of time. The premiums paid are higher than comparable premiums for whole life insurance.

Living trust A trust established by an individual during his or her lifetime. Also known as an inter vivos trust.

Long-term capital gain Gain on the sale of a capital asset that is held for longer than six months.

Marginal tax bracket The percent at which income tax is computed on the last increment of an individual's income. If the last dollar of your income is taxed in the 22 percent bracket, you are said to be in the 22 percent marginal tax bracket.

Marital deduction A deduction for assets passing from one spouse to another during lifetime or on the death of one spouse.

Minimum-deposit insurance The use of loan proceeds from a life insurance policy's cash value to pay for the premiums in whole or in part. Interest must be paid to the insurance company for this "loan," but it is tax deductible.

Minor's trust A trust for the benefit of a minor which provides that unexpended principal and income in the trust will pass to the beneficiary at age 21. Transfers to a minor's trust qualify as gifts of a present interest, although the minor may not receive them until reaching age 21.

Mutual wills Separate wills of two persons that are reciprocal in their provisions.

Nuncupative will An oral will, valid only for the disposition of personal property under limited circumstances; not valid in all states.

OASI Old Age and Survivor's Insurance Trust Fund.

Personalty Personal property.

Pour-over will A will directing that assets in an estate be added to a trust established by the testator during his or her lifetime or on the death of one spouse.

Power of appointment Authority conferred by a will or other instrument upon another person, known as the donee, to determine who is to receive property or its income.

Power of attorney A written instrument by which a person names another as his or her agent (known as the attorney-in-fact) for purposes set out in the instrument.

Premiums Money paid for a contract of insurance.

Probate The process of administering a decedent's estate.

Progressive tax A tax in which the rate increases as the amount subject to taxation increases.

P.S. 58 rates Rates used in computing the cost of employer-provided nongroup pure life insurance protection that is taxable to the employee.

Realty Real estate.

Remainder The portion of an estate that remains after a previous estate has terminated. For example, if a gift is made to Mary for life and then to John, John has a remainder interest (Mary has a life estate).

Reversionary trust Another name for a Clifford trust.

Revocable living trust A trust established by an individual during his or her lifetime that is freely alterable and revocable.

Rollover The changing of a funding medium of an IRA. For example, moving your IRA investment from a stock mutual fund to a bond mutual fund is a rollover.

Settlor The grantor of a trust.

Short-term capital gain Gain from the sale of a capital asset that has been held for less than six months.

Short-term trust Another name for a Clifford trust.

Social Security A retirement system of the U.S. Government in which each generation of workers funds the retirement payments for the previous generation.

Special power of appointment A power of appointment that may not be exercised by the donee of the power in favor of himself, his estate, his creditors, or the creditors of his estate.

Spendthrift trust A trust in which the assets cannot be sold, given away, or otherwise transferred by the beneficiary before they are conveyed to the beneficiary.

Support trust A trust under which the trustee is to pay over to the beneficiary only so much income as is necessary for the beneficiary's support.

Takers in default Those who are designated to take if the donee of a power of appointment fails to exercise the appointment.

Tax avoidance Any legal means of reducing tax liability.

Tax evasion Nonpayment of taxes determined to be due to the government. This is a criminal act.

Tax shelters Any means of shielding or sheltering money or assets from taxation by legal methods.

Ten-year trust Another name for a Clifford trust.

Term insurance A contract of pure life insurance (i.e., life insurance with no investment element). Premiums increase as the insured ages and the risk of death becomes greater.

Testacy Dying with a valid will.

Testamentary trust A trust established by an individual in his or her will.

Testator A person who makes a will. Testator formerly meant a male who makes a will and testatrix a female who makes a will. The growing practice now is to use the term testator for both sexes.

Totten trust A deposit of money in a bank or other savings institution in the name of the depositor, in trust for a beneficiary. The trust is revocable during the depositor's lifetime.

Trust A form of ownership under which one person holds and manages property for the benefit of one or more other persons.

Vested Fixed or absolute. A right that is vested is not subject to being withdrawn.

Whole life insurance A combination of life insurance protection and investment. The face amount of the policy and the premium remain fixed even though the insured ages and the risk of death increases. In the early days of a whole life policy, the premium is higher than for a comparable term life policy. The difference in premium is used to build up a cash reserve, which helps pay for the additional risk in later years.

Will A document providing for the disposition of a person's estate on death.

APPENDIX E

Computing Life Insurance Needs

I. Money needed on your death
   1. Funeral expenses $_____
   2. Debts (including home mortgage
       and mortgages and liens on investments)   _____
   3. Death taxes
       a. State inheritance or estate tax $_____
       b. Federal estate tax   _____
   4. Add lines 3a and 3b   _____
   5. Cost of administration of estate   _____
   6. Aftertax contribution to family
       support   _____
   7. Years remaining before children
       reach 18   _____
   8. Multiply line 6 by line 7   _____
   9. College costs per child   _____
  10. Number of children   _____
  11. Multiply line 9 by line 10   _____
*12. Semester cost of educating
       spouse   _____
*13. Semesters remaining to obtain
       degree   _____
*14. Multiply line 12 by line 13   _____
       14a. Total money needed on
             your death $_____

II. Family resources available
   1. Life insurance $_____
   2. Savings   _____

(continued)

       Asterisked items are optional; include only if appropriate.

  3. Investments (less mortgages and
     liens) _____

  4. Death benefit from employer _____

  5. Number of years spouse would
     work during child rearing _____

  6. Spouse's yearly earning power _____

  7. Multiply line 5 by line 6 _____

* 8. Profit from sale of second car _____

* 9. Profit from sale of home and
     move into smaller home _____

*10. Aid from family (count only
     aid that is certain) _____

 11. Social Security

    11a. Lump-sum death benefit _____

    11b. Benefit for each
        survivor _____

    11c. Maximum family benefit _____

    11d. Benefit for 3 or more
        survivors (enter amount
        on line 11c) _____

    11e. Number of years you
        will have 3 or more
        survivors _____

    11f. Multiply line 11d by
        line 11e _____

    11g. Benefit for 2 survivors
        (multiply line 11b by 2) _____

    11h. Number of years you
        will have 2 survivors _____

    11i. Multiply line 11g by
        line 11h _____

    11j. Benefits for 1 survivor
        (enter amount on line 11b) _____

    11k. Number of years you
        will have 1 survivor _____

    11l. Multiply line 11j by
        line 11k. _____

    11m.Total Social Security
        (add lines 11a, 11f, 11i,
        and 11l) _____

 12. Total family resources available _____

 13. Less contributions to others in
     will (i.e., specific gifts of money
     or property to nonfamily
     members or to charity) _____

 14. Net total family resources
     available after death $_____

Life insurance needs (subtract line 14, part II,
from line 14a, part I) $_____

APPENDIX F

Inventory Form of Information Essential For Estate Planning

GENERAL INFORMATION

_____   _____   _____
Name - Husband   Birthdate   Social Security Number

_____   _____
Employer   Annual Income

Social Security   Yes _____   No _____
AMW   Maximum _____ or $ _____
Veteran   Yes _____   No _____
Civil Service   Yes _____   No _____
    A. If Civil Service, average of 3 highest consecutive years income
        $ _____.
    B. Number of years service _____.

_____   _____   _____
Name - Wife   Birthdate   Social Security Number

_____   _____
Employer   Annual Income

Social Security Yes _____   No _____
AMW   Maximum _____ or $ _____
Veteran   Yes _____   No _____
Civil Service   Yes _____   No _____
      A. If Civil Service, average of 3 highest consecutive years income
        $ _____.
      B. Number of years service _____.

Address
Length of residence in present state _____

Previous marriages and commitments therefrom (copy of decree and settlement papers
Antenuptial Agreement (copy of agreement)

Prospective inheritances.

CHILDREN

Name _____   Birthdate _____   Social Security Number _____

Married Yes _____ No _____   Address (if different from parent) _____

Name _____   Birthdate _____   Social Security Number _____

Married Yes _____ No _____   Address (if different from parent) _____

Name _____   Birthdate _____   Social Security Number _____

Married Yes _____ No _____   Address (if different from parent) _____

Name _____   Birthdate _____   Social Security Number _____

Married Yes _____ No _____   Address (if different from parent) _____

PROPERTY

The form of ownership of your assets is as important as the value and type of asset. For this reason, under the column titled "Ownership," please indicate whether the asset is:

H owned in the sole name of the husband
W owned in the sole name of the wife
J owned jointly by you and your spouse
C community property

PERSONAL PROPERTY

Tangible Personal Property

Type of Property	Ownership H W J C	Value

Securities

No. Shares or DollarAmt.	Company	Type (Bond, Pfd, or Common)	Mkt. Value	Ownership H W J C

No. Shares or DollarAmt.	Company	Type (Bond, Pfd, or Common)	Mkt. Value	Ownership H W J C

Checking Accounts

Bank	Acct. No.	Average Balance	Ownership H W J C

Savings Accounts

Bank	Acct. No.	Average Balance	Ownership H W J C

Insurance

Insured	Owner	Amount	Policy Number	Type	Beneficiary

REAL PROPERTY

Address	Market Value	Mortgage	Net	Ownership H W J C

Residence Property

_____	_____	_____	_____	_____
_____	_____	_____	_____	_____
_____	_____	_____	_____	_____

Other Real Property

_____	_____	_____	_____	_____
_____	_____	_____	_____	_____
_____	_____	_____	_____	_____
_____	_____	_____	_____	_____

PERSON(S) WHO WILL BE GUARDIAN OF THE PERSON OF YOUR MINOR CHILDREN

First Choice - Name   Street Address

Relationship   City, State

Second Choice - Name   Street Address

Relationship   City, State

SPECIAL PROBLEMS

Have any children received large gifts that you wish to have considered as advancements against their share of your estate?

Are any members of your family indebted to you in any significant amount?

How do you wish to treat this debt on your death?
Cancel the debt(s)?
Deduct the debt(s) from the debtor's share?

Are any members of your family spendthrifts?

Is there any significant family tension such as may lead to the possibility of a will contest?

SPECIAL OBJECTS OF BOUNTY

Relatives other than those in immediate family

Servants or employees

Friends

Institutions

Is there anything significant about you, your family, your family situation, or your property that may affect how you should leave your property on your death and that has not been discussed above?

APPENDIX G

Estate and Gift Tax
Valuation Tables

TABLE A. Single Life, Unisex, 10 Percent Showing the Present Worth of an Annuity, of a Life Interest, and of a Remainder Interest.

1 Age	2 Annuity	3 Life Estate	4 Remainder	1 Age	2 Annuity	3 Life Estate	4 Remainder
0	9.7188	0.97188	0.02821	16	9.7815	0.97815	0.02185
1	9.8988	0.98988	0.01012	17	9.7700	0.97700	0.02300
2	9.9017	0.99017	0.00983	18	9.7590	0.97590	0.02410
3	9.9008	0.99008	0.00992	19	9.7480	0.97480	0.02520
4	9.8981	0.98981	0.01019	20	9.7365	0.97365	0.02635
5	9.8938	0.98938	0.01062	21	9.7245	0.97245	0.02755
6	9.8884	0.98884	0.01116	22	9.7120	0.97120	0.02880
7	9.8822	0.98822	0.01178	23	9.6986	0.96986	0.03014
8	9.8748	0.98748	0.01252	24	9.6841	0.96841	0.03159
9	9.8663	0.98663	0.01337	25	9.6678	0.96678	0.03322
10	9.8565	0.98565	0.01435	26	9.6495	0.96495	0.03505
11	9.8453	0.98453	0.01547	27	9.6290	0.96290	0.03710
12	9.8329	0.98329	0.01671	28	9.6062	0.96062	0.03938
13	9.8198	0.98198	0.01802	29	9.5813	0.95813	0.04187
14	9.8066	0.98066	0.01934	30	9.5543	0.95543	0.04457
15	9.7937	0.97937	0.02063	31	9.5254	0.95254	0.04746

(continued)

1 Age	2 Annuity	3 Life Estate	4 Remainder	1 Age	2 Annuity	3 Life Estate	4 Remainder
32	9.4942	0.94942	0.05058	71	5.8914	0.58914	0.41086
33	9.4608	0.94608	0.05392	72	5.7261	0.57261	0.42739
34	9.4250	0.94250	0.05750	73	5.5571	0.55571	0.44429
35	9.3868	0.93868	0.06132	74	5.3862	0.53862	0.46138
36	9.3460	0.93460	0.06540	75	5.2149	0.52149	0.47851
37	9.3026	0.93026	0.06974	76	5.0441	0.50441	0.49559
38	9.2567	0.92567	0.07433	77	4.8742	0.48742	0.51258
39	9.2083	0.92083	0.07917	78	4.7049	0.47049	0.52951
40	9.1571	0.91571	0.008429	79	4.5357	0.45357	0.54643
41	9.1030	0.91030	0.08970	80	4.3659	0.43659	0.56341
42	9.0457	0.90457	0.09543	81	4.1967	0.41967	0.58033
43	8.9855	0.89855	0.10145	82	4.0295	0.40295	0.59705
44	8.9221	0.89221	0.10779	83	3.8642	0.38642	0.61358
45	8.8558	0.88558	0.11442	84	3.6998	0.36998	0.63002
46	8.7863	0.87863	0.12137	85	3.5359	0.35359	0.64641
47	8.7137	0.87137	0.12863	86	3.3764	0.33764	0.66236
48	8.6374	0.86374	0.13626	87	3.2262	0.32262	0.67738
49	8.5578	0.85578	0.14422	88	3.0589	0.30589	0.69141
50	8.4743	0.84743	0.15257	89	2.9526	0.29526	0.70474
51	8.3874	0.83874	0.16126	90	2.8221	0.28221	0.71779
52	8.2969	0.82969	0.17031	91	2.6955	0.26955	0.73045
53	8.2028	0.82028	0.17972	92	2.5771	0.25771	0.74229
54	8.1054	0.81054	0.18946	93	2.4692	0.24692	0.75308
55	8.0046	0.80046	0.19954	94	2.3728	0.23728	0.76272
56	7.9006	0.79006	0.20994	95	2.2887	0.22887	0.77113
57	7.7931	0.77931	0.22069	96	2.2181	0.22181	0.77819
58	7.6822	0.76822	0.23178	97	2.1550	0.21550	0.78450
59	7.5675	0.75675	0.24325	98	2.1000	0.21000	0.79000
60	7.4491	0.74491	0.25509	99	2.0486	0.20486	0.79514
61	7.3267	0.73267	0.26733	100	1.9975	0.19975	0.80025
62	7.2002	0.72002	0.27998	101	1.9532	0.19532	0.80468
63	7.0696	0.70696	0.29304	102	1.9054	0.19054	0.80946
64	6.9352	0.69352	0.30648	103	1.8437	0.18437	0.81563
65	6.7970	0.67970	0.32030	104	1.7856	0.17856	0.82144
66	6.6551	0.66551	0.33449	105	1.6962	0.16962	0.83038
67	6.5098	0.65098	0.34902	106	1.5488	0.15488	0.84512
68	6.3610	0.63610	0.36390	107	1.3409	0.13409	0.86591
69	6.2086	0.62086	0.37914	108	1.0068	0.10068	0.89932
70	6.0522	0.60522	0.39478	109	0.4545	0.04545	0.95455

See footnote to Table B

TABLE B Table Showing the Present Worth at 10 Percent of an Annuity for a Term Certain, of an Income Interest for a Term Certain, and of a Remainder Interest Postponed for a Term Certain

1 Number of Years	2 Annuity	3 Term Certain	4 Remainder	1 Number of Years	2 Annuity	3 Term Certain	4 Remainder
1	0.09091	0.090909	0.909091	31	9.4790	0.947901	0.052099
2	1.7355	0.173554	0.826446	32	9.5264	0.952638	0.047362
3	2.4869	0.248685	0.751315	33	9.5694	0.956943	0.043057
4	3.1699	0.316987	0.683013	34	9.6086	0.906857	0.039143
5	3.7908	0.379079	0.620921	35	9.6442	0.964416	0.035584
6	4.3553	0.435526	0.564474	36	9.6765	0.967651	0.032349
7	4.8684	0.486842	0.513158	37	9.7059	0.970592	0.029408
8	5.3349	0.533493	0.466507	38	9.7327	0.973265	0.026735
9	5.7590	0.575902	0.424098	39	9.7570	0.975696	0.024304
10	6.1446	0.614457	0.385543	40	9.7791	0.977905	0.022095
11	6.4951	0.649506	0.350494	41	9.7991	0.979914	0.020086
12	6.8137	0.681369	0.318631	42	9.8174	0.981740	0.018260
13	7.1034	0.710336	0.289664	43	9.7340	0.983400	0.016600
14	7.3667	0.736669	0.263331	44	9.9841	0.984909	0.015091
15	7.6061	0.760608	0.239392	45	9.8628	0.986281	0.013719
16	7.8237	0.782371	0.217629	46	9.8753	0.987528	0.012472
17	8.0216	0.802155	0.197845	47	9.8866	0.988662	0.011338
18	8.2014	0.820141	0.179859	48	9.8969	0.989693	0.010307
19	8.3649	0.836492	0.163508	49	9.9063	0.990630	0.009370
20	8.5136	0.851356	0.148644	50	9.9140	0.991481	0.008519
21	8.6487	0.864869	0.135131	51	9.9226	0.992256	0.007744
22	8.7715	0.877154	0.122846	52	9.9296	0.992960	0.007040
23	8.8832	0.888322	0.111678	53	9.9360	0.993600	0.006400
24	8.9847	0.898474	0.101526	54	9.9418	0.994182	0.005818
25	9.0770	0.907704	0.092296	55	9.9471	0.997411	0.005289
26	9.1609	0.916095	0.083905	56	9.9519	0.995191	0.004809
27	9.2372	0.923722	0.076278	57	9.9563	0.995629	0.004371
28	9.3066	0.930657	0.069343	58	9.9603	0.996026	0.003974
29	9.3696	0.936961	0.063039	59	9.9639	0.996387	0.003613
30	9.4269	0.942691	0.057309	60	9.9672	0.996716	0.003284

To determine the present value of an annuity, multiply the aggregate amount payable in a year by the figure in colume 2 of table A or B, whichever is appropriate, opposite (in the case of a life annuity) the nearest age (column 1) of the life measuring the duration of the annuity, or (in the case of a term certain annuity) opposite the number of years (column 1) the annuity is to run. This formula produces the present value of an annuity payable annually at the end of the year. If annuity payments are to be made other than annually at the end of the year, an adjustment must be made to the present value obtained. The adjustment is made from the following table.

	FOR AN ANNUITY PAYABLE AT END OF PERIOD Period Certain or life	FOR AN ANNUITY PAYABLE AT BEGINNING OF PERIOD Period Certain	Life
If payment periods are:	Multiply present value of annuity payable annually at end of year by:	Multiply present value of annuity payable annually at end of year by:	Add amount of first payment to value of annuity for a similar period but payable at the end of the period
Weekly	1.0482	1.0502	
Monthly	1.0450	1.0534	
Quarterly	1.0368	1.0618	
Semiannually	1.0244	1.0744	
Annually	1.0000	1.1000	

APPENDIX H

One-Year Term Premiums for $1,000 of Life Insurance Protection

One-Year Term Premiums for $1,000 of Life Insurance Protection (P.S. 58 Rates)

Age	Premium	Age	Premium	Age	Premium
15	$1.27	37	$3.63	59	$19.08
16	1.38	38	3.87	60	20.73
17	1.48	39	4.14	61	22.53
18	1.52	40	4.42	62	23.50
19	1.56	41	4.73	63	26.63
20	1.61	42	5.07	64	28.98
21	1.67	43	5.44	65	31.51
22	1.73	44	5.85	66	34.28
23	1.79	45	6.30	67	37.31
24	1.86	46	6.78	68	40.59
25	1.93	47	7.32	69	44.17
26	2.02	48	7.89	70	48.06
27	2.11	49	8.53	71	52.29
28	2.20	50	9.22	72	56.89
29	2.31	51	9.97	73	61.89
30	2.43	52	10.79	74	67.33
31	2.57	53	11.69	75	73.23
32	2.70	54	12.67	76	79.63
33	2.86	55	13.74	77	86.57
34	3.02	56	14.91	78	94.09
35	3.21	57	16.18	79	102.23
36	3.41	58	17.56	80	111.04
				81	120.57

APPENDIX I

Probate
Jurisdiction
in the 50 States
and the District
of Columbia

Alabama	The probate court in each county has original and general jurisdiction as to probate of wills.
Alaska	The superior court has exclusive statewide jurisdiction of probate. The local practice is to bring actions in the district court where jurisdiction is concurrent.
Arizona	Probate jurisdiction is exercised by the superior court.
Arkansas	Probate courts have exclusive jurisdiction in matters pertaining to probate of wills. For most purposes, probate courts have been consolidated with chancery courts. The judge of the chancery court is judge of probate courts for all counties within his or her chancery district. The circuit clerk is clerk of probate courts in all counties having less than 15,000 population; in more populous counties, the county clerk is clerk of the probate court.
California	Each county has a superior court that sits at the respective county seat and elsewhere in the county as prescribed by statute. Probate jurisdiction is exercised by the superior courts, in designated departments, which sit as courts of probate.
Colorado	Except for the city and county of Denver, probate and estate jurisdiction rests in district courts. In Denver, a probate court has been established with original and exclusive jurisdiction over all probate matters.

Connecticut	Probate courts have jurisdiction in all matters pertaining to probate.
Delaware	Probate courts are called registers' courts. Each register of wills holds register's court.
District of Columbia	Probate proceedings are brought in the probate division of the D.C. Superior Court.
Florida	Circuit courts have exclusive original jurisdiction in all probate matters.
Georgia	Each county has a probate judge who exercises original, exclusive, and general jurisdiction over probate.
Hawaii	Circuit courts have original jurisdiction of all probate matters.
Idaho	The magistrate's division of the district court has original jurisdiction over probate matters.
Illinois	Probate courts were abolished in 1970 and their functions were made part of the circuit courts. The circuit court of Cook County, however, has a county department with seven divisions, one of which is probate.
Indiana	Circuit and/or superior courts have probate jurisdiction in all counties except St. Joseph County. St. Joseph County has a probate court.
Iowa	District courts have general original jurisdiction in all probate maters.
Kansas	Probate courts were abolished in 1977. In each county there is a district court with general original jurisdiction over all probate matters.
Kentucky	District courts exercise exclusive original jurisdiction of all uncontested probate matters. Circuit courts have original jurisdiction in contested probate matters.
Louisiana	In the parish of New Orleans, civil district courts have exclusive original general probate jurisdiction. Outside of New Orleans district, courts have unlimited and exclusive original jurisdiction in all probate matters.
Maine	Each county has a court of probate that has jurisdiction of probate matters. The superior court is the supreme court of probate and has appellate jurisdiction in all probate matters.
Maryland	Orphans' courts in Baltimore City and all counties except Montgomery and Harford have jurisdiction over matters of probate. The circuit courts of Montgomery and Harford Counties sit as orphans' courts for those counties.
Massachusetts	Probate courts have jurisdiction over all matters relating to probate.
Michigan	There are one or more judges of probate in each county or district who have exclusive jurisdiction of all matters relating to probate.

Minnesota	Probate courts are also county courts (in probate division), except in Hennepin and Ramsey counties, where district courts are also probate courts. These respective courts have jurisdiction over all probate matters.
Mississippi	Probate jurisdiction is exercised by chancery courts. The state is divided into 20 districts, each with a chancery court.
Missouri	The probate division of the circuit court has jurisdiction over all matters pertaining to probate.
Montana	Probate jurisdiction is exercised by the district court.
Nebraska	County courts have exclusive original jurisdiction in all matters of probate.
Nevada	Probate jurisdiction is exercised by district courts sitting in probate.
New Hampshire	The probate court has jurisdiction of all probate matters.
New Jersey	The surrogate court of the county where the decedent resided at the time of his or her death may admit a will to probate and grant letters testamentary thereon; but in case doubts arise on the face of the will, or caveat is filed, or a dispute arises respecting the existence of a will, the surrogate must not act except as ordered by the superior court, which court determines the controversy, or probate may be had before a judge of the superior court.
New Mexico	There is a probate court for each county, which has original jurisdiction over informal probate proceedings. The district court has exclusive original jurisdiction over all other probate matters.
New York	There is a surrogates' court in each county that exercises full and complete general jurisdiction in all matters relating to affairs of decedents.
North Carolina	Clerks of the superior court handle probate matters.
North Dakota	County courts have exclusive original jurisdiction in probate matters.
Ohio	Probate jurisdiction is exercised by the probate division of the common pleas court.
Oklahoma	The original jurisdiction of the district courts extends to all matters of probate.
Oregon	Probate jurisdiction is exercised either by circuit courts or county courts, depending on the county for which assignments have been made by the Oregon Revised Statutes.
Pennsylvania	The register of wills handles probate. Appeals are taken before probate by filing with the register of wills. After probate, appeal is to the orphans' court.

Rhode Island	Each city or town has its own court of probate with a licensed attorney as probate judge, except the town of New Shoreham, where the town council is court of probate.
South Carolina	There is a probate court in each county with jurisdiction in all matters relating to probate.
South Dakota	The circuit court has original jurisdiction in all matters of probate and settlement of estates of deceased persons.
Tennessee	Exclusive jurisdiction of probate is vested in chancery courts and chancery clerk and master, except where otherwise specificially provided by statute. In Shelby and Davidson counties, probate jurisdiction is exercised by the probate court and in Dyer County by the law and equity court.
Texas	County courts have general jurisdiction of probate matters. In some larger counties, special probate courts have been created.
Utah	Probate jurisdiction is exercised by the district court. There are seven districts with 1 to 14 judges in each.
Vermont	The probate court has jurisdiction of all probate matters.
Virginia	Probate jurisdiction is in the circuit court. The judge or clerk or deputy clerk has original jurisdiction to admit wills to probate except in cases of persons presumed dead. Appeal of right lies from the clerk or deputy clerk to the judge.
Washington	Superior courts have original jurisdiction in their respective counties of all probate matters.
West Virginia	County commissions have original jurisdiction in all matters of probate.
Wisconsin	Probate jurisdiction is exercised by the circuit courts.
Wyoming	District courts have jurisdiction of all probate matters.

Index

A

C

P

Q

R

S

T

U

Unified credit, 108
  wasting of, 147
Unified transfer tax rate schedule, 112
Uniform Probate Code, intestacy under, 42

V

Valuation of assets, 113

W

Waiver of premium, 204
Whole life insurance, 199
Wills, 55, 71
  attestation clause, 70
  disposition of tangible personal property clause, 63
  execution, 80
  executor, 68
  exordium clause, 60
  formalities, 57
  guardian, 69
  holographic, 58, 75
  identification and definitions clause, 60
  joint and mutual, 82, 151
  no contest clause, 67
  nuncupative, 58
  payment of debts clause, 61
  payment of tax clause, 63
  residuary clause, 65